AN ICE AGE CAUSED BY THE GENESIS FLOOD

by Michael J. Oard

First Printing 1990
Second Printing 2002

An Ice Age Caused by the Genesis Flood

Cover photos courtesy of NOAA.

Institute for Creation Research
P.O. Box 2667
El Cajon, California 92021

Library of Congress Catalog Card Number: 90-83787

ISBN 0-932766-20-X

Cataloging in Publication Data

Printed in San Diego

DEDICATION

To Leo and Mildred Muoth, without whose help this monograph would have been much more difficult to write.

ABOUT THE AUTHOR

Michael J. Oard works as a meteorologist with the National Weather Service, Montana. He received his masters in atmospheric science from the University of Washington.

CONTENTS

LIST OF FIGURES

List of Tables

ACKNOWLEDGMENTS

I especially want to thank my son, David, who drew all the illustrations on his computer. I am indebted to all those individuals who read and offered valuable suggestions to the manuscript. I thank Dr. Robert Brown, in particular, for thoroughly reviewing the manuscript, and liberally supplying much red ink. I appreciate all the comments provided by fellow atmospheric scientist, Dr. Larry Vardiman, and by Dr. Henry Morris, Dr. Steve Austin, Dr. Gerald Aardsma, and Mr. David Unfred. I thank my wife, Beverly, and my children for their patience during the research and writing of this monograph.

FOREWORD

Man's attempts to explain his experience can be classified under two broad headings—materialism and creationism. Materialism accounts for all observations as the consequence of unexplained basic material substance that has the innate properties required for evolution to configurations which produce all that can be observed. Creationism accounts for all observations as the consequence of design by an unexplained intelligence, that has the capability to put its designs into operation. Each of these broad viewpoints encompasses varied subcategories. The subcategory, which incorporates the specifications given in the Hebrew-Christian Scriptures, Biblical Creationism, is often considered to be *Creationism.*

Biblical Creationism has been at a disadvantage in achieving credibility among individuals who are acquainted with the earth sciences. The seventh and eighth chapters of the book of Genesis specify a catastrophe that completely transformed the surface of planet Earth. Data in the eleventh chapter of Genesis, together with additional data in I Kings 6:1; Exodus 12:40,41; Genesis 47:9, 25:26, 21:5, and 12:4, place this catastrophe somewhere between about 4,300 years ago (2300 B.C.) and 5,400 years ago (3400 B.C.), depending on how the statements concerning the Hebrew residence in Egypt are interpreted, and whether the computation is based on the data as given in the Hebrew text of the ninth century A.D. (Masoretic), or as given in the Greek version used by the early Christian church (Septuagint). For the concerns addressed in this book, it is adequate to place the Biblically specified reorganization of planet Earth's surface 5000 ± 500 years ago. Earth's surface contains evidence of ice activity that is widely perceived as impossible to have been restricted to only 5000 years.

According to widely held views among scientific authorities, planet Earth is now in an interglacial interlude which has been preceded by four continental glaciations and three interglacial interludes over the past one-and-one-half million years (the Pleistocene epoch of geologic history). The response of some creationists has been to abandon confidence in the validity of the quantitative historical data in the first 11 chapters of Genesis. Others have preserved their faith in the Biblical data by affirming that planet Earth has never experienced continental glaciation or an ice age; but the evidence for continental glaciation is too clear and too widespread to deny.

On the basis of the principle that the Creator is a model of truthfulness and consistency, it should be possible to find sound interpretations of His works that are fully consistent with the testimony given in His Word. Up to the present, the creationist literature has been critically deficient with respect to such interpretation of the evidence for continental glaciation. Michael Oard has made a major contribution, in opening up vistas for a sound understanding of the evidence for continental glaciation from the perspective of Biblical testimony. He has been equipped for this contribution by his competence as a professional meteorologist, exhaustive study of the scientific evidence related to glaciation, and confidence that Moses recorded only accurate historical data (allowing for the probability that some time lapse data are rounded to the nearest five or ten years, and that the name lists in Chapters 5 and 11 of Genesis are perhaps a representative selection of only ten of the most prominent individuals in a sequence of descendants).

After his presentation of firm evidence that there has been continental glaciation, most readers will be surprised at the evidence Oard gives for the unlikelihood of *any* continental glaciation in a climate that can be modeled by uniform application of scientific principles. The extent to which the evidence for glaciation is evidence for a unique catastrophic interlude in the history of our planet will probably be unanticipated by all readers. The magnitude and precision of quantitative estimates for ice accumulation time, ice volume, ice thickness, glaciated area, and ice retreat time that can be made from meteorological principles, will amaze most readers.

This book should be intensely studied by everyone who is seeking a solution to problems associated with continental glaciation, regardless of what concerns they may or may not have, with respect to related religious issues. In his straightforward treatment of significant data, Oard deals with some incorrect views held by both creationists and uniformitarians concerning ice-age animals. Biblical creationists will be gratified by the detailed extent to which data in the Bible produce a climate model with which he gives a scientifically sound explanation for continental glaciation.

R. H. Brown

CHAPTER 1

THE MYSTERY OF THE ICE AGE

Deposits resembling glacial debris cover the surface of northern North America, northern Europe, northwest Asia, and many mountainous areas of the world where glaciers do not exist today. In the tropics these features are found on the highest mountains, about one thousand meters below existing glaciers. This debris contains rocks of all sizes, chaotically mixed in a finer-grained matrix. End moraines similar to those associated with present-day mountain glaciers are abundant. Streamlined lens-shaped mounds, called drumlins, exist in large numbers. Large areas of North Dakota, Montana, and Saskatchewan are covered by parallel grooves with intervening ridges (Flint, 1971, pp. 104-106). These are best seen from the air. It is difficult to account for drumlins and fluted ground by any means other than glaciers.

Hard rock surfaces are polished, scratched, and grooved. Rock protuberances have one side smoothed and with parallel scratches, while the opposing side has a plucked or sheared surface. The large polished and scratched surfaces are called striated pavements, while the protuberances are called whaleback forms or roches moutonnées. These landforms indicate the passage of a deformable mass that was able to scratch and cut hard rock. There are many other landforms which also indicate glaciation (Sugden and John, 1976). The abundance of the various evidences for glaciation indicates that the mid and high latitudes of the Northern Hemisphere were once covered by large ice sheets.

Requirements for an Ice Age

How much climate change is required to account for these ice sheets? In other words, what are the requirements for an ice age? Scientists have debated these requirements for years, and have reached a reasonable consensus.

Some scientists once thought that colder winters were the main requirement for glaciation. However, winters are already cold enough for glaciation over most areas that were covered by the ancient ice sheets. In fact, winters are now **too cold** in many northern localities. Consider Siberia: The temperatures there average far below zero Fahrenheit in winter, but no glaciers exist. In most high latitude areas, cooler winter temperatures would not produce glaciation. In order to produce an ice sheet, winter snow must survive the summer and continue to accumulate year by year. Therefore, the crucial season for glaciation is **summer**. Summers must be drastically colder than today in order for the snow to survive. This is one of the reasons the snow doesn't pile up in Siberia—summers are too warm.

Probably a more important ingredient is greater snowfall—enough snow must have fallen the previous winter to survive until the next winter. If the snowfall is light, the snow would melt, even if the summer were much cooler. Consequently, sufficient snow must also accompany the lower summer temperatures. Therefore, the requirements for an ice age are a combination of cooler summers and greater snowfall than today (Fletcher, 1968, p. 93).

Inadequacy of a Uniformitarian Ice Age

Now that we have stated the requirements for an ice age, how much summer cooling and annual snowfall are required? Actually, the amount is not exactly known. Only a modest summer cooling and snowfall increase have been suggested by most paleoclimatologists. A few popular science writers have even made an ice age seem so easy that the next one is due relatively soon (Calder, 1974)! A summer cooling over northern Canada of only four to six degrees Centigrade, together with the current precipitation, had been assumed to be adequate (Williams, 1979, p. 445). However, this threshold was never rigorously tested. While the weak astronomical theory of the ice age has been supposedly "confirmed," recent research indicates that much more climate change was needed to glacierize northern North America than had been previously thought (Loewe, 1971; Williams, 1979). A 6°C summer temperature drop is not enough. Loewe (1971) likely was the first scientist to point out the need for a greater climate change. He summarizes: "The origin of the North American ice sheet raises some difficult questions" (Loewe, 1971, p. 332). Although Loewe specifically was referring to the North American ice sheet, similar difficulties would be encountered for other ancient ice sheets, such as the Scandinavian ice sheet in northern Europe and the ice cap that covered the Alps. The focus of this chapter, however, will be primarily on the Laurentide ice sheet of northeast and northcentral North America.

At least two centers of ice sheet growth in northern Canada are assumed by most workers: 1) Keewatin, northwest of Hudson Bay; and 2) Labrador-Ungava, east of Hudson Bay (Figure 1.1). Winters in these areas are now very cold, in fact too cold for significant snowfall. Summers, on the other hand, are relatively warm (except for coastal locations modified by cool water).

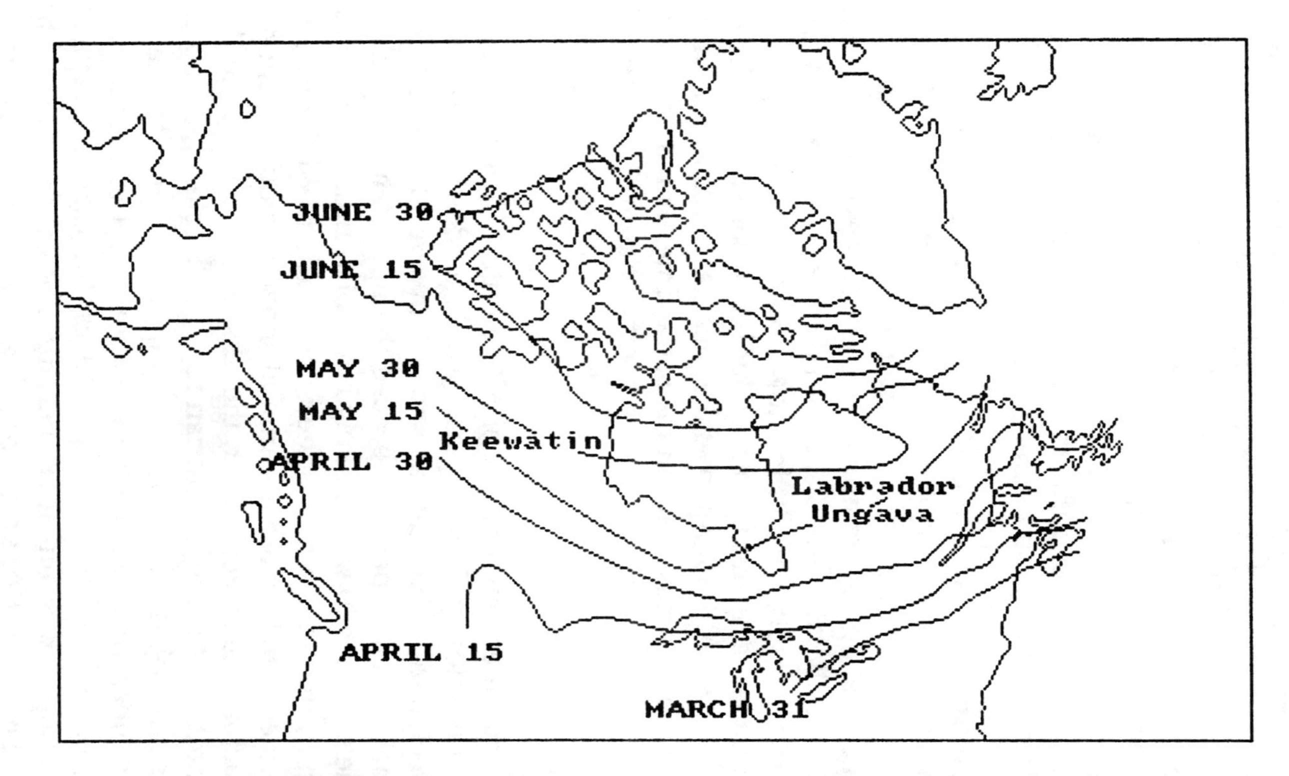

Figure 1.1 Keewatin and the Labrador-Ungava Plateau with the median date for last snow cover of one inch or more for 20 springs in eastern Canada (Redrawn from Potter, 1965).

Currently, the average June-to-September temperature is about 10°C (Loewe, 1971).

According to estimates by geophysicists, Hudson Bay likely was non-existent between ice ages (if there was more than one) due to isostatic rebound (Loewe, 1971, p. 333). Isostatic rebound is the uplift of the earth's crust after the ice melts. When an ice sheet develops, the weight of the ice depresses the crust. Hudson Bay is currently rising, and since it is shallow, it may become dry land before the next supposed ice age. Since Hudson Bay causes a very pronounced regional summer cooling, summer temperatures in the area would have been significantly warmer before ice sheet formation in the standard uniformitarian model.

Current precipitation for the two Canadian ice centers is much different. Labrador-Ungava is wetter, with a yearly average precipitation of about 74 centimeters (29 inches) of water. Keewatin is very dry, a polar desert, with a yearly average of about 20 centimeters (eight inches). But less than half this precipitation actually falls as snow, most falling as summer rain (Loewe, 1971, pp. 339,340). As a result, very little snow accumulates in Keewatin, and, "at present the summer temperatures are so high that the snow easily disappears" (Loewe, 1971, p. 339). Although snowfall is heavier in Labrador-Ungava, winter snow melts over both areas at about the same time, usually by June 15, except for the extreme north, which is not far behind. Figure 1.1 shows the average date of last snow cover of one inch or more for 20 spring seasons in eastern Canada (Potter, 1965, p. 39).

A drop in summer temperature of 6°C would of course cause the winter snow to melt more slowly. This drop also would tend to increase the proportion of annual precipitation that falls as snow. However, the additional snowfall would be smaller than expected, because the upper air temperatures (which determine the snow level) would likely not cool as much as postulated for the ground surface, due to the atmospheric circulation (Williams, 1979, p. 448). The above tendency to increase the annual snowfall would be more than offset by another factor: The cooler the air, the less moisture it can hold. This factor is a serious problem for uniformitarian ice age theories that depend, more or less, on presently observed processes. Figure 1.2 graphs the relationship between air temperature and the water vapor carrying capacity at saturation (Byers, 1959, p. 161). At warm temperatures, the carrying capacity changes rapidly with temperature, but at temperatures below freezing, it changes very gradually. The relationship between air temperature and the water-vapor-carrying capacity is observed between the warm and cold seasons—summer storms drop much more precipitation than winter storms.

If a 6°C summer temperature drop is not enough to bring on glaciation, how much cooling is needed? A computer model that calculates the energy

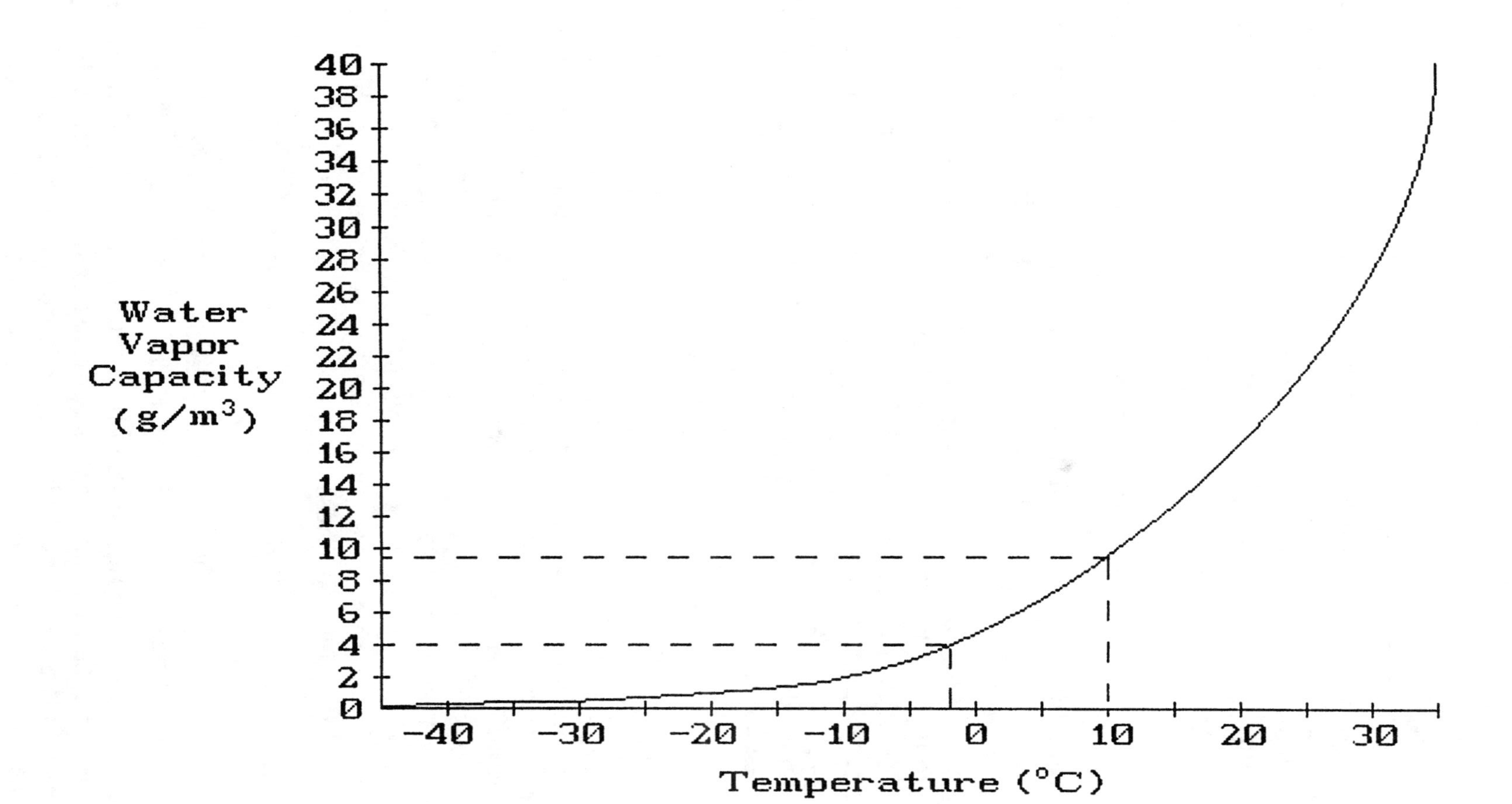

Figure 1.2 Graph of water vapor capacity at saturation (100% relative humidity) versus temperature. Note the 60% drop in capacity as temperature cools from 10°C to -2°C.

balance over a snow cover in northeast Canada has recently estimated the necessary spring and summer cooling (Williams, 1979). The model is realistic. It has a variable albedo (solar radiation reflectivity) for different snow characteristics and makes fairly realistic solar and infrared radiation estimates by taking into account the variations in cloud cover. The proportion of precipitation falling as snow is generously allowed to increase in direct proportion to spring and summer cooling. This computer model closely predicts the observed seasonal changes of the Decade Glacier, on Baffin Island.

One of the purposes of this computer model was to test the astronomical theory of the ice age. In doing so, the summer sunshine was decreased to the presumed solar radiation minimum at 116,000 years ago. Williams began the computer run with the average April-to-August temperature 6°C below normal, and then decreased this value by increments of 2°C until he reached 12°C below normal. Figure 1.3 shows the area permanently snow covered in Canada, after a reduction in average spring and summer temperature of 10 and 12°C. Williams (1979, p. 443) concludes, "...much more climatic change is required for extensive glacierization of either Keewatin or Labrador-Ungava than has been suggested, equivalent to a 10 to 12°C summer temperature decrease...." His model even overestimates perennial snowcover because of two simplifying assumptions.

The scientific basis for this conclusion is that the melting of snow is controlled more by solar radiation, which is abundant at higher latitudes in summer, than by air temperature (Paterson, 1981, p. 313). Researchers have been focusing too much on the latter. At a temperature drop of 12°C, Figure 1.2 shows that the air would hold 60% less water vapor at saturation. This is a large decrease in moisture, which was not taken into account by Williams. Not only that, the above temperature decrease only accounts for a permanent snow cover in northeast Canada. To produce an "ice age," the snow must accumulate year by year, change to ice, and advance down to 37°N latitude in the central United States. More summer cooling than 12°C is likely required. As a result of this temperature criterion, an ice age is extremely difficult to account for, especially when only present processes are allowed.

Possible Solutions to the Difficulty

Some scientists are aware of the magnitude of the difficulty, but most are not. Several possible solutions have been proposed:

One solution is a climate change caused by a modest spring and summer temperature drop that enhances moisture transport to northeast Canada (Barry, 1966; Crowley, 1984). The amount of winter snow would be increased, with a greater chance that the snow cover would remain through the summer. Perhaps this atmospheric circulation of more moist air could be initiated by a temperature drop of only 3°C. (This modest cooling was suggested at a time

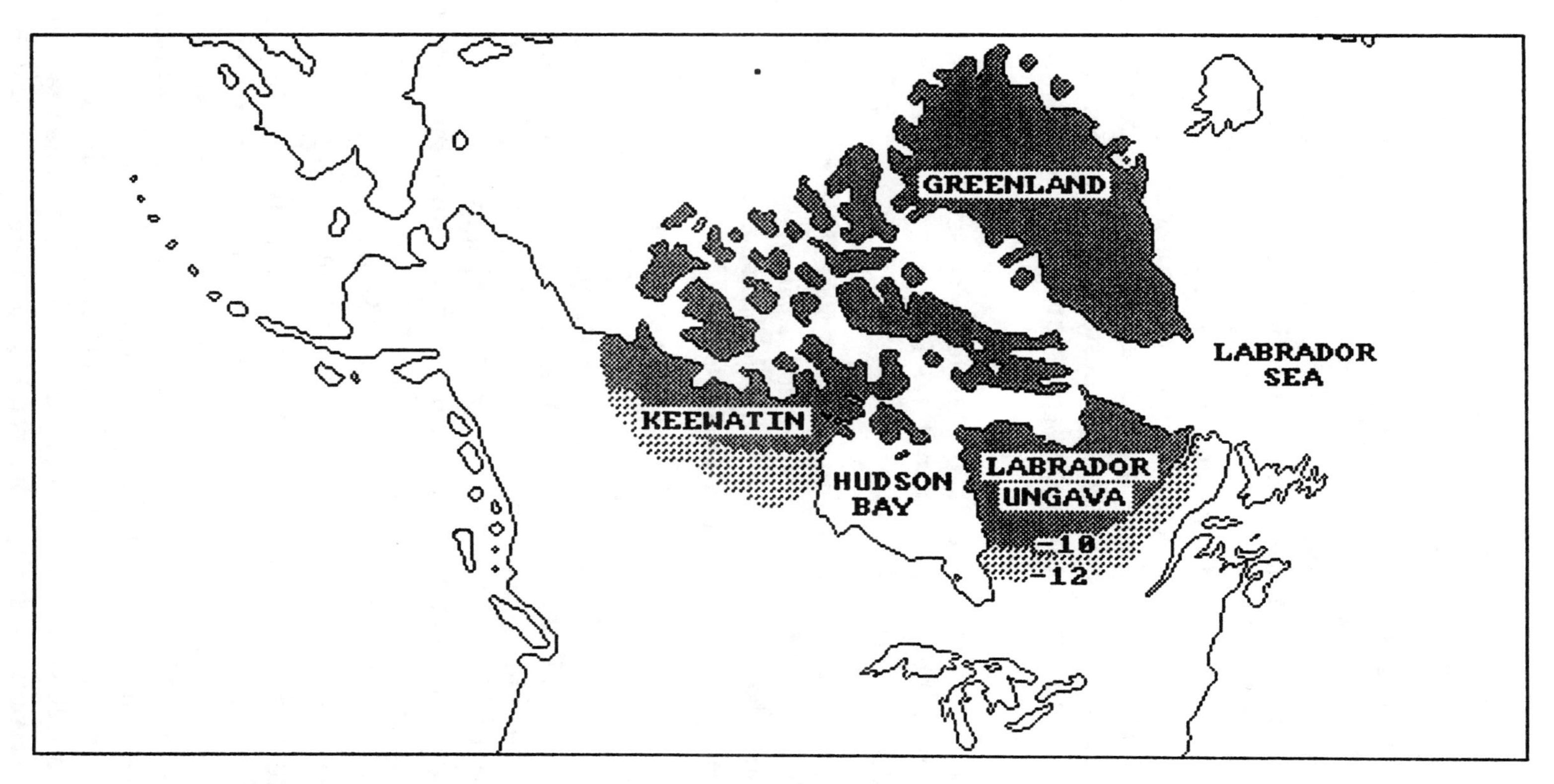

Figure 1.3 Boundaries of permanent snow cover in northeast Canada for a 10° and 12°C spring and summer temperature decrease (Redrawn from Williams, 1979).

researchers believed the threshold temperature drop for glaciation was 6°C.) The main moisture source for this proposal was the North Atlantic.

Support for the above scenario was provided by Lamb and Woodruffe (1970, pp. 36,37), who estimated a 150-300% increase in precipitation for the early ice age circulation. Ruddiman and McIntyre (1979) even calculated that sea surface temperatures in the North Atlantic were 1 to 2°C above normal for about the first half of ice sheet growth, based on geological evidence from deep-sea cores. Warmer sea surface temperatures would evaporate more water vapor and create a larger land-ocean temperature contrast during winter. This would cause the storm track to lie more parallel to the east coast (Ruddiman and McIntyre, 1979). More southerly and easterly winds from storms would then transport more moisture from the North Atlantic to the growing Laurentide ice sheet (Figure 1.4).

Although this proposal seems plausible, a closer examination reveals serious scientific evidence against it. Referring to the more moist Labrador-Ungava, Loewe (1971, p. 338) states:

> *On the other hand, it is not easy to see how a substantial rise of total, or a shift to winter, precipitation can be reconciled with the smaller capacity of the cooler air to hold water vapor. It is also doubtful whether a simultaneous change in general circulation would be able to provide the necessary snowfall.*

Lamb and Woodruffe (1970) based their precipitation estimates on extreme months in the current climate that came closest to the "assumed" pattern at glacial onset. The atmosphere is constantly changing, and it is doubtful if an extreme pattern would last very long, not to mention the thousands of years envisioned for the building of an ice sheet. Barry et al. (1971, p. 417) questioned Lamb and Woodruffe's use of extreme months (which in actuality caused only twice the normal precipitation and not up to three times the normal): "It is doubtful to what extent an extreme circulation pattern may persist for a full season or even more so for a long time interval." So the exaggerated conclusion of Lamb and Woodruffe is clearly not justified scientifically.

The second claim of warmer sea surface temperatures for the first half of a uniformitarian ice age is also contrary to modern observations. How only a 1 to 2°C warmer sea-surface temperature could significantly increase atmospheric moisture is difficult to understand. Actually, observations indicate that sea surface temperatures in the North Atlantic would cool rapidly, due to a colder climate in eastern Canada. In an extensive analysis of sea-surface temperatures for 120 years, Folland and Kates (1984) correlated below-normal, sea-surface temperatures for the Northern Hemisphere with below-normal air temperature, mainly from land. Sea-surface temperature only lagged air temperature by about 15 years, so the cooling response of the ocean is rapid. The relationship is most pronounced in the North Atlantic, where the data are

Figure 1.4 Presumed storm tracks caused by a 1-2°C warmer sea surface temperature in the North Atlantic. Stippled area glaciated (redrawn from Ruddiman and Mclintyre, 1979).

most complete.

Below-normal temperatures in eastern Canada are caused by a little cooler atmospheric circulation (van Loon and Williams, 1976 a,b; Williams and van Loon, 1976). Cooler air blowing off the land over the adjacent North Atlantic Ocean cools the ocean surface. Barry et al. (1975, p. 980) state: "...this evidence suggests that it may be difficult to sustain high sea surface temperatures during the initial phase of a glacial period."

Ruddiman and McIntyre (1979) claim the Labrador Sea would be ice-free for the first half of glacial buildup. However, modern observations indicate that this would not happen any more than would the proposed warmer sea-surface temperature discussed above. Sea ice on Hudson Bay, the Davis Strait, and the Labrador Sea is much more extensive when air temperatures are cooler than average (Herman and Johnson, 1978; Johnson, 1980; Catchpole and Faurer, 1983). Ledley (1984, p. 596) states that sea ice is highly correlated to changes in air temperature, with the following implication: "The extent of sea ice controls the availability of moisture for snowfall. As the sea ice extends farther south during an ice age it caps off the oceans and thus reduces the available moisture." In other words, cooler temperatures will cause more sea ice in the moisture-source regions of Labrador, Ungava, and Keewatin, resulting in further drying. The response is almost immediate (Monastersky, 1987), not thousands of years, as suggested by Ruddiman and McIntyre. Sea ice also reinforces the atmospheric cooling, because of its much higher solar reflectivity than water and its barrier to the escape of the ocean's heat and moisture.

A second possible solution to the difficulty of a uniformitarian ice age is to propose one extreme year of high snowfall in Canada that was caused by a brief change in the general circulation of the atmosphere. Hopefully, this anomaly, combined with a solar radiation minimum (as proposed in the astronomical theory of the ice age), could cause the snow to persist through the summer and start an ice age. Williams (1978) showed that above-normal snowfall in September caused a modest temperature decrease and probably a snow increase in October, in northern Canada. However, in the years he analyzed, it was difficult to tell whether the circulation caused the cooler, wetter Octobers instead of the heavy snowfall the previous month. Besides, only in autumn, the season with the highest snowfall in northern Canada, do such anomalies occur. Early fall is still relatively warm and the air contains more moisture than in winter. The storm tracks are still relatively far north. But once winter arrives, the climatic drying sets in and the storm track is shifted southward, due to very cold temperatures. And even if winters were warmer in northern Canada, winter snowfall could not significantly increase. Figure 1.2 shows that at the winter temperatures of northern and eastern Canada, the air could not hold much more water vapor at warmer temperatures. The largest changes in water-vapor-carrying capacity are at the warmer temperatures during summer, not at the cold temperatures characteristic of Canadian winters.

The deeper autumn snow depth cited in Williams' 1978 investigation was not correlated with cooler summer temperatures. Although late summer and early autumn snowfall was heavy, the annual snowfall during the years of his analysis was only a little above average. For instance, in 1972, heavy, late-summer snowfall resulted in a snowpack only 20% above normal by the end of December (Williams, 1975, p. 289). Assuming this trend for the remainder of the cold season, a 20% increase in snow depth is not significant for glaciation.

Williams (1979) modified his modeling of summer cooling over northern Canada by doubling the cold season snowfall. Even with a 10 to 12°C summer cooling, doubling the snowfall produced only a moderate increase in the perennial summer snow cover. Figure 1.3 has been drawn, taking into account twice the normal snowfall. Williams (1979, p. 443) concludes: "...increased winter snow accumulation (the maximum observed at each station) does not greatly increase the area of perennial snow cover, nor does the possible effect of unrecovered glacioisostatic rebound...."

Just for the sake of argument, let us suppose that some large atmospheric circulation anomaly, by chance, dropped enough snow to last an entire summer, in northeast Canada. Would this start an ice age? No, it wouldn't even be close, because of many other variables that come into play: First, the snow cover and the cooler temperatures accompanying the snow cover would generate less warm-season snow, due to the drier air (Figure 1.2). Therefore, by the time the next spring rolled around, the snow cover very likely would be below normal and would easily melt during the second summer. Even if the snow depth was above normal, Williams (1979) showed that this would not be significant, unless, of course, the snow was five or more times greater.

Hand in hand with the drying tendency from the cooler air, the atmospheric circulation would become unfavorable for an increased buildup of snow. An extensive snow cover has a tendency to cause an upper-level, low pressure system or an upper trough, and a lower-level, high pressure system or anticyclone. This pattern is common over northeast Canada, in winter, but a cooler summer, with a snow cover, would continue this pattern into the summer. Williams (1979, p. 444) states:

> *Because incident solar radiation is mostly reflected from a snow surface, the air above an extensive snow cover is colder, and atmospheric pressure decreases more with altitude in the colder air....This tends to create an upper-air "cold trough" above an extensive snow cover....*

Ruddiman and McIntyre (1979, p. 173) also recognize the problem with expanding an ice sheet (which would be similar to that of expanding an area of snow cover):

> *But the growth of these extensive bodies of ice also implies an expansion of the polar anticyclone normally positioned over ice cover in high latitudes of the Northern Hemisphere. This expansion of dry cold air would reinforce the normal high-Arctic aridity and slow or stop the rapid growth of ice sheets unless opposed by other parts of the climatic system....*

The "other parts of the climatic system" are the 1 to 2°C warmer temperatures for the North Atlantic Ocean, which they believe occurred during the first half of glaciation.

The significance of an upper trough and a low-level anticyclone is that the storm tracks would be suppressed further south and east, resulting in less precipitation for the area. This is observed during the seasonal change from summer to winter in today's climate. As the temperatures in the north cool from late summer to early winter, the average storm track is progressively displaced southward, with the higher latitudes becoming colder and drier. Tarling's (1978, p. 14) statement concerning ice-age theories also applies to the above hypothetic case of increasing an area of year-round snow cover:

> *Apart from the difficulty in isolating different interactive causes, the evidence is always complicated by the strong climatic influences exerted by the ice sheets themselves, as these locally increase the Earth's albedo and create their own atmospheric-pressure zones, with resultant equatorial displacement of pre-existing climatic belts.*

Therefore, the atmosphere and ocean would respond to a summer snow cover, in northeastern Canada, with a tendency to cause drier conditions. And with less precipitation, the snow would easily melt, the next summer, in our hypothetical example.

A third possible solution out of the difficulty of a uniformitarian ice age is to postulate an increase in cloudiness. Increased clouds can cause cooler temperatures, especially in summer. This topic will be discussed further in Chapter 3. However, summers are presently very cloudy in northeast Canada, particularly in Labrador-Ungava (Williams, 1979, p. 454). So, invoking increased cloudiness does not help the problem.

In summary, the proposed solutions cannot provide the sustained cooling and heavy snow to glaciate northeastern North America under essentially uniformitarian conditions. Modern research shows that much more summer cooling than previously thought is a prerequisite. Even doubling the normal snowfall is not sufficient.

A Multitude of Theories

A large number of theories have been exposited to account for the ice age. As of 1968, over 60 theories had been proposed (Eriksson, 1968, p. 68), but all of these theories have serious difficulties. Charlesworth (1957, p. 1532), who has extensively researched the ice age, stated, over 30 years ago: "Pleistocene phenomena have produced an absolute riot of theories ranging 'from the remotely possible to the mutually contradictory and the palpably inadequate.'" The Pleistocene period of geological time is generally the time of the ice age starting about 2,000,000 years ago, and ending about 10,000 years ago. A time span of 10,000 years ago to the present is called the Holocene period, and both eras, combined, are called the Quaternary period. (References to conventional geological time are used for communicative purposes, only, and are not to be construed as indicating belief in the evolutionary/uniformitarian time scale.) Brian John (1979, p. 57), years later, reminiscing on Charlesworth's comment, says the problem has not improved: "Things have become even more confusing since then...."

Ice-age theories are usually classed as either extra-terrestrial or terrestrial. Several of those, which at one time or another have been popular, will be briefly discussed (Imbrie and Imbrie, 1979, pp. 61-68; Tarling, 1978. pp. 14-18).

One obvious extra-terrestrial possibility is a decrease in solar output. Since the sun empowers the climate, researchers have been trying to correlate small fluctuations of the solar "constant" with climatic variables. For instance, atmospheric scientists have developed climate simulation models that are tuned to the present climate. They then decrease or increase solar radiation one to several percent and examine how the model specified changes in climate. This modeling has yielded mixed results, at best. Some mechanism for relatively large changes in solar radiation must be found for the theory to be viable. Furthermore, the solar variations during the past must be known. The theory suffers from a common problem—it can never be proved or disproved, scientifically.

Another extra-terrestrial theory, the galactic dust cloud theory, states that ice ages were caused when the earth passed through cosmic dust, blocking some of the solar radiation. This theory suffers from the inability of astronomers to map areas of cosmic dust and to predict when the earth would have passed through these clouds.

There are a large number of terrestrial theories. One of the most popular is a decrease in the atmospheric gas, CO_2. This gas is transparent to solar radiation but strongly absorbs terrestrial, or infrared radiation at certain wavelengths. Although, the concentration of CO_2 in the atmosphere is very small, a decrease in CO_2 would cause a temperature drop, the opposite of the greenhouse effect. However, some scientists cannot see why or how this would happen, or why CO_2 would be **lower** during ice ages.

Some theories have proposed cooling from volcanic dust. Although volcanic dust and aerosols will cause cooler temperatures, the volcanic activity would have to be much larger than today (Bray, 1976). Each ice age is believed to have lasted 100,000 years; therefore the frequency of very large volcanic eruptions would have to be high and continue for a long time. Since there is no evidence of substantial volcanic activity throughout the 2,000,000 years of the Pleistocene period, the volcanic dust theory is not taken seriously.

Two well-known scientists, several decades ago, proposed that an ice-free Arctic Ocean would greatly increase the moisture over higher-latitude continental areas. A permanent snow and ice cover over land would be formed, increasing the solar reflectivity, or albedo, of the surface (Donn and Ewing, 1968). When temperatures cooled far enough the Arctic Ocean would freeze, and the continental ice sheets would dissipate due to a lack of sufficient atmospheric moisture to maintain them. Subsequently, the climate warms and the ice on the Arctic Ocean melts, and the process begins anew. However, researchers believe that the Arctic Sea icecap has been in place for the past several million years. Thus, this theory is rejected. At least Donn and Ewing recognized the importance for the ice sheets of a moisture source, which is lacking in practically all other theories.

An ingenious theory for glaciation proposes that the West Antarctic ice sheet, which is grounded well below sea level, periodically surges into the ocean due to basal decoupling. This is even a concern today among a few scientists (Denton and Hughes, 1981). This surge would result in increased solar reflectivity over a greater area of the Southern Hemisphere, and may initiate an ice age. There are a number of problems with this theory, one of which is how a small increase in the average reflectivity in the Southern Hemisphere would trigger an ice age in the Northern Hemisphere. Researchers also find no evidence for the resulting catastrophic rise in sea level.

Despite the crude modeling effort of Donn and Shaw (1977), continental drift cannot be invoked to initiate Quaternary glaciation, because the continents have been supposedly in nearly their current configuration since well before the start of the ice age. Then why didn't the ice ages begin much sooner, in the geological time scale? An obvious solution to the problem has been to propose that mountain building in the late Cenozoic initiated icecaps that coalesced to form large ice sheets. Further climatic cooling would cause lower plateau areas to become ice covered (Flint, 1971, pp. 808,809). The problem with this theory is that many mountainous areas are not now draped in snow and ice, and the ancient ice sheet in northeast Canada developed at low altitudes. Even during the ice age when local mountain icecaps developed, for instance, on the Alps and the Tibetan Plateau, the ice did not expand outside the mountainous areas. Other putative mountain-building episodes in the past did not cause ice ages. Even with the high mountains of today, ice ages are extremely difficult to account for (Williams, 1979).

Mountain building has recently been called upon to aid other ice-age mechanisms. Kerr (1989a) reports the modeling effort of William Ruddiman and John Kutzbach, in which the Rocky and Himalayan Mountains are progressively raised, and the resultant climate is compared to the present. When the mountains reach nearly their present height, the astronomical theory (discussed in the next section) is then able to initiate glacial/interglacial oscillations. The mountains deflect the usual west-to-east tropospheric wind currents. Northwesterly winds cause colder air to flow further south in eastern North America. On the other hand, when the upper winds switch to the southwest, warm air is transported farther north. Unfortunately, the model, so far, is able to generate only a very modest 2°C average summer cooling, due to the total uplift of the mountains.

Recent uplift of the mountains is also suggested as a mechanism to decrease CO_2 in the atmosphere, and thus boost the astronomical theory (Horgan, 1988). The mechanism is rather circuitous, and very hypothetical. Higher topography results in greater precipitation and erosion rates. As a result, fresh rocks are more easily exposed. Increased weathering of the exposed rocks produces greater quantities of positively charged ions of sodium, potassium, magnesium, calcium, and others, that are carried to the oceans by streams. The oceans become more alkaline which decreases the amount of carbon dioxide in the water. Since the ocean-surface layer and the atmosphere are in near CO_2 equilibrium, the atmosphere loses CO_2. As will be shown in Chapter 3, even if the above mechanism can significantly decrease atmospheric CO_2, the resulting temperature drop would be very small.

The stochastic ice-age theory has been recently proposed (Hasselmann, 1976). This idea has become popular with some scientists, and is backed up by sophisticated mathematical arguments. It states that since there are random variations in climate on short time scales, there should be large fluctuations inherent in the climatic system over long periods of time. This theory is difficult to test, and essentially relies on random chance.

Revival of the Astronomical Theory

The last theory that will be discussed is the astronomical theory of the ice ages, commonly called the Milankovitch theory, or mechanism. Although this theory does not state how the series of ice ages began, it offers a solution to glacial/interglacial fluctuations. Its popularity has grown immensely during the past 20 years, and there is confidence that the mystery of the ice age has been solved by it (Imbrie and Imbrie, 1979). Therefore, this theory will be discussed in more detail.

The astronomical theory is based upon slight changes in the intensity of sunlight reaching the earth, which are caused by periodic differences in the earth's orbit around the sun. The gravitational pull of the moon and planets causes three orbital variations: 1) slight changes in the eccentricity of earth's orbit, 2) small variations in the tilt of the earth's axis with the plane of the ecliptic, and 3) the precession of the equinoxes. Only the first variation will be discussed, since it is considered the main cause of glacial/interglacial oscillations.

The earth's orbit is not a perfect circle, but is slightly elliptic. The orbit changes from nearly circular to slightly elliptic, and back to nearly circular about every 100,000 years. A measure of this change is the eccentricity of the orbit. The eccentricity varies from zero for a perfect circle, to one for an orbit completely flattened to a line. Figure 1.5 (exaggerated to show the slight difference) illustrates the present earth's eccentricity of 0.017, which results in the earth being 3,000,000 miles closer to the sun in Northern Hemisphere winter, than in summer. Less sunshine at higher latitudes in summer supposedly causes cooler temperatures that trigger an ice sheet. Since the variations are periodic, ice ages, separated by interglacials at regular intervals of 100,000 years, are postulated.

The theory was first proposed in the late 1800s and helped persuade scientists to believe in multiple ice ages, as opposed to just one. According to the theory at that time, the last ice age ended about 70,000 years ago. Scientific evidence was marshaled to prove this date. The astronomical theory was not well developed until the 1920s and 1930s, when Milutin Milankovitch worked out many of the details. According to the revised astronomical theory, the ice age peaked about 18,000 years ago, and data now "prove" this date. The theory was later discarded, for good reasons, during the 1950s and 1960s.

Before the Milankovitch theory once again became popular, in the 1970s, West (1968, p. 213) stated how the theory could be tested: "If there was a correlation between a Milankovitch-type curve and the geological evidence for climatic change, then the point might be decided." In the 1970s, the astronomical theory was revived, due to the influence and persistence of several eminent scientists. The theory was "proved," by matching the earth's orbital variations with slight differences in the oxygen isotopic composition of small planktonic shells that have settled on the bottom of the ocean (Hays, Imbrie, and Shackleton, 1976). As many as 20 or 30 ice ages, separated by complete melting, are now assumed to have developed in succession, over the past several million years (Kennett, 1982, p. 747).

Many serious problems, which have been overlooked in the enthusiasm for this theory, are discussed elsewhere (Oard, 1984a,b, 1985). A few brief

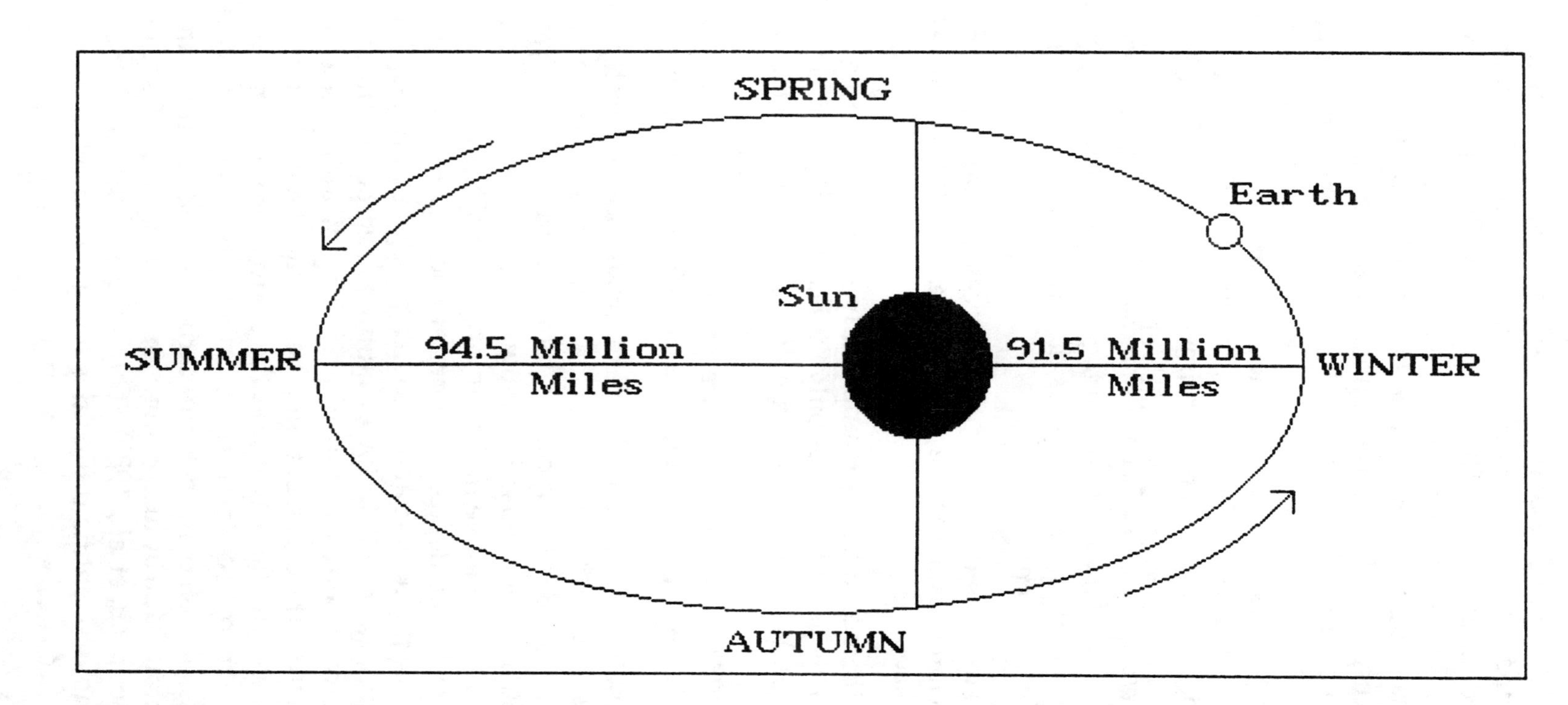

Figure 1.5 Present eccentricity of Earth's orbit (flatten to illustrate the phenomenon). Seasons are in reference to the Northern Hemisphere.

comments are in order. The changes in summer sunshine at higher latitudes, postulated by the theory are actually small—too small to cause the dramatic changes needed for an ice age. The "proof" is only a statistical correlation with geological data. The theory does not tell how each ice sheet actually developed. Furthermore, heating at higher latitudes depends only partially on sunshine. Northward transport of heat by the atmosphere and oceans is also important, but is mostly neglected by proponents of the theory. This transport would lessen the cooling at higher latitudes, caused by reduced sunshine. Meteorologists have known the weaknesses of the theory for a long time, and these weaknesses contributed to its earlier downfall. Famous astronomer, Fred Hoyle (1981, p. 77), expresses his sentiments with the following words:

> *If I were to assert that a glacial condition could be induced in a room liberally supplied during winter with charged night-storage heaters simply by taking an ice cube into the room, the proposition would be no more unlikely than the Milankovitch theory.*

The night-storage heaters are the other processes that supply heat to higher latitudes in winter, and the ice cube represents the slight cooling of the astronomical theory.

Data from the ocean bottom supposedly show that ice ages repeat every 100,000 years. This period matches only the eccentricity variation of the earth's orbit (Figure 1.5). However, this particular orbital variation is the smallest of the three variations by far, changing the solar radiation on earth, at most, 0.17% (Fong, 1982, p. 4). Scientists are greatly perplexed, and are seeking a secondary mechanism to boost the weak orbital variations.

The ocean bottom data should be examined more critically. Many poorly known processes can influence the oxygen isotopes in plankton shells (Berger and Gardner, 1975). For instance, the temperature of the water in the past, when the shell formed, must be known within one or two degrees. The planktonic animals often live in the surface layer of the ocean, which exhibits seasonal changes of ten degrees or more at mid and high latitude. Adding to the confusion, the planktonic animals change depths at times. Since the ocean cools with depth, especially at lower latitudes just below the surface, a large unknown source of error is introduced. For meaningful oxygen isotope measurements from the ocean bottom, the sediment must lie undisturbed since deposition. However, shells lying on the bottom of the ocean are commonly subject to erosion by ocean currents, mixing by abundant bottom-feeding worms, and dissolution of the calcium carbonate. Dissolution can even change the oxygen-isotope ratio by dissolving thinner shells that are isotopically lighter (Erez, 1979; Bonneau et al., 1980). Thus, the astronomical theory does not escape the serious scientific difficulties encountered by all other theories, in explaining the ice age.

What about Climate Simulations?

Although a uniformitarian ice age seems meteorologically impossible, and proposed solutions to the problem are inadequate, atmospheric climate simulations have recently shown that the small changes in solar radiation proposed by the astronomical theory supposedly do cause ice ages. Since climate simulations have been analyzed elsewhere (Oard, 1984a), they will only be summarized here. Interestingly, the small changes in solar radiation, presumed to have generated ice ages, have been considered adequate only after the astronomical theory was "proven" by correlations with deep-sea cores. The desired results are actually the consequence of radiation-sensitive initial conditions, such as ice sheets already in place, uncertain values for input variables, and by inexact "parameterizations" in the models. A parameterization is simply the statistical representation of a poorly understood variable, in terms of another, better-known variable (Schneider, 1984, pp. 853,854). For instance, the complex process of energy loss to space by infrared radiation is typically parameterized in terms of surface temperature, by comparing present radiation with seasonal and latitudinal variations in temperature.

One variable that is favorable for the development of an ice age in these models, is the albedo of snow, which is too high. It is usually treated as a constant with a value of about 0.7 (Suarez and Held, 1979, p. 4829). This is a good value for dry, winter snow, but is much too high for melting snow, and is especially high for exposed, glacial ice. The albedo of melting snow drops to 0.4 in about two weeks (U.S. Army Corp of Engineers, 1956, Plate 5-2, Figure 4). The albedo of ice ranges from 0.2 to 0.4 (Paterson, 1981, p. 305). In addition, there are positive feedback mechanisms that aid the melting of snow or ice. These will be discussed further in Chapter 6. They can lower the albedo below the 0.2-to-0.4 range.

Ice-age models have generally used unreasonably high values of precipitation. A common value seems to be 1.2 meters/year for northeastern North America (Birchfield and Others, 1981, p. 130; Hyde and Peltier, 1985, p. 2179). This precipitation rate is almost twice the average value for the Labrador-Ungava plateau, and is six times too high for Keewatin. With such extremely high values for snowfall and snow albedo, it should not come as a surprise that these models predict an ice age due to small changes in radiation that are correlated to the Milankovitch oscillations. One model even predicts that we should be in an ice age at present (Suarez and Held, 1976, 1979)!

There is a very basic problem with all of these climate models. Although causal mechanisms may be tested, even the most sophisticated general circulation model is still too crude for anything but qualitative results. And these results may be severely distorted by some of the considerations noted above. In other words, we still do not have sufficient knowledge to justify confidence in climatic reconstructions. Bryson (1985, p. 275) states: "In general, physical models of the atmosphere-hydrosphere-cryosphere system are not yet sufficiently advanced, nor is our knowledge of the required inputs, to allow for climatic reconstruction, per se."

A New Paradigm Needed

On one hand, extensive glacial deposits cover the surface of mid and high latitude continents, providing undeniable evidence for extensive past glaciation. On the other hand, atmospheric science and related disciplines strongly suggest that an ice age, which depends upon present processes, (uniformitarianism) is nearly impossible. The only other possible solution is with a catastrophic mechanism. Such a mechanism is, by definition, dramatic, and out of the range of normal experience, but many scientists are now convinced that a catastrophic mechanism has much scientific support.

The model presented in this monograph is based on the historicity of the Bible, especially in its account of Creation and the Genesis Flood. Both scientific and religious implications are involved. Most men of science, 150 to 200 years ago, accepted the first 11 chapters of Genesis as historically valid. Furthermore, these chapters have never been **proved** wrong. They have been arbitrarily rejected by a newer generation of scientists who preferred the theory of evolution and the uniformitarian principle (Gould, 1987). If the reader has difficulty accepting this starting point, at least evaluate the following presentation with an open mind. If one does not know both sides of an issue, he really cannot say he is truly educated on that issue. All possibilities should be examined carefully.

The solution proposed is tantamount to a paradigm shift in glaciology and the historical sciences. A paradigm is, essentially, a supermodel, or a set of foundational principles, which determine what is science in a particular field (Kuhn, 1970). It also determines the way research is conducted, and what problems will be tackled. Paradigms have advantages for scientific research, but they rarely motivate scientists to examine the basis of the paradigm. Usually, data that don't agree with a prevailing paradigm are overlooked, ignored, or forced to fit. Thomas Kuhn (1970, p. 24) writes:

> *Mopping-up operations are what engage most scientists throughout their careers. They constitute what I am here calling normal science. Closely examined, whether historically or in the contemporary laboratory, that enterprise seems an attempt to force nature into the preformed and relatively inflexible box that the paradigm supplies. No part of the aim of normal science is to call forth new sorts of phenomena; indeed those that will not fit the box are often not seen at all.*

Paradigms are engrained into scientists early in their careers, while they are students. Young scientists tend to accept theories, not on the evidence, but on the authority of the teacher or text, since they usually do not know the alternatives or have the competence to make an independent choice (Kuhn, 1970, p. 80). A wrong paradigm, or, more commonly, one based on half truth, can dominate for a considerable time, especially if the paradigm supports the desires of prominent individuals. A large number of significant anomalies must build up to invoke a crises sufficient to make scientists recognize new foundational principles. Thomas Kuhn gives examples from the physical sciences, his expertise, to demonstrate this. There are just as many examples in the biological sciences.

What about the **facts**? Aren't they scientifically solid? Yes, if facts are observed, and "all" the observations are adequately described. This last point may not be appreciated. Unfortunately, it is common practice, in science, not to publish negative or inconclusive studies (Peterson, 1989). The facts on record may just be a biased sample. We must be careful, even when using "observational" data.

The problem of understanding the ice age is not the "facts," but the interpretation of those facts. There is rarely just one way to view a given body of data. "Philosophers of science have repeatedly demonstrated that more than one theoretical construction can always be placed upon a given collection of data" (Kuhn, 1970, p. 76). So there may be other frameworks within which to place a set of data. Before new ideas can be entertained and/or accepted, a revision of basic assumptions or a shift to a new paradigm may be needed. This shift is basically a different way of viewing the data. Kuhn (1970, p. 85) writes:

> *One perceptive historian, viewing a classic case of a science's reorientation by paradigm change, recently described it as "picking up the other end of the stick," a process that involves "handling the same bundle of data as before, but placing them in a new system of relations with one another by giving them a different framework."*

New paradigms practically always advance scientific knowledge, and the change comes about in a revolutionary manner. Such a change is needed in order to solve the mystery of the ice age. The uniformitarian paradigm in glaciology and historical sciences has been long dominant. Paradigms in historical science are much more difficult to change than those in the observational sciences, because it is almost impossible to objectively test the former. Because of the many anomalies that have cropped up, some scientists have already opted for a neo-catastrophism that allows local catastrophes. The data from geologic investigations are making strict uniformitarianism more and more difficult to believe (Ager, 1973). The theory of evolution—the basis for most of mainstream historical science is coming under attack, even from non-Christian scientists and intellectuals (Himmelfarb, 1962; Macbeth, 1971; Zuckerman, 1971; Grassé, 1977; Fix, 1984; Denton, 1985).

In view of this trend, we will take another look at the global Genesis Flood and see if it provides a basis for a catastrophic ice age. This will be a paradigm shift, but making use of previously available data. Parker (1980, p. 186), in a review of the popular book on the astronomical theory *Ice Ages: Solving the Mystery* states:

> *The earlier chapters make mention of the conflict of religious belief and scientific theory. The authors would have done well to state that the conflict is one of basic principles, not of conflicting observations. The basis of all scientific research into the distant past is the principle of 'uniformitarianism', i.e. that the laws of nature have always been the same as they are now. Research could not proceed without such an assumption, and the results should be taken as true in so far as that assumption holds. Belief in God's creative and other activities in the past is not intellectual suicide but the choice of a different set of basic principles.*

The solution to the ice age mystery requires a multidisciplinary endeavor. The author's expertise is in atmospheric science, and that will generally be the focus of this book. However, information from related fields will be brought together to develop a reasonable synthesis.

CHAPTER 2

CAUSE OF THE ICE AGE

Obviously, the Bible is not a textbook of science, at least as currently understood. The Bible was not meant to be taken that way. It is a book about God, man, their relationship, and truth. Truth covers religious truth and the history of God's more important interactions with man. It is in the context of this history that the Bible describes how the universe, the world, man, and everything in the world came into existence. The Bible tells how evil arose in mankind and how the great worldwide Flood was needed to destroy a hopelessly wayward generation. These events have something to say to science, just as an ancient city in Israel buried below the sand has something to say to archeology.

The reader must be aware that events which occurred in prehistory cannot be verified by science. Scientific verification requires observations, whether directly, by the five senses, or with the aid of an instrument such as a telescope or microscope. Observational verification cannot be applied to the so-called historical sciences. This has been admitted by several evolutionary scientists (Birch and Ehrlich, 1967, p. 352; Peters, 1976). Consequently origins, whether by evolution, creation, or abrupt appearance, really is not a scientific subject, according to several definitions of science. It mainly comes under the classification of history, philosophy, or theology, although it can be included under some definitions of science (Bird, 1989). What one believes about origins will depend mostly on what one believes about life, God, and other ultimate considerations. If a person does not believe in God, he surely will not believe the events recorded in Genesis. Information obtained from observational science will only be interpreted in terms of one's belief. One's reconstruction of the past will be based on the foundation of his view of origins.

Does this mean that events which happened in the past cannot be studied by science? Plausible scenarios or hypotheses concerning prehistory can be studied by science—but they cannot be absolutely verified. Such study is in the domain of historical science, or origin science. The possibility of Creation or any extraordinary manifestation of God, is appropriate for intellectual treatment (Thaxton et al., 1984, pp. 6-9,204-206; Bird, 1989). The ice age is thus categorized as historical or origin science, since this event is outside modern observations. An hypothesis in historical or origin science is plausible in proportion to its ability to reasonably account for mysteries of the past, with the minimum of assumptions and additional hypotheses. I shall focus attention on this aspect of plausibility.

Evolutionary scientists hold a position of authority in this country, and in most other countries. They can be expected to make every effort to defend this position. They discount the historical reality or even possibility of Creation and the Genesis Flood as a valid starting point for answering questions concerning origins. Biblical considerations are excluded from their thought system by their initial premises. They have not realized that their own evolutionary/uniformitarian assumptions are of the same presuppositional character as belief in the Bible. No matter what scientific information is discovered that may appear contrary to their foundational assumptions, those assumptions are never seriously challenged by adherents. For some individuals, these foundational assumptions are considered as basic "facts." Yet, as we have seen, these assumptions do not work well when considering the ice age.

In view of these considerations, it is intellectually valid to use the foundational principles of Creation and the Genesis Flood, in combination with modern scientific observations, in an effort to reconstruct a more reasonable history and solve more mysteries of the past than can be achieved otherwise. It is the purpose of this book to construct a model of the ice age on the basis of what can be inferred from the Bible, combined with what evidence can be garnered from science. The Biblical considerations are the subject of this chapter.

The Flood Catastrophe

At this point, some readers may object to the Genesis Flood as a starting point for an ice-age theory. One may think that although the current paradigm of historical science is seriously flawed, the old theory of the Genesis Flood need not be revived. After all, haven't scientists proved long ago that a flood of this magnitude did not occur? Not only that, couldn't the Flood in the Bible have been just a local event?

The principle of uniformitarianism is one of the key assumptions of the current paradigm in historical sciences. This was not always so. More than 150 years ago, many scientists believed the rocks on the earth's surface were laid down and fashioned by the Genesis Flood. The geological evidence that overthrew the Biblical explanation was not well developed at that time. Geological data, alone, did not usher in the current paradigm. The main force behind the rise of uniformitarianism was the desire to eliminate God as Creator and as Initiator of the Flood (Gould, 1965, 1987). In general, the 1800s were a period of revolt against religious authority and the Bible. The Bible was attacked as full of errors, and of limited value for an enlightened, modern age.

Since then, archaeology has demonstrated many historical details in the Bible to be accurate. For example, in the fifth chapter of the Book of Daniel, the writing-on-the-wall incident describes Belshazzar as the last king of Babylon. Archaeology, in the 1800s, had a record that Nabonidus was the last king. Skeptics claimed the Bible contained an unresolvable error. With the discovery of the Nabonidus Chronicle and other clay tablets, it became apparent that Belshazzar was the oldest son of Nabonidus, and co-ruler of the empire. Belshazzar was left in charge of the empire, while Nabonidus was attending other business. According to Daniel 5, Belshazzar was so shaken by the writing on the wall, he promised the translator the position of third ruler in the kingdom. Why third? Archaeology tells us the answer—Belshazzar was already the second ruler. Would this detail have been mentioned in the Bible if the book of Daniel was written hundreds of years after the event, as skeptics claim? The historical accuracy of the Bible is amazingly verified by this incident. This is not to say that all Biblical questions have been answered, but that many have. We should at least be open to the possibility that the Bible is historically true, including the first 11 chapters of Genesis.

Scientists, in the 1800s, deliberately chose to exclude the Genesis Flood by substituting uniformitarianism at a time when the science of geology was in its infancy. The Genesis Flood, consequently, was never proved wrong—just denied. Since the current uniformitarian paradigm has not solved the mystery of the ice age, the time is ripe to reevaluate the Genesis Flood as a basic foundational assumption for earth history. Bringing back a once-discarded theory is not particularly unusual in geology. Charlesworth (1957, p. viii) states: "...one cannot be sure that any hypothesis has been finally relegated to the geological dustbin....Even exploded theories have a habit of being resurrected." I must add that this is especially true when the theory is rejected for other than scientific reasons.

It should not escape our notice that strict uniformitarianism has been in decline for more than a decade. Many of the leading geologic thinkers now call themselves "neo-catastrophists," espousing local and even regional catastrophism to explain geologic deposits of the past. Leading the way in this shift was the acceptance of a catastrophic origin for the channeled scablands of the northwestern United States, as well as a study of the rapid geologic processes present in recent local catastrophes such as the eruption of Mount St. Helens in 1980. A similar shift can be seen in the biological sciences also, for slow and gradual neo-Darwinism has been substantially replaced by the punctuated equilibrium model.

Of course, scientists who held to a belief in Biblical creation have long pointed to the weaknesses in uniformitarian thinking, and the necessity of past processes operating at rates, scales and intensities far greater than those in operation today, to account for most of the world's geologic deposits. The Flood of Noah's day provided the framework for geologic interpretation.

Some believe the Genesis Flood was just a local, or regional event. However, the language of Genesis strongly states the Flood covered the entire world (Genesis 7:19-23). The purpose was to kill all mankind because of the extreme depravity which had developed. All but eight people and representative pairs of landbased animals perished. How could all the people in the world at that time be killed in a local, or regional flood? Why would a representative of each kind of animal need to be on the Ark, if the Flood was not worldwide? In fact, why would God send the animals to the Ark in the first place, if the Flood was local? The animals, as well as man, could flee to higher ground. The covenant of the rainbow makes no sense if Noah's Flood was only local, since many local floods have occurred since then. Thus, under the circumstances of God's wish to destroy a hopelessly evil generation, a worldwide flood is the most reasonable interpretation of Genesis 6-8.

Over 100 traditions of a large or worldwide flood from tribes and ancient peoples across the earth imply a gigantic flood early in history. Not surprisingly, many of these stories are far-fetched, and incorporate polytheism and nature worship. For instance, the proportions of the boat in the Bible, are very close to modern-day ships, but the closest non-Biblical version, the Babylonian Epic of Gilgamesh, has a cube-shaped boat. A cube would be toppled many times in rough seas, from a catastrophic, global flood. However, taken as a whole, these traditions likely reflect a true event that became distorted with time. But since the Biblical version is the most reasonable, it must be the original, testifying either to Moses' direct revelation from God, or his access to records previously written by the patriarchs, or other reliable eye-witnesses.

The Vapor Canopy

A world-wide Flood has important implications for the field of historical geology. Unfortunately, the Bible tells us very little about the Flood. We must piece together a reasonable model, from the limited information at hand. Most of this information is recorded in the early chapters of Genesis, but some is added at other locations in the Bible, such as in Psalm 104:5-9. Before describing the events of the Genesis Flood that relate to the subsequent climate, the climate before the Flood will be postulated, since that climate may relate to the initial conditions for a post-Flood ice age.

Genesis implies that the pre-Flood climate was likely much different than is that of today. Genesis 1:7 is best interpreted to indicate that water was placed above the atmosphere on the second day of creation. Genesis 2:5,6 seems to show, although vaguely, that the pre-Flood world possessed a different hydrological system. The verses seem to say that at one time there was no rain on the earth, and that a mist, together with a system of underground streams, watered the surface.

One of the mechanisms of the Flood, described in Genesis 6-8, is the 40 days and nights of rain, or the opening of the "floodgates of the heavens." This implies heavy rain, presumably of worldwide extent. Within the field of atmospheric science, it is well known that an average of about two inches of precipitable water exists in the atmosphere, and the atmosphere cannot hold significantly more, at saturation. Two inches would be depleted in a matter of hours in such a catastrophe. Consequently, some other source for the rain must have existed. Many creationists believe the additional rain came from water that was placed above the atmosphere, according to the interpretation of Genesis 1:7. This water is called the vapor canopy, since it would most likely be in a gaseous state. The vapor canopy must not have contained too much water vapor, or the light of the stars would have been blocked out (Genesis 1: 14-19 indicates that the stars could be seen).

Another source of Biblical evidence comes from Genesis 9:8-17, the covenant of the rainbow. God promised not to send another flood like the one experienced by Noah. Since a rainbow needs rain, many believe the reason a rainbow wasn't seen until this time was because there was no liquid water droplets in the atmosphere before the Flood. Adding up all these pieces of circumstantial information leads to the theory of the vapor canopy.

From a meteorological point of view, a vapor canopy likely would cause a generally uniform climate at the surface (Vardiman, 1986). Water vapor strongly absorbs solar and infrared radiation and would be very warm. The downward, re-radiated infrared radiation would keep the surface of the earth warm, even at high latitudes, like a blanket warms a person while sleeping. Small latitudinal and diurnal difference in temperature would undoubtedly exist, due to differences in solar radiation. The lower atmosphere, with a high relative humidity, warms and cools slowly. An atmosphere with a weak latitudinal temperature change would have a weak north-south pressure difference, and hence produce weak winds. As a consequence, no large-scale synoptic storms could generate because they need substantial horizontal temperature differences to develop. Since the vapor canopy would be very warm, likely even hot, a strong temperature inversion would exist in the atmosphere below. This inversion would suppress all small-scale or convective precipitation mechanisms, and could prevent the development of conditions that would produce rain. These considerations begin to make sense of Genesis 2:5,6, as descriptive of a continuing phenomenon until the Flood.

An interesting model of the vapor canopy, how it could maintain itself, and some of its climatic implications, has been constructed by Joseph Dillow (1981). As is understandable for such a large, complex project, this model needs further development (Oard, 1982). Dillow's model has a vapor canopy with the equivalent of 40 feet of precipitable water (Dillow, 1981, p. 137). This corresponds to 40 days of rainfall at the rate of half an inch per hour, which is classified as heavy rain, by National Weather Service definition.

Some creationists do not hold the theory that the pre-Flood earth had a vapor canopy, since there are a number of scientific problems with the theory (Morton, 1986, pp. 37-44). For instance, the latent heat released by the condensing water vapor, in Dillow's model, would have been too hot for Noah and his crew. It remains to be seen whether this problem can be solved.

The fossil record shows a large amount of supporting evidence for a much more uniform climate in the past. Palm-tree fossils have been found in Alaska, and coal in Antarctica. Fossils of reptiles, for instance dinosaurs, that cannot live in a very cold climate, have been found in today's polar regions. These fossils would be a result of the Flood, and they probably represent animals that lived in areas near their present location.

Consequently, whether polar warmth was caused by a vapor canopy or by some other mechanism, the pre-Flood ocean must have been significantly warmer than today. The deep ocean today is cooled, at higher latitudes, by the cold atmosphere. The water in contact with the cold atmosphere cools and becomes more dense. It sinks and maintains cold water in the deep ocean, even to the tropics, up to 100 meters or so below the surface. If the higher latitudes were relatively warm before the Flood, the deep ocean would not have cooled as much as it does now. Therefore, the average temperature of the oceans before the Flood most probably was warmer than today. (Even if there was no vapor canopy, the temperature of the pre-Flood deep ocean could have been higher than it is today. Relatively more ocean at higher latitudes, and relatively more land at lower latitudes, would reduce temperature extremes and produce a warmer deep ocean than at present.)

The vapor canopy model specifies destruction of the canopy during the Flood. As previously stated, this vapor would be very warm. The water would condense out of the canopy and end up in the oceans, adding to the average temperature of the post-Flood ocean. Compared to the heat already stored in the oceans, this would only be a minor addition, because of the small amount of water held in the canopy.

Fountains of the Great Deep

The second mechanism of the Flood which has post-Flood climatic consequences is the fountains of the great deep specified in Genesis 7:11. There is little information in the Bible as to what these were. The Bible says all of them burst open on the first day of the Flood, and that enough water was available to cover all the mountains all over the earth (Genesis 7:19). Since the amount of water in the vapor canopy was too small for a global flood, the water from the fountains, which would be part of the ocean today, would need to be considerable. However, this water did not have to cover the high mountains of today because the mountains before the Flood were lower (Psalm 104:5-9), which will be discussed later. A recent uplift of the mountains is supported by geological evidence which shows that practically all the mountains on the earth today are sedimentary rocks, and are fresh looking. The sediments in the high mountains contain marine fossils, which indicate they were below sea level at one time, and were thrust up thousands to tens of thousands of feet, and not too long ago!

Although the actual height of the pre-Flood mountains was probably low in comparison with the modern situation, the amount of water needed to cover them would have been substantial. Where could this water have come from but below the ground or ocean? (Whitcomb and Morris, 1961, p. 9). Any water erupting from this source (the deep) would move out, under pressure from the crust, and hence would shoot up into the air. The ejected water would produce fountains. In order to release the necessary amount of water, many holes and cracks in the earth would have opened. A worldwide eruption of the fountains of the *great* deep would be expected to be accompanied by extensive tectonic and volcanic activity. The tectonic activity would cause immense tidal waves and churning of the water, as the ocean level rose above the mountains. The 50,000 or more volcanoes and seamounts, on the earth, are likely relics of the tectonic activity during and after the Flood.

The large amount of water coming from the fountains of the great deep originated from "deep" within the earth. How deep, no one knows. This water would have been very warm, because the interior of the earth is hot, and the temperature increases downward through the crust at an average of about 30°C per kilometer (Cook, 1973, pp. 163-171). When this water was added to the pre-Flood ocean, the net result was an even warmer ocean at the end of the Flood. Even if there was no vapor canopy, as some creationists believe, and the pre-Flood ocean was not warm, this added water from the deep would be sufficient to raise the temperature of the ocean much higher than the present average of 4°C.

Draining of the Flood Waters

The Flood waters drained from the earth in about 150 days. Many creationists believe Psalm 104:5-9 is a description of this process. In the New American Standard translation of the Bible, verse eight describes this event as the mountains rising and the valleys sinking down. Anybody in a boat during such an event would see the land rise out of the water. However, there is controversy over the exact meaning of these verses. Some believe they refer to the third day of creation when God caused the dry land to appear out of the water that surrounded the earth, since verse five refers to the creation. There is good evidence on both sides (Raaflaub, 1984; Lang, 1984). The Flood interpretation of verse eight is favored for the following reasons. Verse six describes the water as standing above the mountains. If those verses described events on the third day, why even mention the water covering the mountains? They could not be seen if they were there in the first place. The mountains would likely have developed on the third day, when God caused the dry land to appear. More persuasive evidence comes from verse nine, when God set a boundary for the waters so that they may never return to cover the earth. Thus, the previous verses surely must refer to the Genesis Flood.

As the water receded steadily from off the earth, God caused a wind to pass over the earth, according to Genesis 8:1. The meaning of this verse is obscure, but from a meteorological point of view, as the water drained and more and more land became exposed, the wind would increase. The atmosphere would respond quickly to the increasing area of land and height of the mountains. With no protective vapor canopy, the surface in mid and high latitudes and the atmosphere would cool quickly, due to the loss of infrared radiation. Horizontal temperature differences would cause the wind to increase at the surface and aloft. In an atmospheric simulation experiment which began with conditions similar to those which probably prevailed before the Flood waters were drained, the model atmosphere changed from a uniform temperature to nearly the present temperature distribution in only forty simulation days after the many heating and cooling processes in the present atmosphere were introduced (Mintz, 1968).

At the end of the Flood, Noah and his family would find themselves at a higher elevation above sea level, assuming the Ark grounded near the top of the present mountains of Ararat (modern-day Mt. Ararat is composed of two peaks). Since Mt. Ararat is in the mid latitudes, the wind increases with elevation. The current average wind velocity at 14,000 feet at the latitude of Mt. Ararat is about 15 mph in summer and 30 mph in winter (Lorenz, 1967, pp. 34-37). God would still be the cause of the wind (Genesis 8:1), by letting nature take its course.

Whether Psalm 104:8 refers to the Flood or not, the Flood water must have drained by the mechanism described there. In order to drain a worldwide flood, sections of the earth would have to move up, while others moved down. The water could not go back into the earth, because it would move against the pressure difference that brought it out. The pre-Flood subterranean water storage areas, whether caverns, voids in the rocks, or in minerals, would have disappeared or changed during the Flood. The elevation of the present-day, fresh-looking mountains indicates that great vertical changes occurred not too long ago. The general lack of sediments on the ocean bottom are likely evidence for the recent drop in the ocean basins. These vertical changes would cause further tectonic activity, volcanism, erosion, and sedimentation.

An important point with regard to post-Flood climate change is that the ocean water would have been well mixed from this radical change in geography, as well as from the previous tectonic activity during the Flood. The bottom of the oceans and the surface layer of the polar seas would have been relatively warm, and, as a result, the ocean would have been almost uniformly warm from top to bottom and from pole to pole. This condition would have a dramatic climatic consequence following the Flood.

Summary

The picture that emerges at the end of the Flood catastrophe is a barren world with no trees, plants, animals, or birds (except in the Ark). All air-breathing, land-based animals had died and were fossilized, or were in the process of being fossilized, in the sediments of the Flood. The oceans would be about 40 meters higher than today, because the Antarctic and Greenland ice sheets had not yet developed. The newly-formed stratosphere would contain a thick shroud of volcanic dust and aerosols, due to the extensive volcanic and tectonic activity during the Flood. It probably was a dark, depressing world. The oceans would be uniformly warm. The initial conditions would be established for a second, much-lesser catastrophe—a post-Flood transition to the present-day climate. This would be a post-Flood ice age.

CHAPTER 3

BEGINNING OF THE ICE AGE

The requirements for an ice age are a combination of much cooler summers and greater snowfall than in today's climate. As discussed in Chapter 1, these requirements are very difficult to meet with uniformitarian theories. Washburn (1980, p. 648), understating the problem, writes:

> *Yet the mechanism and quantitative adequacy of the effect [discussing the astronomical theory] pose major difficulties, and the nature of the climatic changes responsible for the present ice sheets and for the growth and decay of the Pleistocene glaciers are still problematical. The moisture sources and mechanisms permitting the growth of the Northern Hemisphere ice sheets also remain to be established...*

But can these requirements be met by the climate after a worldwide Flood? This chapter will show how these requirements are indeed met in the post-Flood climate.

Volcanic Dust and Aerosols

The newly-emerged land, with high mountains, would have already cooled significantly in the mid and high latitudes, by the end of the Flood. At the most, the present distribution of climate would have resulted, which is unable to support continental ice sheets, except on Antarctica and Greenland. (Once the Antarctic and Greenland ice sheets developed, the present climate can maintain them. But they may not have been able to develop in the present climate.) Thus, additional mechanisms, other than those created by post-Flood geography, are needed to produce cooler summers. Volcanic dust and aerosols remaining in the atmosphere following the Flood would provide one such mechanism. This mechanism has been recognized by many creationists (Whitcomb and Morris, 1961, p. 294; Clark, 1968, p. 174; Coffin, 1969, pp. 237-240). The abundant layers of lava and ash, mixed with sedimentary rocks around the world, attest to extensive volcanism during the Flood.

Uniformitarian scientists do not accept a volcanic cooling mechanism, because of their greatly expanded time scale. Since glacial geologists believe each ice age lasted around 100,000 years, volcanism is seen as an insignificant factor. However, the possibility that high volcanic activity could initiate continental glaciation is acknowledged: "...volcanic explosions would need to be an order of magnitude more numerous than during the past 160 years, to result in continental glaciation equivalent to the Wisconsin glacial episode" (Damon, 1968, p. 109). The Wisconsin glacial episode is the last glaciation in the standard ice-age chronology. Bray (1976) has suggested that a period of high volcanism may indeed have triggered glaciation, by causing cooler summers for a few years, which, in turn, resulted in an extensive summer snow cover. The snow cover then reinforced the initial cooling, and an ice age started. Bray (1976, p. 414) states: "I suggest here that such a [snow] survival could have resulted from one or several closely spaced massive volcanic ash eruptions." I believe he has a point.

Volcanic dust and aerosols act like an "inverse greenhouse," by reflecting solar radiation back to space, while still allowing infrared radiation to escape the earth's surface (Figure 3.1). This has been shown by modern-day eruptions, which are very limited, compared to those during, and soon after, the Flood. The eruption of Krakatoa, in 1883, was estimated to have deposited 30 to 100 million tons of dust into the global stratosphere. The effect was noticable worldwide, and lasted several years. The direct-beam solar radiation was decreased about 25%, but 85% of this was regained by diffuse radiation reflected back to the earth from the dust particles. The net loss, therefore, was four percent (Oliver, 1976, p. 936). Mass and Portman (1989, p. 567) report that modern-day eruptions reduce total solar radiation five percent to seven percent in polar latitudes, for about one year. The dust and aerosols from the eruption of Mount Agung, in 1963, caused an observed-surface cooling of about 0.4°C in the tropics for several years (Hansen et al., 1978).

The large eruption of Tambora, in 1815, is believed responsible for abnormally cold weather in New England and adjacent Canada the following year or two. During the summer of 1816, an unprecedented series of cold snaps chilled the area. Heavy snow fell in June, and frost caused crop failures in July and August. Sea ice was extensive in Hudson Bay and Davis Strait that summer (Catchpole and Faurer, 1983). Europe simultaneously experienced abnormally cold weather. The year 1816 is called the year without a summer (Hughes, 1979). The unusually cold weather likely was caused by the volcanic dust from Tambora, although some researchers question this claim (Flam, 1989; Mass and Portman, 1989, pp. 588,589).

Acidity measurements in ice cores from Greenland are apparently a measure of past volcanic activity. These measurements can be roughly correlated to northern hemispheric temperatures for the past 1400 years (Bradley, 1985, pp.

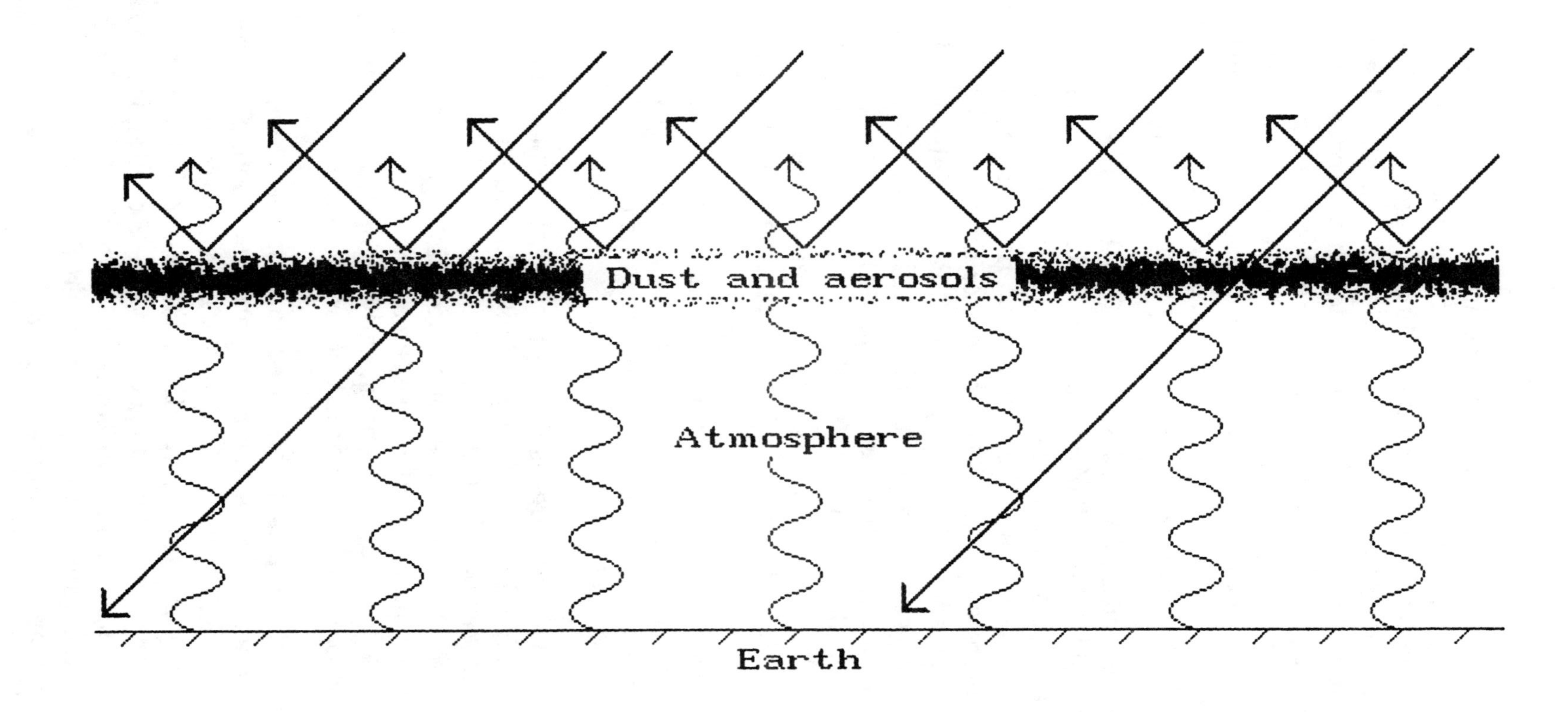

Figure 3.1 The inverse greenhouse. Straight lines are solar radiation, partly reflected back to space by dust and aerosols. Wavy lines are infrared radiation.

142-145). This is because sulfuric acid is the main volcanic aerosol in the stratosphere. This aerosol is spread around the hemisphere, and possibly the whole world, by upper atmospheric winds. As the aerosol slowly descends back to the surface, some of it falls onto the extant ice sheets. Measurements on ice cores indicate that periods of high volcanic activity correspond to times of cooler temperatures, and low volcanic activity to warmer temperatures. For instance, there was a relative lack of volcanism in the ice cores between 1920 and 1960, which was a time of probable warmer temperatures in the Northern Hemisphere. Other glaciers, in both hemispheres, likely have fluctuated in response to the volcanic activity of the past 100 years (Porter, 1981).

Data from ice cores must be used with caution. The upper portion of ice cores, which represents 1000 or 2000 years, is probably reasonably well dated by counting annual layers. Acidity measurements from these levels probably are reliably correlated with time. The very bottom five percent of the long ice cores supposedly represents about 90% or more of the total time interval. Its time sequence is based on inexact glacier flow models. Furthermore, equilibrium between accumulation and ablation is assumed for the entire Pleistocene period. Consequently, the uniformitarian time scale is automatically built in (Bradley, 1985, pp. 147-150). Equilibrium assumes that the ice sheet probably was built up before the Pleistocene, and that ice has flowed through the ice sheet from near the surface to deep within the ice sheet, and then out into the ocean. Dating the bottom of the core, can, therefore, be hazardous, and time scales derived from such dating have differed widely. However, when push comes to shove, the bottom of long ice cores are generally dated by simple curve-matching to oxygen isotope fluctuations from deep-sea cores (Bradley, 1985, pp. 152,153).

The middle portion of the cores is within the transition between counting annual layers and dating, by glacial flow models. Consequently, this portion likely presents a number of difficulties that make an extension of counting annual layers from the top unreliable. One uncertainty is introduced by the presumed amount of "thinning" of the seasonal layers in order to blend in smoothly with glacial-flow models. Consequently, there is much room for error in the interpretation of the middle portion of long ice cores.

Although increased volcanism correlated to decreased temperatures has been established numerous times, the strength of the cooling has remained controversial (Angell and Korshover, 1985, p. 937). Several complicating factors have surfaced in the 1980s (Schneider, 1983; Ellsaesser, 1986). For instance, several major eruptions apparently did not produce a cooling response. The 1982 eruption of El Chichón, in Mexico, is an example. Not only that, the average annual temperature record is so variable that temperature dips in "nonvolcanic years" are of the same magnitude as dips just after major eruptions.

Recent investigation of the settling rate of a thick layer of volcanic dust suggests that volcanic dust may coagulate and fall to the ground much faster than previously thought (Carey and Sigurdsson, 1982; Devine et al., 1984, p. 6320; Rampino et al., 1985). Accordingly, the cooling effect from the dust itself is probably short lived, on the order of several months (Toon et al., 1982, p. 188). But research has also shown that aerosols, especially sulfur and possibly halogen compounds, remain in the stratosphere much longer than the dust, and are, therefore, more responsible for volcanic cooling (Devine et al., 1984). Volcanic cooling of the global atmosphere is estimated to last about two to three years following an eruption, but can range from one year to more than five years (Angell and Korshover, 1985, p. 946). Summer and autumn temperatures are the most influenced by volcanic eruptions (Bradley, 1988). These are the most important months for producing an ice age.

Some of the observational complications are being resolved by more sophisticated analytical techniques. By using superposed epoch analysis (Panofsky and Brier, 1965, pp. 159-161), in which the years before and after each major eruption are composited, a statistically significant cooling trend has been established (Angell and Korshover, 1985, p. 947). Superposed epoch analysis smooths most of the nonvolcanic climate variability. Furthermore, individual eruptions need to be examined closer, because the latitude of the eruption, as well as its magnitude, determine the distribution of the cooling effect (Anonymous, 1986; Budyko and MacCracken, 1987, p. 242). For example, the dust, and probably the aerosols from the El Chichón eruption in Mexico remained in the tropics for about six months, before spreading into higher latitudes. As a result, the cooling from El Chichón was slight in polar latitudes. Mid-latitude eruptions are the most important for mid and high-latitude cooling needed for an ice age (Bradley, 1988).

Although some analysts have claimed a quick tropical cooling from El Chichón, others have not detected any significant effect (Angell and Korshover, 1985). The lack of significant cooling probably was due to a compensating warming, caused by a strong El Niño that year (Angell, 1988). An El Niño is a rather sudden warming of the central and eastern equatorial Pacific Ocean, which warms the tropical air and possibly the atmosphere in the extratropics, as well. El Niños have been associated with other large volcanic eruptions (King, 1987, p. 347; Angell, 1988). Evidently the cooling caused by tropical volcanism may be masked by other short-term variables that cause warming (Angell and Korshover, 1985, pp. 947,948).

Interest in the climatic effect of dust and soot from nuclear war has produced extensive research on the "nuclear winter" concept. A "nuclear winter" has been compared to the effect of very large prehistoric volcanic eruptions, and to the hypothesized asteroid extinction of the dinosaurs. Climate models indicate that a nuclear winter would likely involve mid-latitude surface temperature drops, in continental interiors, to well below freezing in a matter of days, in either summer or winter (Toon et al., 1982; Turco et al., 1983; Covey et al., 1984, p. 308). Toon et al. (1982, p. 197) speculate:

> *Sub-freezing temperatures for 6 months over the entire globe could possibly lead to extensive snowfield buildup over large areas of the continents. Such snowfields would greatly increase the albedo of the Earth and could sustain themselves indefinitely.*

Nuclear winter models have produced much controversy, mainly because of the simple parameterizations and assumptions involved. More sophisticated models have recently shown that the climatic catastrophe would be less disasterous—more like "nuclear fall" (Beardsley, 1986). The climatic consequences of atmospheric dust in such scenarios is still significant, and is analogous to very large volcanic eruptions. Thus, research on nuclear winter indicates that heavy volcanic dust and aerosol loading following the Genesis Flood, would have caused strong continental cooling with the rapid establishment of a snow cover. There would also have been cooling in the tropics, due to less sunshine. Volcanic cooling was likely the cause of tropical mountain glaciation that has occurred at significantly lower altitudes than the elevations of the present glaciers there. Lower tropical mountain glaciation may be nearly impossible to explain by uniformitarian theories.

In the immediate post-Flood climate, volcanic dust would have caused very little cooling of the warm oceans. The reason for this is the large heat capacity and circulation of the ocean. Temperature changes on land are rapid, but a relatively large heat gain or loss is required to significantly change the temperature of the ocean. Toon et al. (1982, p. 187) state that in a nuclear winter, "...the oceans cool by only a few degrees owing to their large heat capacity." Therefore, the warm ocean, following the Flood, would be influenced very little from the volcanic dust, while the land would cool substantially.

Snow-Cover Cooling

Volcanic dust and aerosols would initiate an extensive snow cover on mid and high-latitude continents. Once a snow cover has become established, summer cooling would be strongly reinforced (Budyko, 1978, pp. 94,95). In other words, the snow cover acts as a positive feedback mechanism to a temperature drop. A positive feedback mechanism acts to reinforce the initial perturbation, in this case summer cooling from volcanic dust. Cooling from a snow cover is the strongest positive feedback mechanism the climate offers, and the one invoked the most often by ice-age researchers to reinforce any cooling they can generate from their theories. The biggest problem in applying this positive feedback mechanism is the initial establishment of a permanent snow cover.

Table 3.1. Solar albedo (reflectivity) of various surfaces

Surface	Reflectivity
Fresh snow	0.70-0.90
Old or wet snow	0.40-0.60
Glacier ice	0.20-0.40
Very dirty snow	.15
Cloud tops	0.40-0.90
Forests (no snow)	0.05-0.20
Forests (snow covered)	0.20-0.30
Bare soil	0.10-0.25
Grass	0.15-0.25
Desert sand	0.25-0.40
Water (with a high sun)	0.05-0.10

The snow cover further cools the atmosphere by increasing the reflectivity, or albedo of the surface to solar radiation. Table 3.1 lists the albedos of various surfaces. Fresh snow has an albedo of about 0.8, which means that 80% of the solar radiation is reflected back to space. The albedo of the earth's surface that is not covered by snow or ice is variable, but averages about 0.15. Consequently, five times more sunlight is reflected back to space from a fresh snow cover, than from bare ground, under clear skies. Clouds will decrease this difference by variable amounts since clouds are highly reflective. For a present-day average cloud cover of 52% over the earth, the average earth/atmosphere albedo is approximately 0.33. So, under average cloudiness, a fresh snow cover will reflect about 2.5 times more sunlight back to space. With less sunlight absorbed at the surface, infrared radiation loss causes the air temperature above the snow to dip much lower than without the snow cover. Furthermore, snow is a good insulator, and will shield the cold atmosphere from the warmer ground.

The effect of a snow cover is illustrated by the following hypothetical example:

> *Thus, if snow and ice covered the whole surface of the Earth even for a short period of time, its mean temperature (equal now to 15°C) would be reduced by approximately 100°C. This estimate shows what an enormous effect snow cover can exert on the thermal regime (Budyko, 1978, p. 95).*

Toon et al. (1982, p. 197) concur: "The problem of the ice-covered Earth has been investigated many times, and it has been generally concluded that with the present solar luminosity an ice-covered Earth represents a stable climatic condition...."

The albedo of snow can change rapidly with age and/or melting, as will be discussed in Chapter 6. The albedo of old or wet snow is 0.4 to 0.6, and for ice, is only 0.2 to 0.4—significantly less than that for fresh snow (Paterson, 1981, p. 305). So the amount of sunlight reflected from the snow surface will especially depend on the quality of the snow. During glaciation, ice would rarely be exposed at the surface, and if snowfall remained heavy in summer, the snow surface would generally continue fresh, with a high albedo. Thus, heavy summer snow is required for the positive feedback mechanism to work the best. A snow cover, especially if it was fresh, in the post-Flood climate would also compensate for periods of volcanic lulls that allowed more sunshine to penetrate the surface.

Barren Land

Barren land acts as a reinforcement for snow-cover cooling. Note in Table 3.1 that a snow-covered plain will reflect back to space about three times as much sunlight as a forested surface with a snow cover. The darker color of the trees and bushes is responsible for the greater absorption of solar radiation (Otterman et al., 1984). Immediately following the Flood, the land was completely barren. Once a snow cover was established, the high albedo of fresh snow on barren land would cause greater cooling than would be the case in areas that are presently tree covered.

Trees and bushes present additional problems for ice age theories, such as the astronomical theory, that depend upon present processes. Trees and bushes now cover most of the areas of Europe and North America that were formerly glaciated. In the uniformitarian model, a similar vegetation pattern should precede each ice age. To overcome the higher solar absorption of vegetation-covered terrain, a uniformitarian ice age would need an even greater summer chill and higher snowfall than Williams (1979) has estimated (see Chapter 1).

According to glacial scientists, an ice sheet developed in the far north and then moved slowly into the northern United States. According to the evidence available, at least one ice sheet had to move as far south as 37°N in the central United States. If this were true, all the trees and vegetation in its path would die and end up in the glacial till. The same scenario would be repeated 20 to 30 times. Abundant evidence of these past forests and vegetation should be found mixed in with the glacial till. However, Charlesworth (1957, pp. 225,226) states that fossil flora are rare:

> *Evidence has been found which suggests that the ice in places advanced over standing and probably living forests in which the annual rings show a marked decrease in the rate of growth only during the last twelve years before death occurred. Nevertheless, the ice may generally have invaded a barren, timberless and storm-swept country .... The rarity of vegetation in the drift suggests that the preglacial material was carried beyond the limits of glaciation.*

According to the model presented in this book, a post-Flood ice age developed on barren land. It would have begun immediately in most areas that became glaciated, including the central United States. Those areas not immediately glaciated were close to the warm ocean. When the initial conditions ameliorated, the ice and snow in the central United States would have melted first, because of its southerly latitude. Trees and vegetation within the till are normally not expected in this post-Flood model. The trees and vegetation that are rarely found can be explained as later glacial oscillations engulfing forests that grew south of the ice sheets.

Charlesworth presents two possible explanations for the rarity of trees in glacial drift. One suggestion is that the trees all died and disappeared well before the glaciers descended from the north. His explanation may be possible within the uniformitarian framework. However, if the climate was that cold and harsh, conditions probably would have been too dry for an ice age. Trees likely would have died in a colder climate, in advance of an ice sheet in most of Canada (Ball, 1986), but the argument would hardly hold in extreme southern Canada and the United States. In these areas, conditions likely would not have been too cold for at least the more hardy trees, such as spruce and birch, to grow, unless the climate was too dry. The rare occurrence of fossil trees that show growth for 12 years before burial indicates that trees and vegetation did grow south of the ice sheets. The trees did not decompose and disappear, before inundation by ice. If a substantial number of trees had existed and decomposed before glaciation, their existence should be apparent from organic residue in the till.

Charlesworth's second suggestion seems very unlikely. It is hard to understand how a majority of existing trees could be carried beyond the limits of glaciation by meltwater streams, after the trees had been buried in glacial drift. Regardless of whether uniformitarian scientists can satisfactorily explain the scarcity of trees and shrubs, the rarity of organic remains in glacial debris is more in accord with an ice sheet that developed rapidly over denuded land.

More Cloudiness

Another mechanism reinforcing cooler mid and high-latitude summers is an increase in cloudiness. Until recently, the effect of clouds on climate was unknown (Stephens and Webster, 1981). The problem was that clouds reflect a significant proportion of solar radiation back to space, while they absorb infrared radiation and re-emit it back to the ground. The two effects were believed to be compensatory, so that a change in cloudiness would have little effect on surface temperatures. Recent satellite measurements of the solar and infrared radiation balance have revealed that clouds do exert a major influence on the surface temperature. A regional increase in cloudiness causes cooler surface temperatures, and vice versa (Ramanathan et al., 1989; Monastersky, 1989a, p. 6). These results are preliminary, but solid. Other variables, like cloud height, type, and structure, modulate the magnitude of the temperature change.

The radiative effects of clouds have several interesting variations with latitude. In the tropics, the sunlight reflection and infrared radiation from clouds actually balance each other, causing no net change in ground temperature. In other words, a change in cloud cover apparently makes no temperature difference in the tropics. However, clouds significantly influence surface temperatures in the mid and high latitudes. Cloud changes are most effective over the oceanic storm tracks. The most surprising result of this new research is the large magnitude of surface cooling that results from increased cloudiness. A change in cloudiness is much more effective than a change in CO_2—a subject of much modern concern and research. Ramanathan et al. (1989, p. 57) write:

> *The greenhouse effect of clouds may be larger than that resulting from a hundredfold increase in the CO_2 concentration of the atmosphere .... Hence, small changes in the cloud-radiative forcing fields can play a significant role as a climate feedback mechanism.*

How does this new result reinforce cooler summer temperatures from other mechanisms? The post-Flood oceans at mid and high latitude were quite warm. The warmer the water, the more rapidly water vapor would have been evaporated from it. Cloudiness and precipitation will increase as the water vapor in the air is increased. Accordingly, the immediate post-Flood era should have had greater cloudiness and cooler summers than is characteristic of the present.

Carbon Dioxide

A reduction of the greenhouse gas, CO_2, would make a delayed contribution to cooler summer temperatures. Carbon dioxide is a minor constituent of the atmosphere, but it absorbs infrared radiation at certain wavelengths, while being more or less transparent to solar radiation (Budyko, 1978, p. 108). CO_2 is a greenhouse gas, like water vapor, but not as significant as the latter. An increase in carbon dioxide will increase temperatures, and a decrease will lower temperatures. This concept is theoretically sound, but its magnitude is disputed, because of possible compensating or negative feedback mechanisms. Climate models have consistently predicted a global temperature increase from 1.5°C to about 5.5°C for a doubling of CO_2 (Brewer, 1978, p. 16; Manabe and Broccoli, 1985a; Ramanathan et al., 1989, p. 62; Monastersky, 1989b, p. 234). One investigator believes that changes in carbon dioxide may have little atmospheric temperature response (Idso, 1987). The reason for the differing conclusions is that current models are too simple to adequately describe all the many interacting processes related to CO_2 in the atmosphere and ocean.

Much has been learned, in recent years, about atmospheric CO_2 and its interactions with the ocean and biosphere. This increased understanding is the result of research prompted by fears of carbon dioxide climate warming, due to deforestation and the burning of fossil fuels. A few scientists believe a climate warming may cause the West Antarctic ice sheet to either disintegrate or surge into the ocean, raising sea level, and destroying many seaport cities.

A lower level of atmospheric CO_2 has been invoked recently, to boost the weak Milankovitch theory for starting an ice age (Kerr, 1988, p. 532):

> *But the variations in the tilt and direction of Earth's axis of rotation and the shape of its orbit could not fully account for the magnitude of the chilling during an ice age. Within the past few years, marine sediments and glacial ice have yielded evidence that carbon dioxide, through its greenhouse effect, acts as an essential amplifier of the climate effects of Earth's orbital variations.*

Support for this thesis comes from the discovery of reduced CO_2 in air bubbles trapped in the deeper ice of the Greenland and Antarctica ice sheets (Sundquist, 1987). This ice was presumably deposited during the last glaciation. Scientists claim that the level of carbon dioxide during the ice age was about 200ppm (parts per million), which compares to a pre-industrial value of about 275ppm and a current value of 350ppm (Anonymous, 1988). The value of 200ppm is likely not significant enough to compensate for the deficiency of the Milankovitch mechanism. The average world temperature since preindustrial times is believed to have warmed on the order of only 0.5°C for the 25% increase in CO_2. On this basis, a 25% decrease to presumed glacial CO_2 values would likely cause a temperature drop of only 0.5°C, which is hardly significant (see Chapter 1).

There is doubt whether the average world temperature has really increased 0.5°C since pre-industrial times. If there has been no increase, or an increase of less than 0.5°C (which is more likely), the influence of carbon dioxide changes on temperatures is even less significant than has been proposed. The reason for the doubt is because many variables, which have not been taken into account, have influenced temperature records. One systematic variable not related to climate change that would cause warmer temperatures at weather stations is the urban heat island effect. As cities grew during the 20th century, more heat was given off by buildings and homes, and more solar radiation was absorbed by concrete and asphalt. This warming can be substantial for big cities, where weather stations are often located. A recent report analyzes this complex and incompletely understood variable. Karl and Jones (1989, p. 265) conclude that the urban heat island effect has warmed average temperatures in the United States anywhere from 0.1°C to 0.4°C during the 20th century, although the former value is thought best (Jones et al., 1989). This is a substantial fraction of the 0.5°C temperature rise that has been presumed to be due to carbon dioxide warming. Karl and Jones (1989, p. 269) state: "The magnitude of the urban bias in two global, land-based data sets was found to be a substantial portion of the overall trend of global and regional temperatures."

Another significant variable that may be responsible for the presumed worldwide temperature change during the past 100 years is volcanic dust. A large number of volcanic eruptions, from 1880 to 1915, most likely cooled temperatures at that time (Budyko and MacCracken, 1987, p. 242). Less volcanic activity, after 1915, could be responsible for warmer temperatures. Support for a general decrease in volcanic dust and aerosols in the Northern Hemisphere comes from acidity measurements in Greenland ice cores and from Northern Hemisphere glacier mass balance (Porter, 1981).

Therefore, there is a high probability that other variables besides CO_2 increase have caused the presumed 0.5°C-20th-century temperature increase at weather stations. Consequently, the impact of a 25% decrease in CO_2, postulated as a booster in uniformitarian ice age modeling, is miniscule.

Before discussing how atmospheric carbon dioxide decreased during the post-Flood ice age, we need a brief overview of the important variables influencing atmospheric CO_2. The natural sources and sinks of carbon dioxide are extremely complex, and are not worked out in detail (Trabalka and Reichle, 1986). However, the general features of the carbon cycle are well enough understood to allow a good qualitative estimate of the change in carbon dioxide associated with a post-Flood ice age.

The concentration of atmospheric CO_2 depends largely on the terrestrial and oceanic biosphere and the oceanic reservoir of inorganic carbon. Table 3.2 presents the current estimates of carbon in the most important carbon reservoirs (Bolin, 1986, p. 408). About four times as much carbon is stored in wood, vegetation, soil, peat, and decaying surface detritus as in the atmosphere.

Table 3.2. Approximate carbon inventory (units of 10^{12} kilograms) estimated in various reservoirs (after Bolin, 1986)

Carbon Reservoir	Total Inventory
Atmosphere	720
Soil and surface detritus	1,460
Peat	500
Wood and vegetation	830
Ocean surface layer	930
Intermediate ocean layer	8,250
Deep ocean	28,700
Carbonate sediments	20,000,000

The ocean contains a very large amount of dissolved carbon dioxide, especially in the deeper ocean. The ocean surface and the air are constantly exchanging CO_2, depending mostly upon the difference in the CO_2 partial pressure between the ocean and the air, as well as the wind speed (Fung, 1986, pp. 464,465). If the partial pressure is lower in the ocean, carbon dioxide is transferred from the air into the water. The partial pressure of CO_2 in the ocean surface layer depends upon surface temperature, salinity, upwelling of rich CO_2 waters, and biological activity (Trabalka and Reichle, 1986). At a constant salinity, the amount of CO_2 dissolved in the surface water increases with decreasing temperature (Brewer et al., 1986, p. 366). The reason for this inverse effect is the lower partial CO_2 pressure due to greater CO_2 solubility at cooler temperatures (Brewer, 1978, p. 15). Consequently, cooler water absorbs more CO_2 from the atmosphere.

Immediately after the Flood, the amount of CO_2 in the atmosphere and ocean likely was relatively high. A large CO_2 content could have been associated with the large pre-Flood biosphere. Decomposition of this biosphere would have generated a large CO_2 input. Mixing of the ocean waters during the Flood would have distributed the CO_2 between atmosphere and ocean. Higher carbon dioxide levels in the atmosphere immediately after the Flood would have resulted in warmer temperatures, if there were no variables causing cooler temperatures. However, CO_2 would have decreased rapidly during the ice age. This decrease would reinforce summer cooling over land, possibly when some of the other mechanisms, like volcanic dust, may have been waning. The reason for this decrease is the rapid development of vegetation, soil, and peat on a barren earth, taking CO_2 out of the air. Recent research shows the initial rate of decrease of CO_2 would have been relatively rapid. Schlesinger (1986, p. 196) writes: "When vegetation colonizes a newly available land surface, that is, primary succession, there is often a rapid accumulation of organic carbon in the soil." Current inventories of terrestrial carbon from Table 3.2 indicate how much CO_2 has been taken out of the air after the Flood. Most of this terrestrial carbon likely built up during the ice age.

The post-Flood oceans would have had a high CO_2 partial pressure at first, due to a large amount of decaying organic material from the Flood, and to the warm temperature of the water. A higher partial pressure in the ocean would cause a corresponding higher atmospheric CO_2 content. As the oceans cooled during the ice age, the partial pressure would have decreased with concomitant transfer of CO_2 from the air into the ocean. Abundant nutrients dissolved in the ocean during the Flood, and an overturning ocean (see Chapters 4 and 8) would have resulted in very large post-Flood rates of phytoplankton and zooplankton growth. The plankton would fix some of the oceanic CO_2 in their structures, decreasing, further, the oceanic and atmospheric partial pressures of CO_2. It is apparent that many factors would contribute to a large decrease in atmospheric CO_2, as the ice age progressed. The decrease would be much larger than the meager 75ppm decrease surmised for uniformitarian models. At the end of the ice age, when the ice sheets would be melting and the atmosphere colder than now (see Chapter 6), the CO_2 content of the atmosphere likely would be lower than it is today.

Storm Tracks

The climate soon after the Flood would be characterized by cold continents, especially at mid and high latitudes, due to volcanic dust, an extensive snow cover over barren terrain, and greater cloudiness than at present. The ocean adjacent to these continents would be relatively warm, due to the very warm "fountains of the great deep" during the Flood. The cooling mechanisms would hardly affect the warm ocean. Consequently, isotherms, which are lines of equal temperature, would parallel the coasts of mid and high-latitude continents. The greatest horizontal change in temperature would be along the shore line. A secondary area of packed isotherms (area of rapid change in temperature perpendicular to the isotherms), would develop just south of the building ice sheets. The postulated annual average isotherms at the beginning of the ice age for Northern America, are depicted in Figure 3.2. Notice the strong packing of isotherms along the east coast of North America and in the southeast United States.

From meteorological principles, the wind speed would increase rapidly, with altitude above these areas of strong packing. The wind direction would be mostly parallel to the isotherms, with the coldest air to the left of an individual with his back to the wind. Figure 3.3 depicts this relationship between a north-south horizontal temperature difference and the change in the west wind aloft. This relationship is expressed by the thermal wind equation for the east-west component of the wind (Hess, 1959, p. 191):

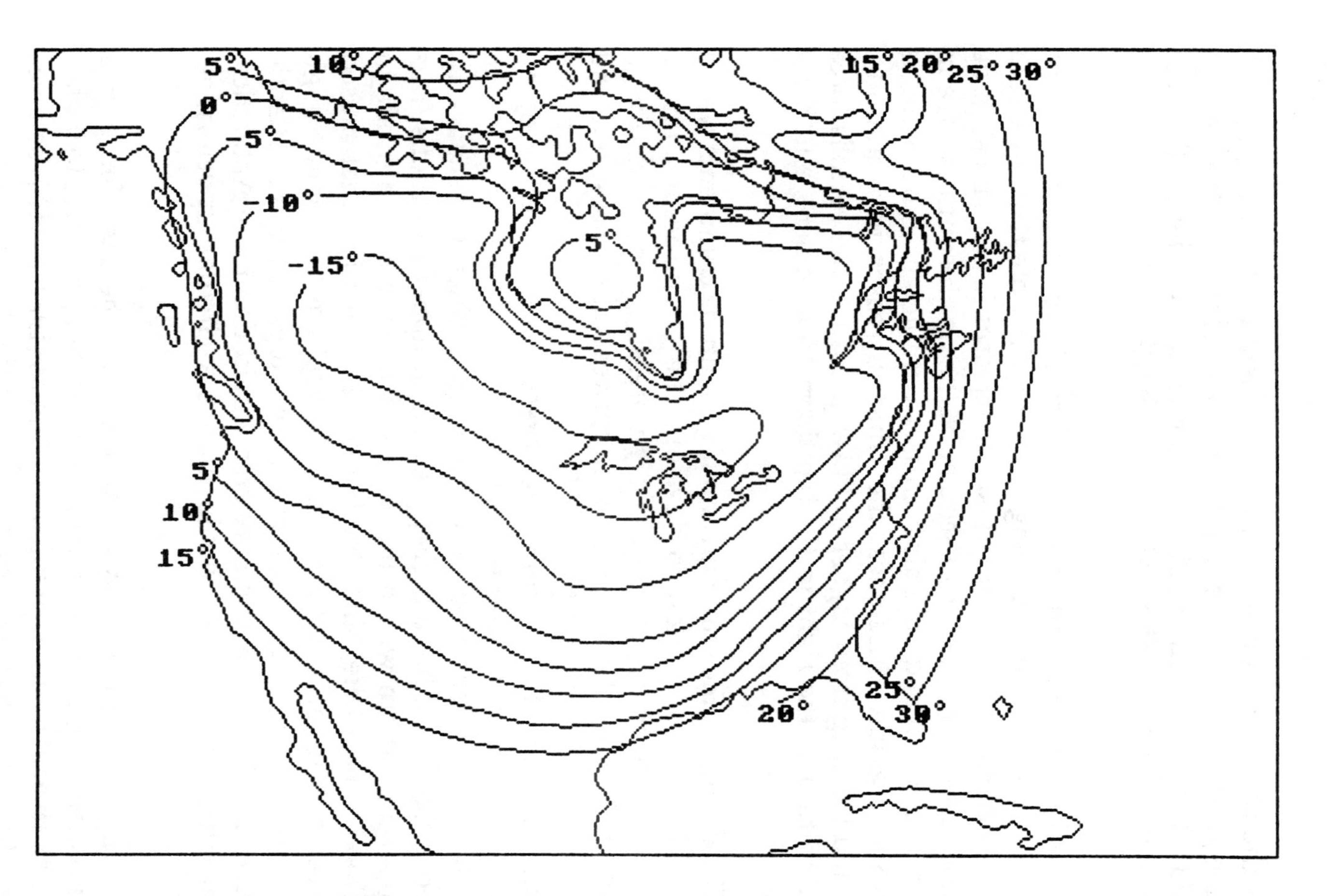

Figure 3.2 Postulated annual temperature (° C) for North American at the beginning of a post-Flood ice age.

$$\frac{\Delta u}{\Delta z} \approx -\frac{g}{fT}\frac{\Delta T}{\Delta y} \tag{3.1}$$

where $\Delta u/\Delta z$ is the change in the east-west component of the wind, u, with altitude, z; g is the gravitational constant; f is the coriolis force; T is the average temperature; and $\Delta T/\Delta y$ is the change in the temperature in the north-south direction, y. An analogous expression exists for the north-south component of the wind.

The thermal wind relationship may be difficult for the layman or non-meteorologist to understand. Referring to Figure 3.3, note that since cold air to the north has a higher density, the pressure decreases faster with altitude than in the warmer air to the south. Consequently, the north-south change in pressure between and warm and cold air increases with height. Since wind is proportional to the pressure difference, the wind increases with altitude. Instead of the wind blowing from higher to lower pressure, the coriolis force causes the wind to turn to the right in the Northern Hemisphere, and blow parallel to the isotherms.

In the post-Flood climate, the cold mid and high-latitude continents would cause a trough of low pressure aloft to develop. The warm oceans, on the other hand, would induce an upper ridge of high pressure. An upper trough is a pattern in which the wind blows from the northwest on the west side and southwest on the east side of the trough axis. An upper ridge has the opposite wind configuration (Figure 3.4). The upper high pressure ridge over the ocean is caused by the warm ocean heating the atmosphere by contact and by the release of latent heat of condensation from evaporated water. Consequently, the warm air above the oceans has a higher pressure at upper elevations. This trough-ridge upper-air pattern would likely extend to very high altitude in the early post-Flood atmosphere, since the low-level mechanism that caused it would have been so strong. In the Northern Hemisphere, an upper trough would lie over North America and Asia and upper ridges over the Atlantic and Pacific Oceans. An upper low-pressure area would dominate Antarctica, while the warm surrounding ocean would induce a circular upper ridge, offshore.

The forcing of high pressure aloft by a warm ocean is the basis for Jerome Namias's work in correlating above-normal sea-surface temperatures to higher pressure aloft, and seasonal weather prediction. Namias (1972, p. 1174) believes "The physical mechanism of feedback from sea to air, in this case, appears to have been ... due to anomalous, differential heat supply from the underlying water." However, the mechanism involved is only partially understood, and some researchers believe that the higher pressure aloft may actually have induced the warmer sea-surface temperatures (Wallace and Blackmon, 1983, pp. 74-77). The sea-surface temperature anomalies in the present climate are

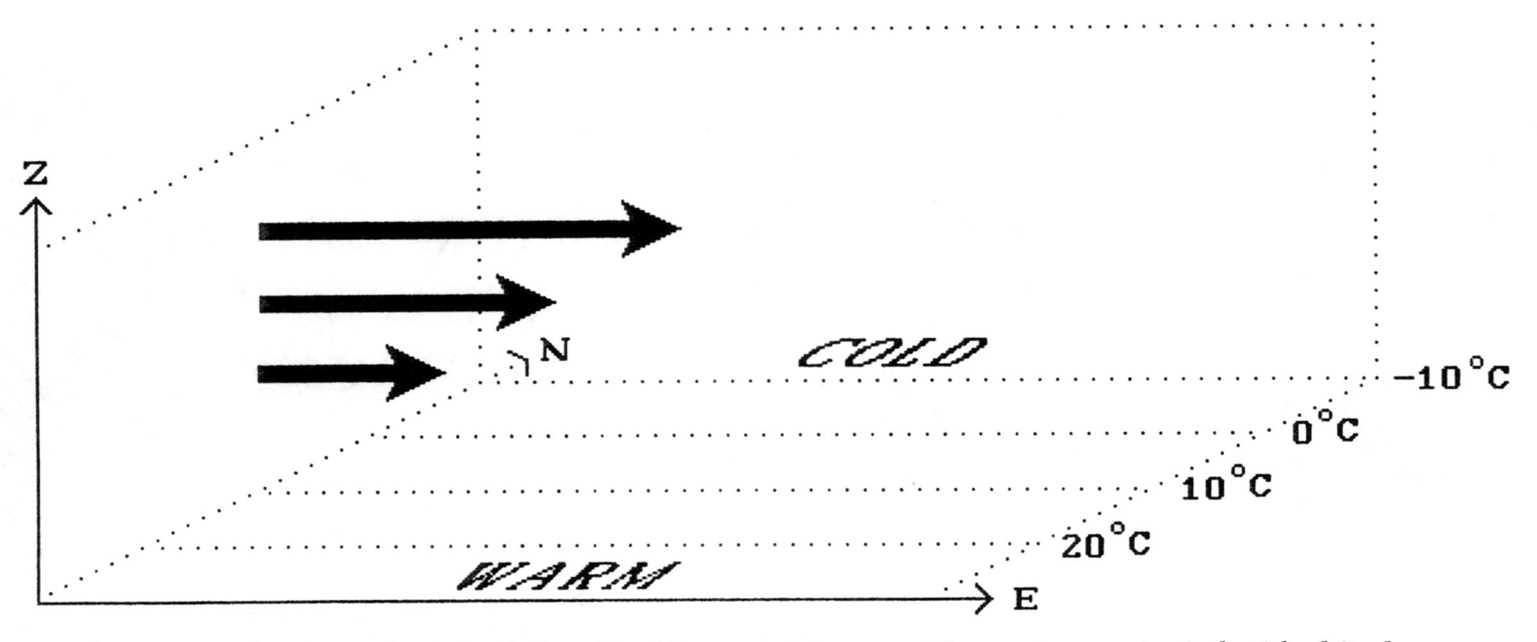

Figure 3.3 The thermal wind relationship. The arrows represent increasing west wind with altitude (Z direction). The dotted lines are east-west isotherms.

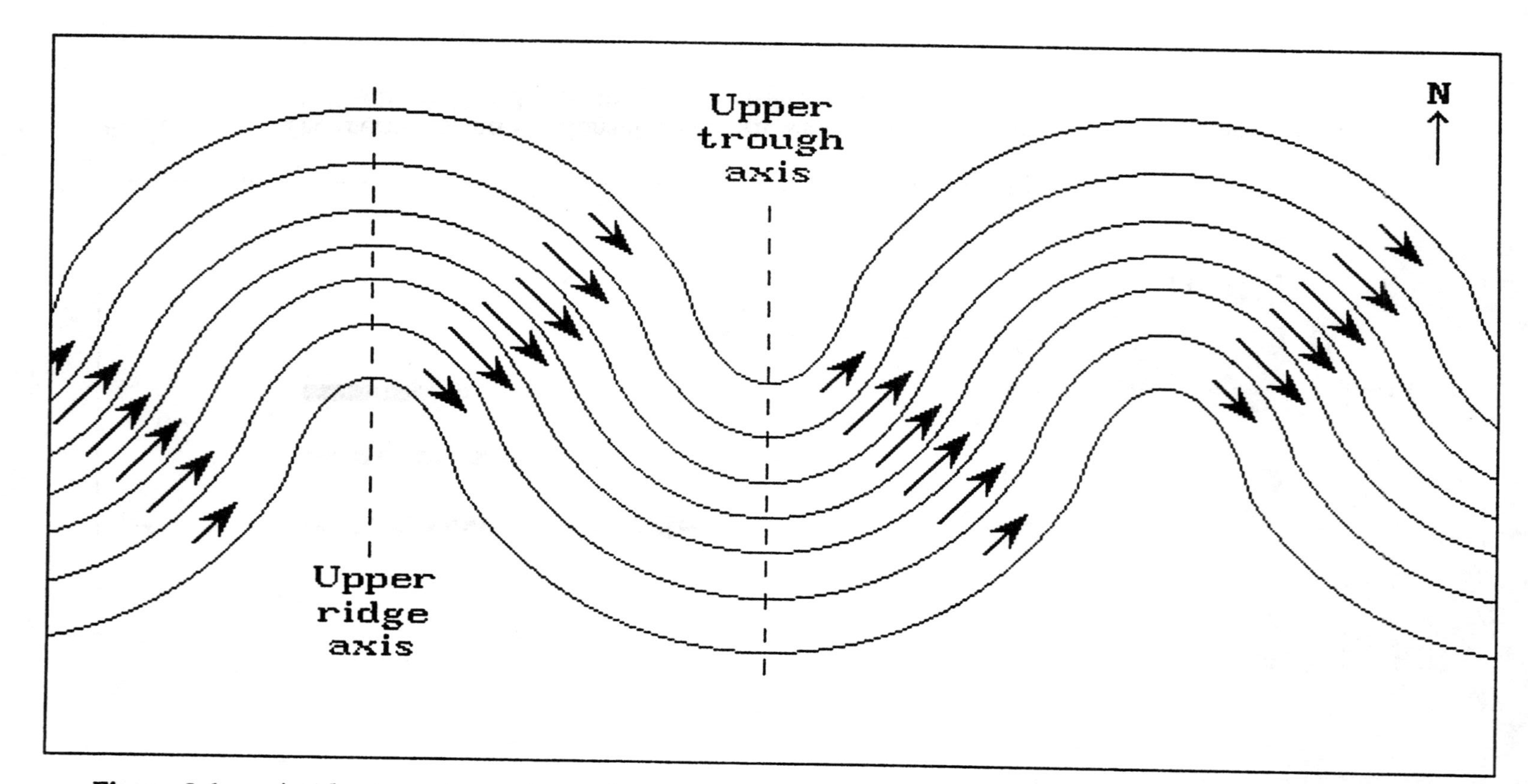

Figure 3.4 A ridge-trough couplet in the mid and upper atmosphere. The lines are of equal pressure. The arrows represent wind direction.

small—on the order of a few degrees Celsius or less. This is probably the reason the sea-air forcing has been difficult to substantiate from atmospheric models.

In the post-Flood climate, sea-surface temperatures would be much warmer than any anomalies in the present climate. Atmospheric models have indicated that a radical sea-surface warming would cause a substantial atmospheric response. Namias and Cayan (1981, p. 871) write, in referring to model behavior with present sea surface temperature anomalies: "The responses found were generally small except when unrealistically large SST [sea-surface temperature] anomalies were imposed." In a general circulation computer simulation, the sea-surface temperature in the mid latitudes, over much of the western Pacific Ocean was raised 3 to 12°C (Chervin et al., 1980). Such a strong sea-surface temperature anomaly caused a significant temperature and pressure increase high in the atmosphere, with stronger storms developing in the southwest portion of the anomaly area and tracking northeastward. This experiment adds credence to the unique trough-ridge pattern of the post-Flood climate.

Thermal forcing by cold continents and warm oceans is only one of two main influences on the upper-air pattern. Orographic, or mountain forcing by predominantly westerly winds aloft over the Rocky and eastern Asian Mountains, is the second. North-south temperature differences across these mountains would exist in the post-Flood climate (Figure 3.2), as in the present winter climate, due to the cold mid-latitude continents and the warm subtropics. By the thermal wind relationship (equation 3.1), relatively strong west winds aloft would be induced. This forcing tends to cause an upper trough about 1,000 miles downstream to the east (Held, 1983), somewhat similar to a boulder in a stream causing a downstream wave. Although there is disagreement on the subject, thermal and orographic forcing are probably of equal importance in the present atmosphere (Chen, 1986). In the post-Flood climate, mountain forcing would reinforce the thermal forcing in eastern North America, making the upper trough especially strong in this area. However, the Himalayas and other ranges in eastern Asia, which are much higher than the Rocky Mountains, would not only exert a stronger influence on the upper circulation, but also would tend to shift the upper trough off the east coast of Asia. According to these considerations, the upper trough, induced by the westerly winds flowing over the eastern Asian mountains, would be out of phase with the thermal forcing caused by the cold Asian continent and the warm North Pacific ocean. This difference in forcing, by the two mountain ranges, is most likely important for the subsequent distribution of ice in the ice age.

Before one can draw the average storm tracks due to cold continents and warm oceans in the early post-Flood climate, the effect of a very warm Arctic Ocean needs evaluating. The Arctic Ocean would be too far north to have much impact on the mid-latitude westerly flow. However, it would add large amounts of heat and water vapor to the atmosphere near the North Pole. As a result, the general north-south temperature difference at high latitude would be reversed, from today, since the continents to the south would be colder (Figure 3.2). An easterly wind flow would likely be induced aloft parallel to the shore line of the Arctic Ocean, especially at the lower levels. The warm Arctic Ocean likely is a key factor in the development of ice over normally very dry Keewatin.

Areas of strong horizontal temperature change are areas of baroclinic instability in meteorological jargon (Holton, 1972, pp. 161-210). In these areas, small surface-pressure perturbations grow into storms. Baroclinic instability and storm development are especially favorable in the strong southwest flow downstream from an upper trough. Based on statistics of time-filtered data, the storm tracks in the present climate are predominantly downstream, and slightly poleward of the upper tropospheric jet stream maximum (Hoskins, 1983, p. 190). Figure 3.5 is a schematic of the relationship between the upper-air pattern and the area of storm development.

Storms are steered by the strongest winds aloft, i.e., by the jet stream. (This is why so much space has been dedicated to explaining the winds aloft in the post-Flood climate.) In the present atmosphere, the jet stream meanders around the globe. The storm belt likewise shifts with the jet stream, preventing any one location from receiving an over-abundance of precipitation. However, some areas in the mid latitudes do receive relatively large amounts of precipitation, due to a higher frequency of storms.

In the post-Flood climate, the thermal and mountain forcings would be more or less permanently fixed year-round. Consequently, storms in this unique climate would follow similar tracks all year long. For instance, storms would commonly develop along the east coast of the United States, and off the east coast of Asia. In the current climate, a storm develops in a baroclinic zone every one to three days. This could also have been the frequency in the post-Flood climate. Storms would often develop and track northeast along and off the east coasts of North America and Asia, where the strongest baroclinic zone exists. The storms would tend to weaken, moving into the higher latitudes, due to a weaker horizontal temperature contrast. Consequently, the major storm tracks along the east coasts in the Northern Hemisphere would splay out into minor storm tracks in various directions. Minor storm tracks would also develop just south of the developing ice sheets, due to the stronger north-south thermal difference. Figure 3.6 presents the major and minor storm tracks postulated for the Northern Hemisphere at the beginning of the ice age.

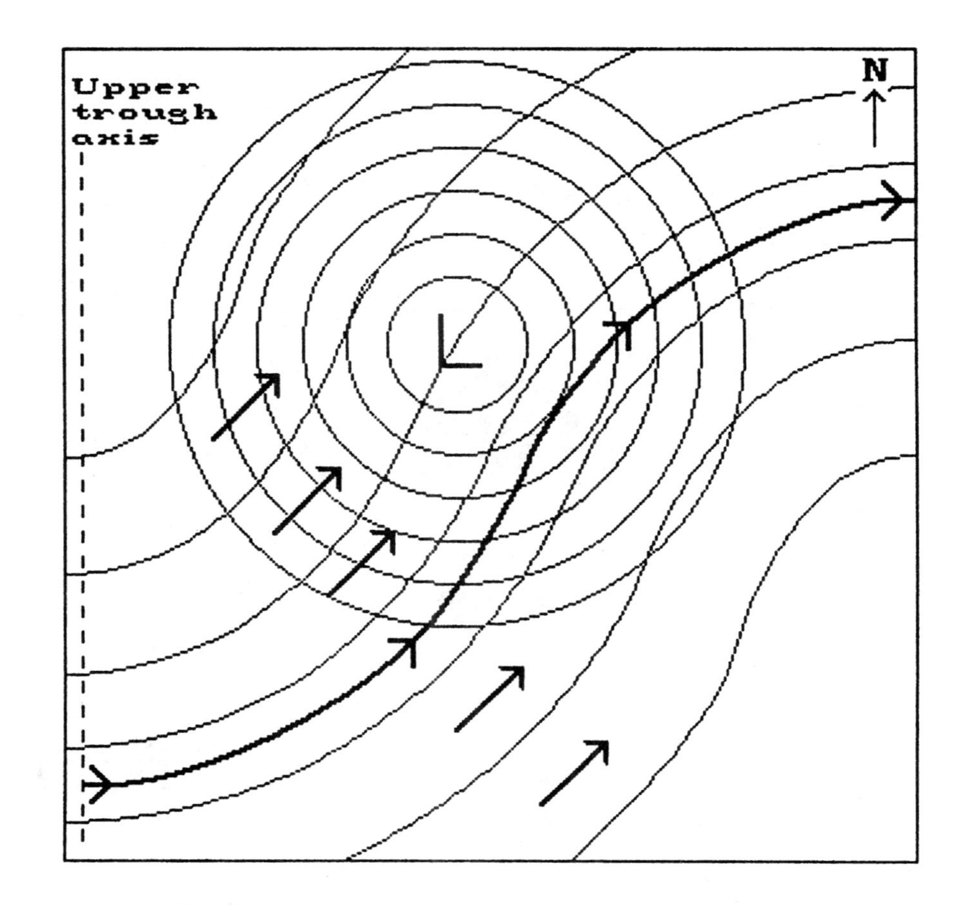

Figure 3.5 The normal location of a surface low pressure system in relationship to the upper trough-ridge pattern and jet stream. The center of the jet stream is depicted as an accented line.

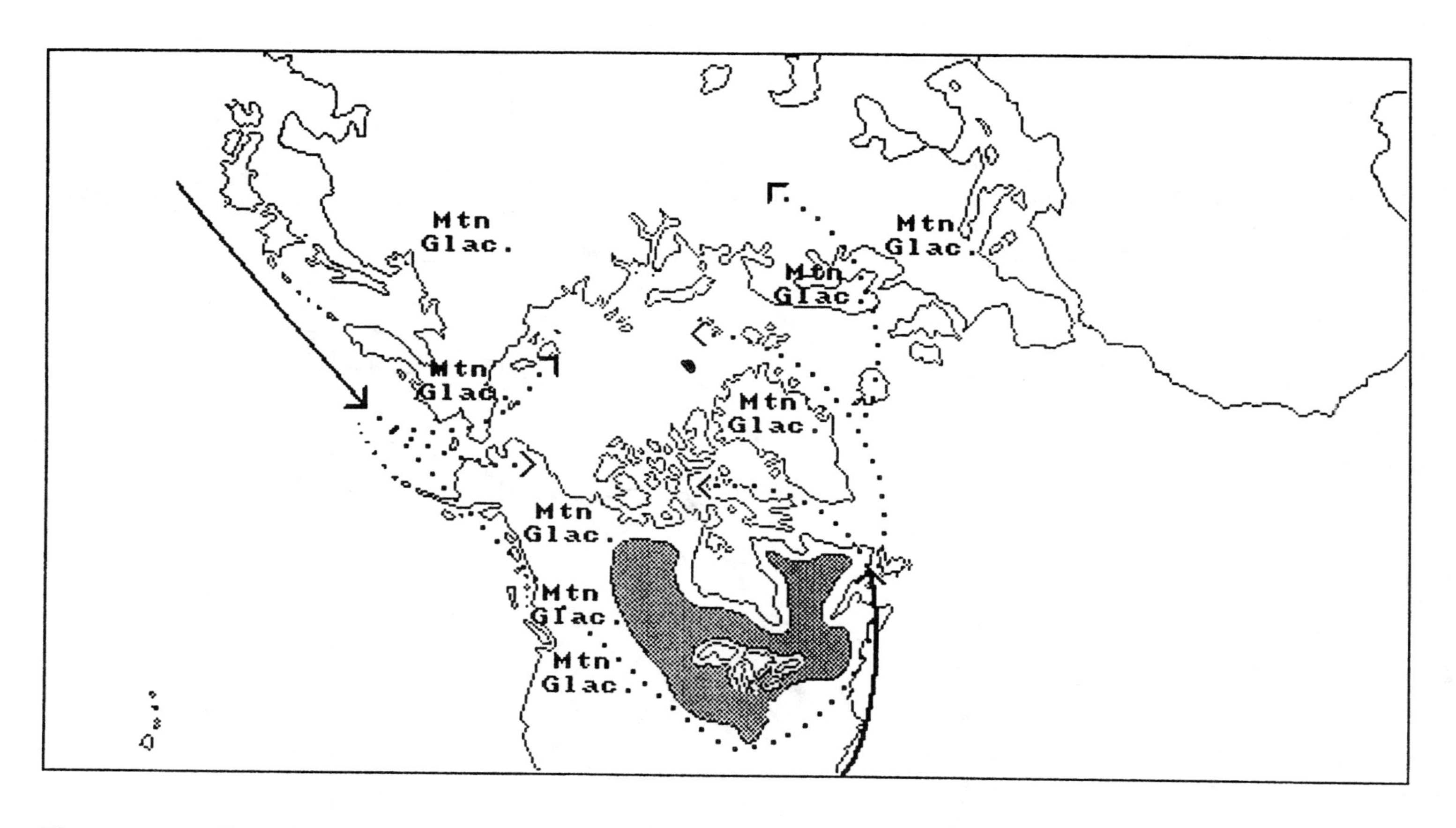

Figure 3.6 Postulated major and minor storm tracks and snow cover in the Northern Hemisphere at the beginning of a post-Flood ice age. Solid lines represent major storm tracks and dotted lines represent minor storm tracks. Mtn. Glac. means mountain glaciation.

In the Southern Hemisphere, the post-Flood jet stream and the average storm track would be much simpler. A cold continent near the South Pole, and encircled by a warm adjacent ocean, would have storms tracking eastward along the coast (Figure 3.7). But since West Antarctica, at that time, would have been mostly ocean with mountainous islands, storms would more often circle around East Antarctica, which would have been mostly a low-lying flat plain (Bentley, 1965, pp. 263,267).

Snowblitz

So far it has been shown that the mid and high-latitude continents in the early post-Flood climate would be much cooler in summer, and the approximate position of the storm tracks has been indicated. One more ingredient remains for the development of a post-Flood ice age, and that is the moisture for the snow. An abundant supply of moisture is probably the most serious difficulty for uniformitarian ice age theories. Can the post-Flood climate generate the needed moisture?

The needed moisture is evaporated from a much warmer ocean. Evaporation from the ocean surface can be estimated from the bulk aerodynamic equation for evaporation (Bunker, 1976, p. 1122):

$$E = \rho\, C_E(Q_s - Q_{10})U_{10} \tag{3.2}$$

where E is the average evaporation, ρ is the air density, C_E is the empirically derived exchange coefficient for water vapor, Q_s is the saturation mixing ratio corresponding to the sea surface temperature, Q_{10} is the average mixing ratio at ten meters above the ocean, and U_{10} is the average wind speed at ten meters, which is usually the ship anemometer level. The mixing ratio is the actual amount of water vapor present in the air per unit mass, usually expressed in grams of vapor per kilogram of dry air. Equation 3.2 indicates that evaporation is mainly proportional to the wind speed and the air-sea surface mixing ratio difference. When the air temperature is colder than the sea surface temperature, which would practically always occur in the higher latitudes, the exchange coefficient, C_E, varies little, and for all practical purposes, can be considered constant (Bunker, 1976, p. 1126). Bunker's equation was empirically based on ship observations over large areas, and could be inaccurate. But a recent experiment, using sophisticated technology in measuring the evaporation from the ocean, indicated very close agreement with his equation (Donelan, 1986, p. 1282).

The air-sea surface difference in the mixing ratio (Q_s - Q_{10}) is proportional to the sea-surface temperature. The greater the sea-surface temperature, the greater will be the mixing ratio difference and evaporation, all other variables remaining equal. For instance, at an air-sea temperature difference of 10°C,

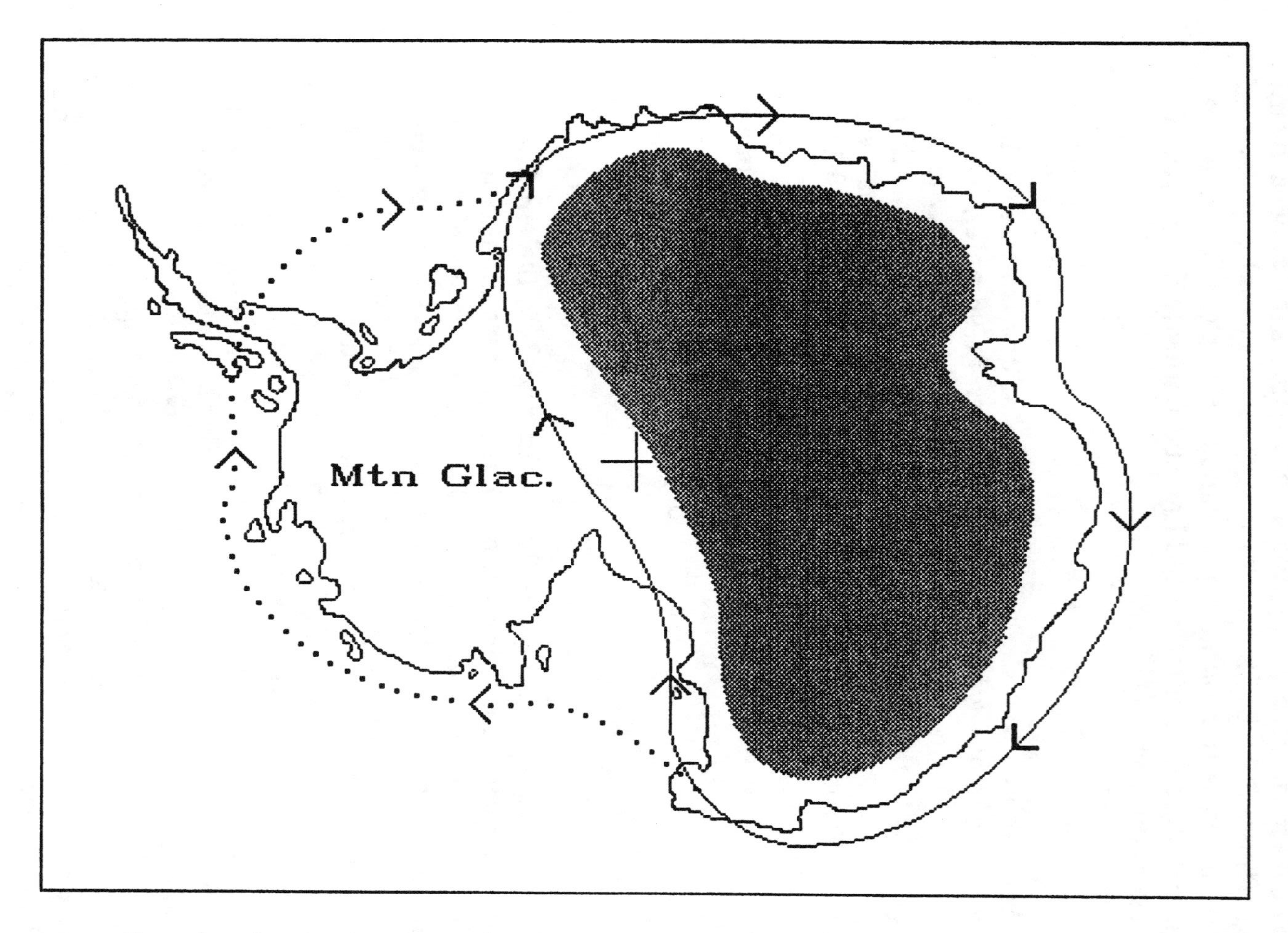

Figure 3.7 Postulated major and minor storm tracks and snow cover over Antarctica at the beginning of a post-Flood ice age. Notation the same as in Figure 3.6.

and a relative humidity of 50%, the term (Q_s - Q_{10}) would be 20.5 grams/kilogram at a sea-surface temperature of 30°C and only six grams/kilogram at a sea-surface temperature of 10°C. If the sea-surface temperature was 0°C, the term (Q_s - Q_{10}) would be approximately three grams/kilogram, which is one-seventh the value at 30°C. This example illustrates the strong dependence of sea-water evaporation on water temperature.

The mixing ratio difference (Q_s - Q_{10}) is especially high when cold, dry air blows over warm water. The stronger the wind, the higher the evaporation. Consequently, the highest evaporation in the post-Flood climate would be over the ocean east of Asia and North America. In the present climate, the greatest evaporation in the world is located in the same areas (Bunker, 1976, pp. 1129-1133; Budyko, 1978, p. 88). The evaporation is greatest in winter, when the land-ocean contrast is highest and the wind speed more intense. In the area of strongest evaporation over the Gulf Stream, 2.4 meters of water is evaporated in the fall and winter. Barnett (1978, p. 29) states:

> *Strong areas of heat uptake by the atmosphere occur during the winter off the eastern margins of the Northern Hemisphere continents, when cold, dry air suddenly encounters a relatively warm ocean.*

The high evaporation in the northwest Atlantic is in an advantageous location for rapid development of the Laurentide ice sheet.

The east coasts of Asia and North America also coincide with the major storm tracks in the post-Flood climate. The strong evaporation in these areas is mostly caused by east coast storms, because storms have strong cold and relatively dry west-to-northwest winds south of the storm center, as depicted in Figure 3.8. Once the cold, dry air encounters the warm water, the air is warmed and moistened rapidly, and quickly accumulates a large amount of water vapor. Since the air-sea temperature and mixing ratio differences decrease along its trajectory, the air soon looses its ability for evaporation. A recent atmospheric experiment, called GALE (Genesis of Atlantic Lows Experiment), off the east coast of North America, is trying to discover why storms moving out over the Gulf Stream become more intense than expected (Dirks et al., 1988). The extra intensification is probably caused by the latent heat energy released from the evaporated water. As expected, very high evaporation was measured in these storms, and the cold, dry air was rapidly modified along its trajectory over the warm water. Sometimes evaporation was so rapid that steam or "sea smoke" reduced the visibility to zero (Raman and Riordan, 1988, p. 163).

Figure 3.9 presents the average evaporation for the early post-Flood climate in the Northern Hemisphere, as determined from postulated major and minor storm tracks and values for the variables in Equation 3.2. High evaporation

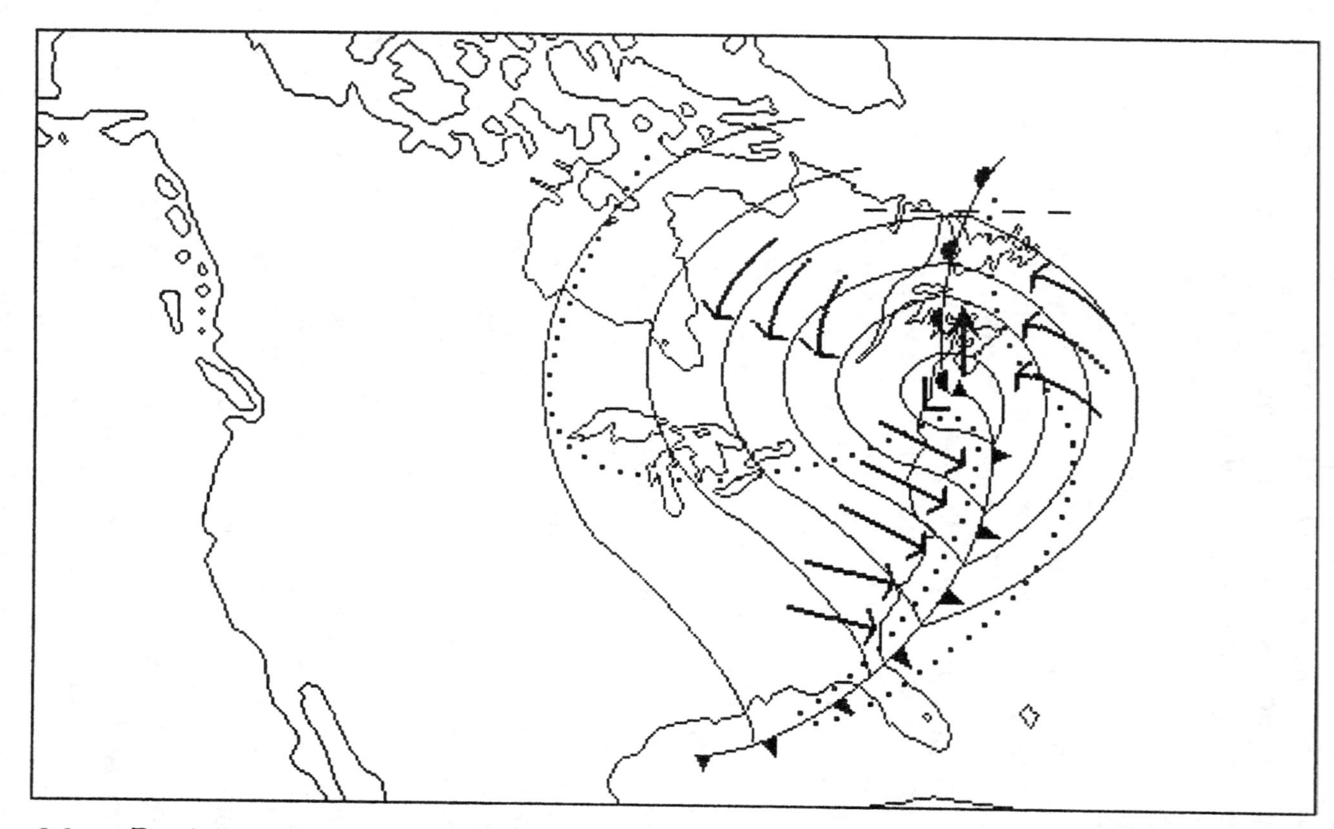

Figure 3.8 Precipitation and wind around an ice age northeaster. L is the storm center, the solid arrows are wind direction, and the dotted lines are the precipitation boundry. The dashed line is the location of the cross section in Figure 3.10.

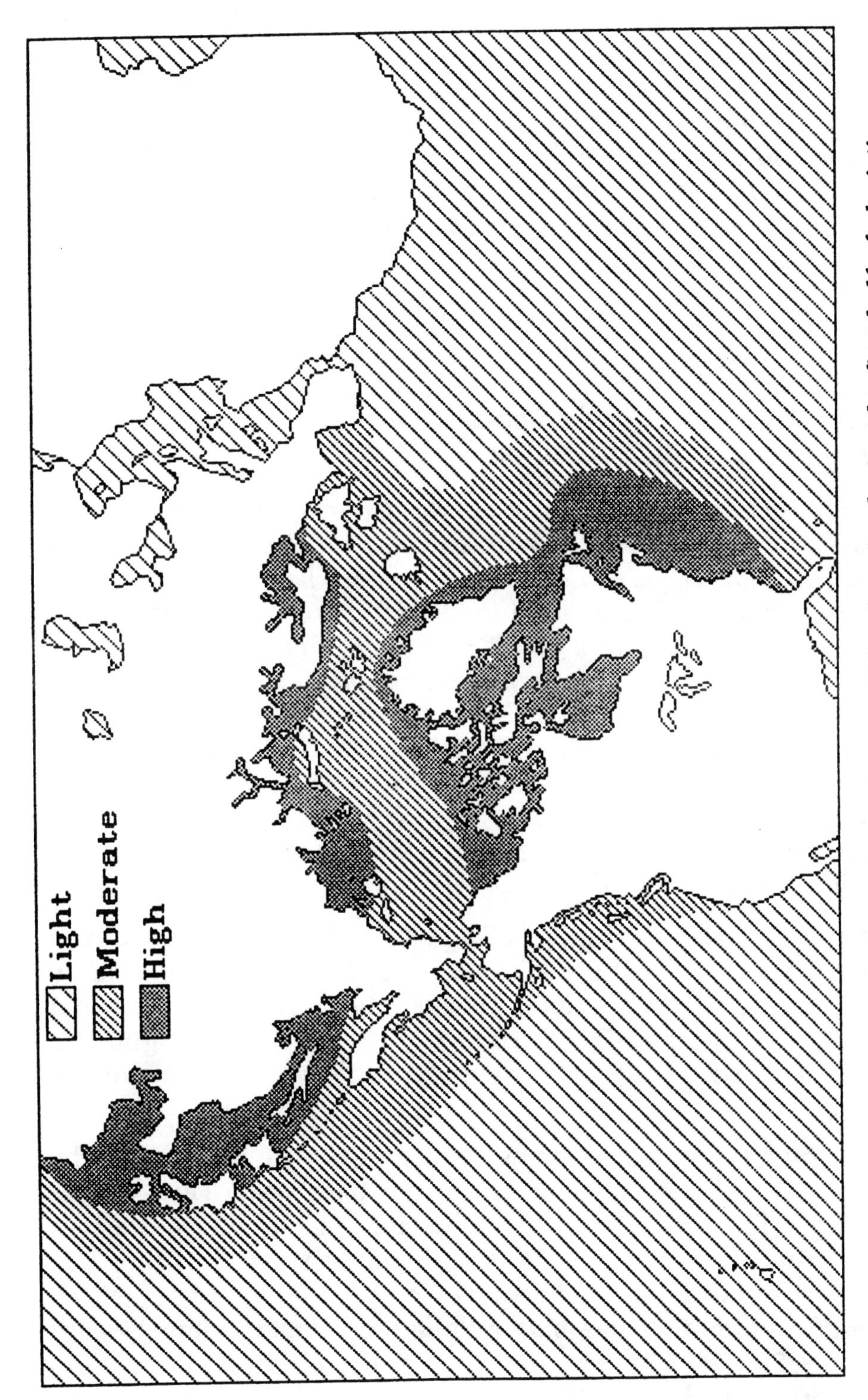

Figure 3.9 Postulated evaporation from the post-Flood ocean during the first half of glaciation.

would occur just east of Asia and North America. Due to a lack of intense storms, the Arctic Ocean would likely have mostly moderate evaporation, especially in areas farther from colder land. Light evaporation would be characteristic of the open ocean. The west coast of North America would likely have a light-to-moderate evaporation rate. This is because the predominant wind direction is westerly, which is too warm and moist for significant evaporation. In the Southern Hemisphere, cold air flowing off East Antarctica would cause high evaporation. This moisture would circulate around the storm center, and condense as snow over the continent. Thus, the greatest evaporation would be just off the Antarctic coast.

We are now ready to consider the snowblitz. The snowblitz is the concept that a snow cover or an ice sheet develops over **large** areas all at once, instead of in local mountainous areas, from which it subsequently flows outward (Sugden and John, 1976, pp. 129,130). One science writer (Calder, 1974, pp. 118,121) describes the snowblitz as follows:

> *In the snowblitz the ice sheet comes out of the sky and grows, not sideways, but from the bottom upwards. Like airborne troops, invading snowflakes seize whole counties in a single winter. The fact that they have come to stay does not become apparent, though, until the following summer. Then the snow that piled up on the meadows fails to melt completely. Instead it lies through the summer and autumn, reflecting the sunshine. It chills the air and guarantees more snow next winter. Thereafter, as fast as the snow can fall, the ice sheet gradually grows thicker over a huge area .... The cold comes instantly, but then the snow piles up for 5000 years at perhaps 18 inches a year. 'Instantly' may mean a hundred years or a single bad summer. So ice ages can start very suddenly — that is the implication of this research and of the snowblitz theory.*

The snowblitz method of glaciation is not very popular among scientists, even for northeast Canada, because the method is based on simplified energy assumptions and is close to catastrophic. However, the snowblitz is just what would have occurred in the post-Flood ice age, and would have engulfed a far larger area than that envisioned by the most radical proponents of the snowblitz theory.

In the post-Flood snowblitz, storms would often develop near the southeastern coast of the United States, and move northeastward. These storms would be very much like present-day "northeasters" that wrack the eastern seaboard of the United States and southeast Canada every year (Figure 3.8). Northeasters cause crippling ice, heavy snow, and gale force winds, with a resultant loss of life and more than a billion dollars in property damage each year (Dirks et al., 1988, p. 148). In these storms, cold, dry air south of the storm center becomes more unstable with time (Bryan, 1978, p. 23). The air moistens, warms, and circulates counterclockwise around the low-pressure center. It is then lifted up and over the denser, cold air to the north and west. The boundary between the cold and warm air is called either a cold or warm front, depending upon whether the cold air is displacing the warm air or vice versa. This boundary slopes westward, north and west of the storm center. The warm, moist air overrunning the cold air would be forced to precipitate, as depicted in Figure 3.10. This is a potent mechanism for heavy snow in the cold air over northeastern North America. In a typical winter-time storm, most of the precipitation falls in the colder air portion of the storm, with a narrow band of showers along the cold front. The air southwest of the low center is usually dry, unless close to the low-pressure center. This general precipitation pattern is depicted in Figure 3.8. As a result, most of the precipitation in post-Flood storms would fall over the cold land.

In the post-Flood climate, northeasters would carry much more water vapor, extend over a larger area, and develop much more frequently than they do today. To illustrate the potential for a snowblitz that turns into an ice age, we can conservatively assume that only one northeaster a week developed and moved up the east coast of North America. Let us assume that each storm dropped five centimeters (two inches) of water equivalent of snow over a broad area, which is only twice the snow in modern northeasters. At this rate, with no summer runoff, almost three meters of ice would accumulate in a year. In 200 years, the depth would be 580 meters (1,900 feet) over favorable areas of northeastern North America.

Ice would form from the snow by either of two mechanisms (Paterson, 1969, pp. 5-27). Snow in a cold environment slowly transforms to ice, at depth. The process involves mutual displacement of crystals, changes in size and shape of the crystals, and internal deformation. In the present-day Greenland ice sheet, this transformation is complete at about 100 meters. The second mechanism is the refreezing of meltwater during the warm season. This process operates on temperate glaciers, and would be more characteristic of the early post-Flood ice sheets while the ocean was still warm. Snow is changed to ice at shallow depths by this mechanism, once an adequate depth of snow and ice accumulate to absorb the latent heat of freezing, which is 80 calories/gram. On the Seward Glacier of Alaska, ice begins at a depth of 13 meters in the water-soaked zone, but higher up the glacier, in the dry, cold zone, it begins at a depth of 80 meters (Paterson, 1969, pp. 15-17). Once ice develops, it will tend to spread by flow, and gradually cover a larger area.

Early Distribution of Snow and Ice

From a consideration of the post-Flood climate, it has been established that cool, cloudy continents would exist adjacent to warm, higher-latitude oceans. The storm tracks would generally be locked in place, and snow would fall in the same localities time after time. An ice age would develop, but due

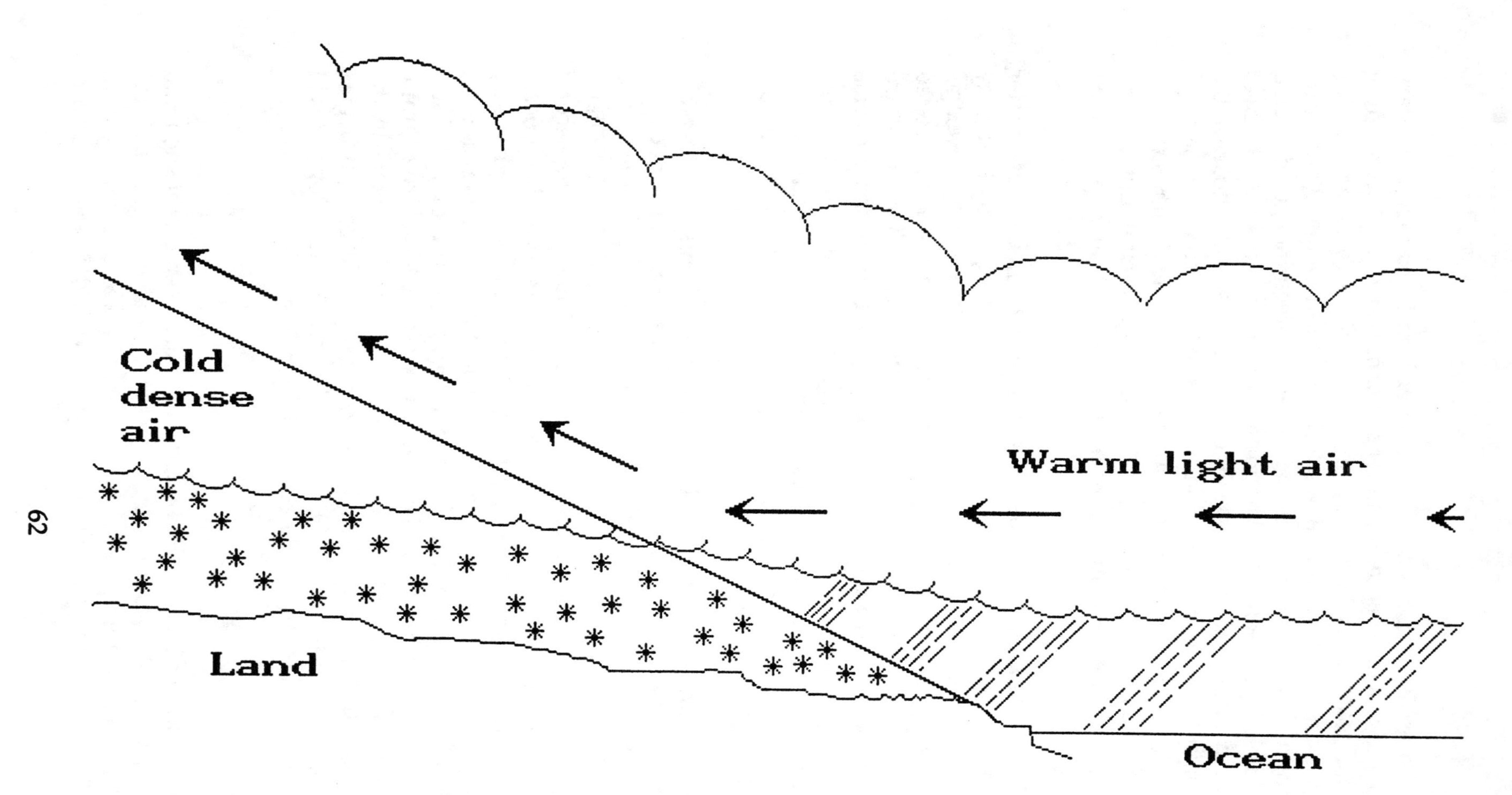

Figure 3.10 An atmospheric cross section through the northern part of a northeaster. The straight angled line is the boundary between cold and warm air.

to the unique climate, it would not develop in all areas at once. Figures 3.6 and 3.7 show the major areas of snow and ice accumulation early in the ice age, for the Northern and Southern Hemispheres, respectively.

High and mid-latitude continents close to a storm track would begin glaciating immediately after the Flood. Eastern Canada would be most favored, from the start. The interior of Canada would develop a permanent, but thinner snow cover. At this time, the north-central United States, down to 37°N latitude, would acquire a snow cover that would eventually turn into a thin ice sheet. This area would be cold in the summer, and located relatively close to the major storm track along the coast and a minor storm track just to the south. Volcanic activity immediately following the Flood would continue high. (High volcanism at the beginning of the ice age will be explored in Chapter 4.) High volcanism would be correlated to the coolest temperatures and highest precipitation in the north-central United States.

Lowlands, close to the warm ocean water, would not be glaciated at this time. Such areas would include the British Isles and northwest Europe, which would be bathed in warm westerly winds at the beginning of the ice age. Many mountainous regions in these areas would develop icecaps. The higher mountains of Scandinavia, the initial source for the Scandinavian ice sheet, would receive heavy snow, but the low elevations would be snow-free at the beginning. Scandinavia, moreover, was not in a favorable storm track at the beginning of the ice age. Figure 3.6 indicates that Scandinavia would receive decaying storms from a minor storm track to the west. Eventually, a short minor storm track would be induced just south of Scandinavia, due to the developing north-south temperature contrast.

Greenland and West Antarctica, although located at high latitude, would possess only mountain glaciers at this time. Greenland is mostly a low-level plain punctuated by mountains (Fristrup, 1966, pp. 237-248). Warm water would surround Greenland, keeping the lower elevations snow-free in summer. West Antarctica is made up of several mountain ranges, which after the Flood would be mountainous islands in warm water, even considering isostatic uplift (Bentley, 1965, p. 267). East Antarctica would mostly be above sea level (Bentley, 1965, p. 263), and would have a rapidly developing ice sheet at the beginning.

Many mid-latitude mountains would develop a snow cover due to their altitude, for instance, the Alps, the coastal mountains of western North America, the Rocky Mountains, and the southern Andes. The high tropical mountains would become glaciated at lower altitudes than the levels of their present glaciers, due to cooler tropical temperatures from volcanic dust and aerosols.

The warmth of the Arctic Ocean would cause the surrounding lands to be warmer and more moist than at present. This ocean would be a moisture source for cold continental areas further south, such as Keewatin, that are normally dry in the current climate.

Alaska and eastern Asia would be unique. The main storm track would be further off the east coast of Asia than the corresponding storm track over eastern North America. The cold, continental air from Asia would therefore be modified by the warm water north and west of the storm track. The heaviest precipitation would mostly fall in the ocean. In addition, the mountains of eastern Asia are much higher than in eastern North America. Continental air, forced down these mountains by predominantly west winds, would tend to warm and dry considerably. This is basically the principle behind the chinook or foehn wind. These conditions would combine to make eastern Asia an unfavorable area for an extensive lowland snow cover, although the mountains would be glaciated. Due to the warmth of the large North Pacific Ocean and the upper ridge over it, storms would be steered into Alaska. By the time they arrived, they would have lost most of their thermal contrast, due to the factors mentioned above for Asia, and also due to the warm Arctic Ocean. Consequently, the lowlands of Alaska would be bathed in relatively warm air, but the mountains would receive heavy snow. Figure 3.11 shows the above variables that would combine to cause only mountain glaciers in Alaska and eastern Asia.

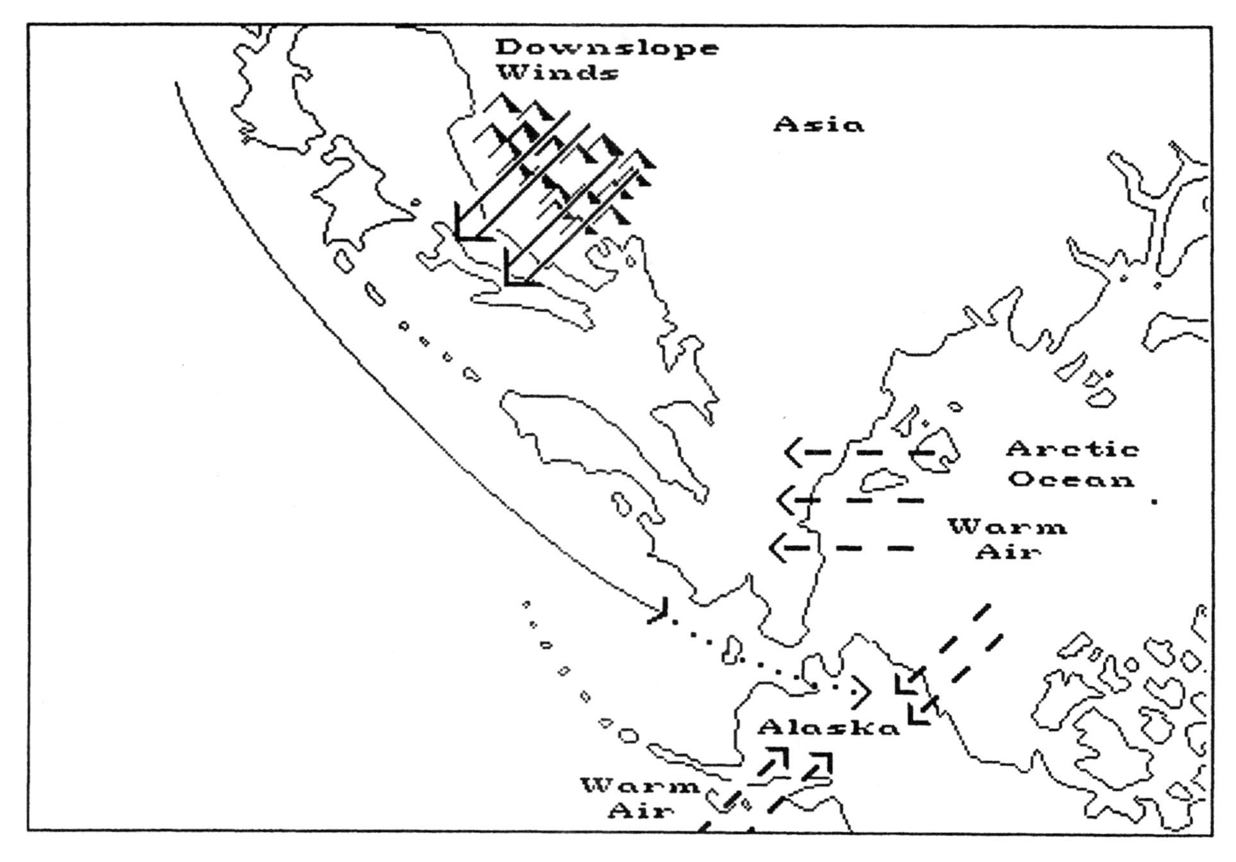

Figure 3.11 Schematic illustrating reason why lowlands of Alaska and eastern Asia were not glaciated. Solid line represents the main storm track and dotted line a minor storm track. Double arrows represents westerly winds sinking down the mountains of east Asia. Dashed lines indicate the average movement of warm moist air.

CHAPTER 4

PROGRESSION OF THE ICE AGE

Earlier we established that a rapid initiation of a snow cover and a thin ice sheet was caused by the unique climate immediately following the Genesis Flood. But, for a full-blown ice age, cooler summers and much higher snowfall must be sustained. Can these conditions be maintained for a lengthy period? This chapter will focus on the continuing climate from the initial inception of glaciation to nearly the time of glacial maximum. As the ice age progressed, unusual plant and animal associations occurred, and the woolly mammoth found a suitable home in Siberia and Alaska.

Volcanic Reinforcement

The volcanic dust and aerosols that initiated the post-Flood ice age would gradually settle out. But the earth may be expected to have continued tectonically unstable, with a high level of volcanism for years after the Flood, similar to the aftershocks from a large earthquake. Figure 4.1 depicts the postulated volcanism from the time of the Flood to glacial maximum, which is defined as the time the largest volume of ice covered the land. Since volcanic eruptions are episodic, peaks and lulls would be superimposed on a gradual decline as the earth slowly returned to the present level of geophysical equilibrium. High volcanism would reinforce the initial cooling immediately following the Flood.

Surface sediments deposited soon after the Flood attest to extensive tectonic movements and volcanism. Charlesworth (1957, p. 601) writes: "... signs of Pleistocene vulcanicity and earth-movements are visible in all parts of the world." In the context of the Flood model, Whitcomb and Morris (1961, p. 312) add:

> *Evidently the tectonic and volcanic disturbances which played such a large part in the initiation of the Flood, as well as in the uplift of the land at its close, continued with only gradually lessening intensity for many centuries thereafter.*

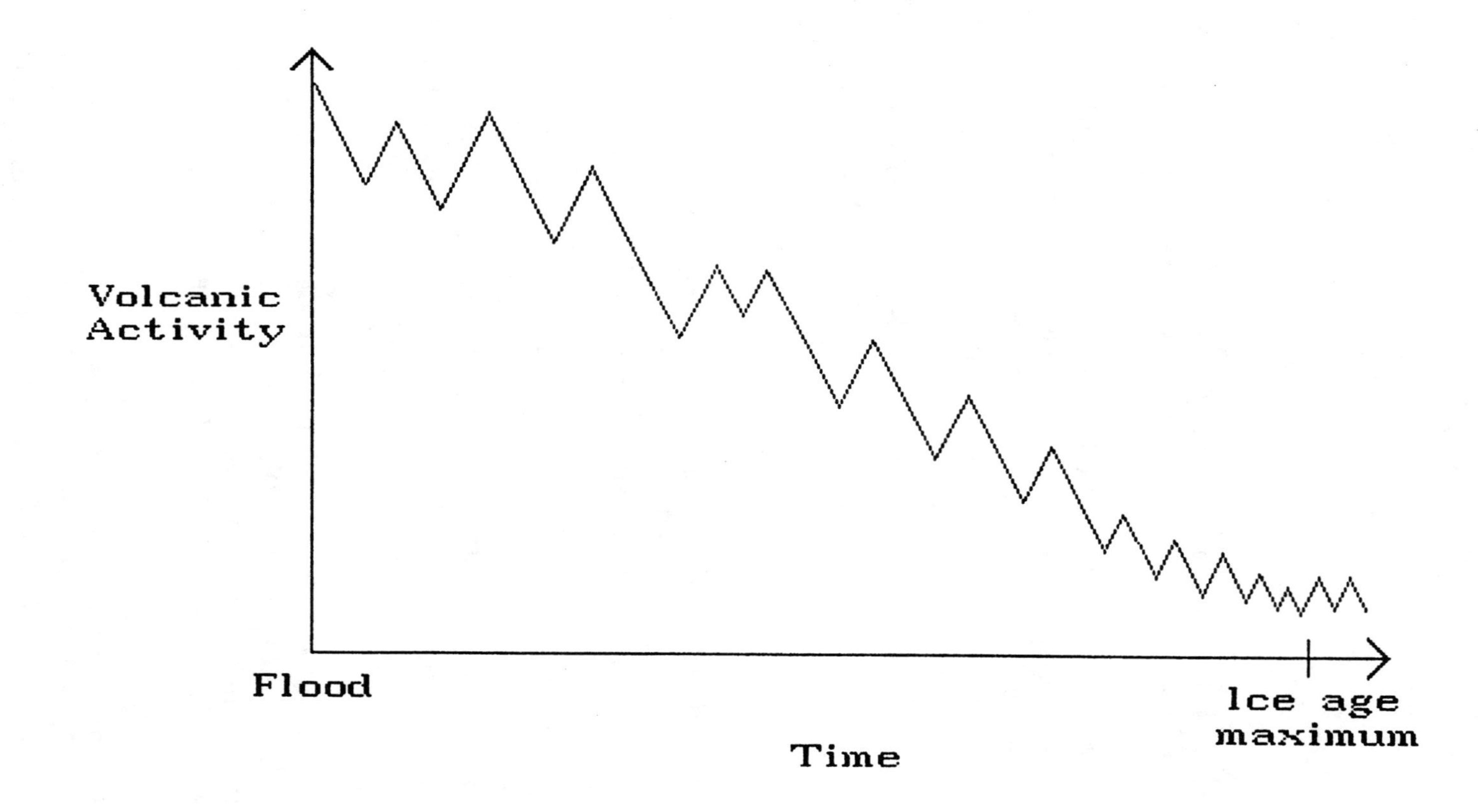

Figure 4.1 Postulated post-Flood volcanism.

Although people have been impressed by recent volcanic eruptions, these are insignificant compared to post-Flood eruptions (Kerr, 1989b, p. 128). Mount St. Helens, which erupted in 1980, seemed impressive. A dry "fog" traveled as far eastward as central Montana that blocked out much of the sunlight for two days. However, Mount St. Helens was small compared to other eruptions of the past 300 years. The largest of these eruptions include Laki, Iceland, in 1783; Tambora, in 1815; and Krakatoa, in 1883. But these modern eruptions are considered so insignificant compared to volcanic explosions in the more remote past, that the volcanic ash transported away from the immediate vicinity of their vents is not expected to be discernible in the future (Froggatt et al., 1986, p. 578).

The ice age volcanoes left huge deposits of ash. In the western United States alone, more than 68 ash falls, coinciding with the ice age, have been recognized (Izett, 1981). The size of the ash beds indicate that some of these eruptions were gigantic. An exceptionally large ice age eruption was recently discovered in New Zealand (Froggatt et al., 1986). This eruption spread a distinct layer of ash over at least ten million square kilometers of the South Pacific Ocean. Based on correlations with modern volcanic eruptions, the dust and aerosol loading from the largest post-Flood volcanoes was on the order of the atmospheric contamination postulated for the worst nuclear winter scenarios. In these scenarios, almost all sunlight is blocked out over the entire world (Rampino et al., 1985; Froggatt et al., 1986, p. 581). The popular interpretation extends all these ice age eruptions into a time span of several million years, and hence obscures their significance for an ice age. Telescoping all the ice age eruptions into a short period after the Flood assures that cool summer temperatures, due to volcanism, would continue over mid and high latitude continents.

Another likely source of volcanic dust and aerosols is basaltic lava flows, such as those found on the Columbian Plateau in the northwest United States. These flows are now believed to have introduced significant amounts of aerosols into the upper atmosphere, partly by local explosive volcanism. It is estimated that a total of around 200,000 km^3 of basalt accumulated rapidly from up to 150 flows on the Columbian Plateau (Hooper, 1982). For instance, the Roza member of the Columbian sequence is estimated to have spread to a distance of 300 kilometers in just a few days.

Earlier investigators assumed that emission plumes from these relatively quiet basaltic eruptions did not remain in the atmosphere long. Modern evidence suggests this is not true (Stothers et al., 1986). The Laki basaltic fissure eruption on Iceland, in 1783, produced a long-lasting dry fog in northwest Europe. The sulfuric acid haze from Laki has been estimated to be the cause of famine and epidemics resulting from a 5°C cooling of the Northern Hemisphere (Schneider, 1983; Devine et al., 1984; Weisburd, 1987). The highest acidity level in Greenland ice cores over the past 1,000 years corresponds to the Laki eruption (Bradley, 1985, pp. 143,144). The acidity level represents the amount of aerosols placed in the upper atmosphere by volcanic eruptions.

Strong atmospheric convection currents, similar to those that occur in thunderstorms, generated by the hot lava flow, together with the explosive activity that did occur, are the likely mechanisms for introducing volcanic dust and aerosols into the upper atmosphere (Devine et al., 1984, p. 6321; Stothers et al., 1986). Furthermore, debris from this type of eruption contains about ten times the amount of sulfur compounds per cubic meter than does debris from the more explosive eruptions. Thus, basaltic lava flows may have even more potential for causing climatic cooling than the more explosive eruptions.

There is a question as to whether large basalt lava plateaus, which are found in many areas of the world, are Flood or post-Flood deposits. Standard geological dating places these basaltic plateaus in the pre-Quaternary portion of the standard time scale—the portion containing what the creationist model considers to be Flood deposits. The huge Deccan lava flows in India are six times the size of the Columbian Plateau flows, and cover an area the size of France. They are not precisely dated, but according to potassium-argon dating, they range from 30 to 80 million years old in the standard time scale (Weisburd, 1987). Within the Creation-Flood model, at least some of these flows may be post-Flood. If they are fresh looking and show no surface signs of being erupted under the sea, such as the existence of pillow lavas, they probably are post-Flood. Any one lava plateau may have begun during the Flood, and continued forming afterwards. Nevins (1974) believes the volcanic strata of the John Day Country of northeast Oregon, which is part of the Columbian Lava Plateau, is post-Flood, although geologists date it from 10,000,000 to 50,000,000 years old (Baldwin, 1964, p. 104).

In summary, sufficient extended volcanism likely continued after the Flood, to provide adequate volcanic dust and aerosols for centuries of glaciation (Figure 4.1). During volcanic lulls, more sunlight would penetrate to the surface, but the higher albedo of greater cloudiness than at present, and of fresh snow, as well as the effect of decreasing carbon dioxide, would modify the heating of the atmosphere to a minor increase. Variable volcanism would play a significant role at the margins of the ice sheets, by causing fluctuations of the ice edge. High volcanic dust and aerosol loading would cause glacial advances, while low volcanism would cause glacial retreats.

Post-Flood Ocean Circulation

During glaciation, not only would the mid-latitude continents continue cold, but, also, the adjacent oceans would remain warm. As a result, strong evaporation, especially during storms, would ensure progressive buildup and expansion of the ice sheets. A warm North Atlantic Ocean is a phenomenon that can only be hoped for by uniformitarian scientists, but its importance as the moisture source for glaciation is recognized (Ruddiman and McIntyre, 1979).

Why would the oceans adjacent to cold continents remain warm? At the beginning of the ice age, the oceans, as a result of mixing during the Flood, were generally the same warm temperature from top to bottom, and from pole to pole. As surface water cooled and became denser at mid and high latitudes, the water would sink, and be replaced by lighter, warm water from below, causing warm surface water temperatures to prevail at mid and high latitudes for a long time.

Oxygen isotope changes in foraminifera indicate that the bottom water temperature was likely relatively warm at the end of the Flood and also during the beginning of the ice age: "The oxygen isotope and other data point to the startling conclusion that the deep ocean was much warmer than now during most of the last 100 million years" (Anonymous, 1978, p. 40). For example, Paleocene ocean-bottom temperatures are claimed in uniformitarian calculations to have been as warm as 55°F. Late Cretaceous oceans are specified a little warmer than Paleocene (Frakes, 1979, p. 190). Normally, pre-Quaternary sediments are classified as Flood deposits. However, the foraminifera shells are unconsolidated on the bottom of the ocean, and likely were deposited in the late stages of the Flood, and in the ice age (see Chapter 8). Although warmer than the present ocean, these temperatures are significantly cooler than claimed, in this monograph, for the ocean temperature at the beginning of the ice age (see Chapter 5). Given the many variables and assumptions in oxygen isotope temperature estimates, we should not use the uniformitarian numbers quantitatively, but would consider their qualitative trend to be in the right direction.

The cooler water, formed at the surface in the post-Flood oceans, would continue to sink and spread out along the bottom, gradually filling all the ocean basins in the world (see Figure A1.1). This overturning would be more rapid than at present, because of the large density contrast between the chilled and highly saline (due to evaporation) surface water, and the warm water below the surface. In today's climate, the cold water found worldwide just below the thermocline, is formed at the surface in two areas of the world—just off the coast of Antarctica and in the Norwegian and Greenland Seas of the North Atlantic Ocean (Kennett, 1982, pp. 250-257). The northern North Pacific does not form cold deep water, because the salinity, which also determines the water density, is too low. The deep-Pacific cold water is maintained by Antarctic bottom water. The areas of deep water formation are relatively small, and the cold water is generated mainly during winter. As a result, the turnover time of the ocean is very slow at present—about 1,000 years.

In the early post-Flood climate, the downwelling of ocean water would occur over a much broader area of the mid and high-latitude ocean than it does at present. Generally, this area would correspond to the area of moderate-to-high evaporation, as estimated in Figure 3.9. This high rate of downwelling must be balanced by concomitant large upwelling in other areas of the ocean. This rapid turnover of ocean water would be significant for the production of biogenic sediments on the ocean bottom. These sediments appear to be a creationist problem because of the presumed long time to form them, according to present rates (Roth, 1985). But, the post-Flood ocean circulation can potentially account for most of these sediments (see Chapter 8).

At the same time, as the ocean mixes vertically, a surface circulation would be induced by the low-level atmospheric winds, that would transport warm water into the area of the main storm tracks off the east coast of North America and Asia. Average low-level winds, which are usually parallel to the storm tracks, are the primary driving force for modern-day surface ocean currents (Kennett, 1982, p. 240). Currents similar to the Gulf Stream, the Kuroshio Current off the east coast of Asia, and the Antarctic Circumpolar Current, would be generated in the post-Flood climate. More storms, all year long, off the east coasts of North America and Asia, and probably stronger surface winds in these storms due to a greater temperature difference, likely would cause stronger ocean currents off the east coasts. These strong currents would also be aided by the intensified vertical circulation. Due to the coriolis force, the Gulf Stream and the Kuroshio Currents would tend to turn clockwise and form the eastern portion of large circular gyres, similar to the present situation in the North Atlantic and North Pacific Oceans. Figure 4.2 shows the likely ocean circulation and areas of sinking and upwelling water in the North Atlantic Ocean during the post-Flood climate.

Because of the vertical and horizontal water exchanges, warm water would remain juxtaposed with the developing ice sheets for a considerable time. But, during this time, the higher latitude ocean surface would gradually cool as colder water accumulated in the ocean depths. Surface cooling would slowly spread to the mid latitudes, as the ice age progressed. As a result, the storm tracks would slowly shift. The ice-accumulation rate would diminish slowly in areas that were near the initial storm tracks—for instance, over the eastern Laurentide ice sheet. The shifting storm tracks would increase the snowfall on Greenland, the British Isles, and Scandinavia.

Warm, Ice-free Arctic Ocean

At the beginning of the ice age, the temperature of the Arctic Ocean would be warm. Because of its polar location, it would quickly lose heat by evaporation and conduction to the atmosphere, resulting in rapid turnover. Large amounts of heat and moisture would be added to the Arctic atmosphere

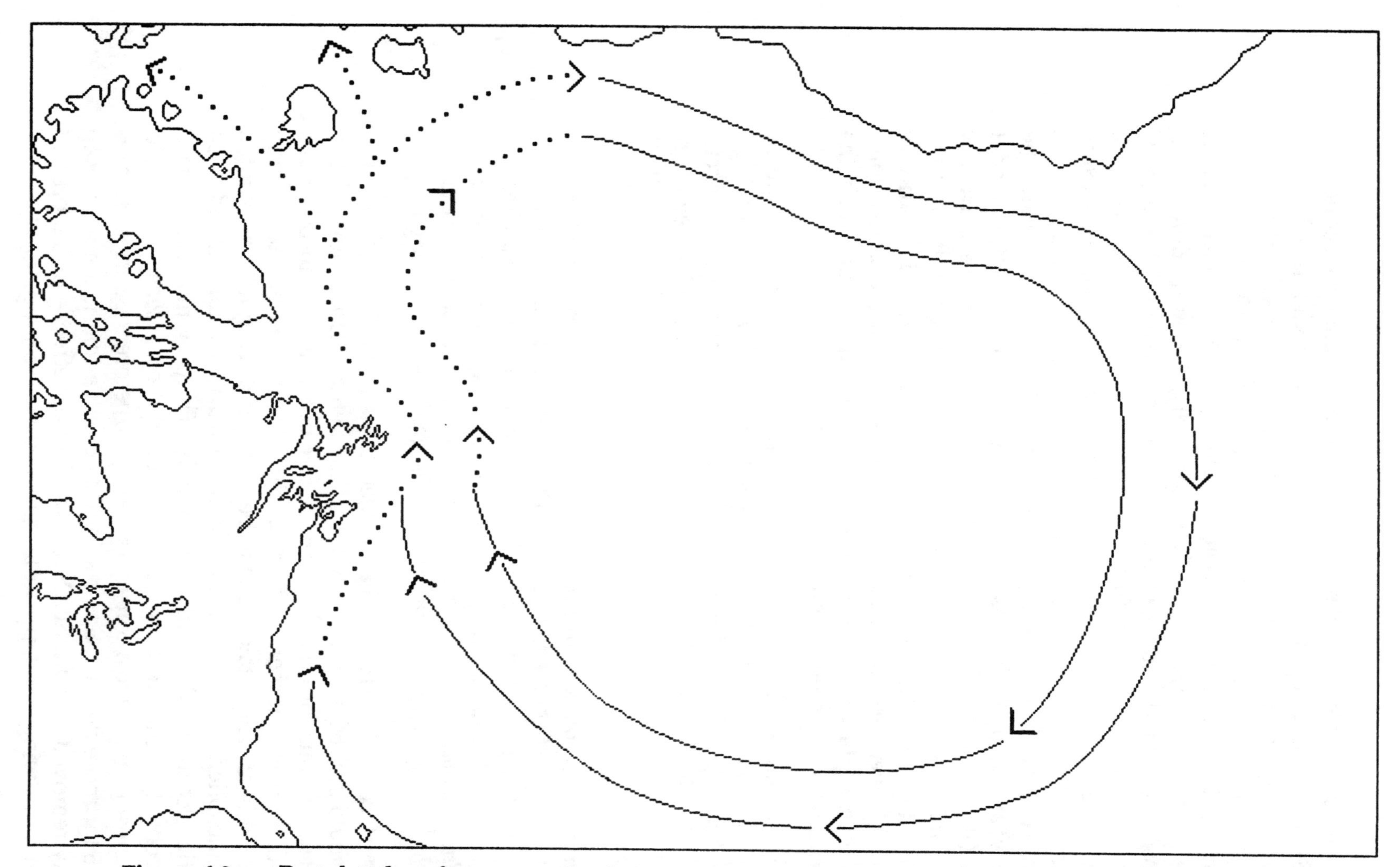

Figure 4.2 Postulated surface ocean circulation and areas of sinking and upwelling water for the North Atlantic during the post-Flood ice age. Dotted lines represent sinking water and solid lines represent upwelling water.

for an extensive time. This would have impressive climatic consequences. Newson (1973) experimented with a general circulation model, in which the Arctic Ocean sea icecap was removed. The ocean temperature was held constant at the freezing point of sea water. The results were dramatic. The winter-time air over the Arctic Ocean warmed 20 to 40°C, while the air over Canada and Siberia warmed 10°C to 30°C (Figure 4.3). Unexpectedly, the simulation caused about a 5°C cooling over the mid-latitude continents between 30 and 50°N latitude. Decreased westerly wind from a weaker north-south temperature difference, and more stationary weather systems were suggested as the reason. A reduced westerly flow results in less warm air penetration from the ocean, and more infrared radiational cooling of the continental interiors during the winter. Warshaw and Rapp (1973), using a different general circulation model than Newson (1973), reported similar findings. The atmosphere markedly decreased in stability over the Arctic Ocean, which would result in much greater precipitation. In the early post-Flood climate, the high-latitude warming would be even more significant than indicated by these simulations, because the ocean surface temperature would be much warmer than the freezing temperatures assumed in making the simulations.

The more the evaporation, the more the precipitation, and this would be more pronounced in the higher latitudes. This is the basis of Donn and Ewing's (1968) ice-age theory briefly mentioned in Chapter 1. A warm, ice-free Arctic Ocean can explain glaciation in high latitude "polar deserts," like Keewatin, which are problematical for uniformitarian theories. Donn and Ewing (1968, pp. 102,103) state:

> *It is difficult to imagine a source of moisture for the maintenance of the prominent northwestward extension [to the Keewatin district] of the Canadian ice sheet in view of the pronounced barrier effect of the large Laurentide ice sheet to the south. It is also difficult to explain the presence of fairly thick ice over the northwestern portion of the archipelago [Queen Elizabeth Islands] by simple movement from the south as has been argued.*

After the surface of the Arctic Ocean cooled to near the freezing point of sea water, it would still take a relatively long time before sea ice would form. There are several reasons for this. First, an ice-free ocean would absorb much more solar radiation in summer, and warm significantly above the freezing point. This stored heat would take time to be released during fall and winter. Second, the atmosphere in winter would be much warmer than it is today, so that the Arctic Ocean would cool more slowly. Third, when the surface temperature cooled to the freezing point during the cold season, the cold surface water must be mixed to a considerable depth, before the surface freezes (see Chapter 6 for more details). Some scientists believe that if the sea icecap were suddenly removed, the Arctic Ocean would not refreeze in the present climate (Donn and Ewing, 1968, pp. 101,102; Fletcher, 1968, pp. 98,99).

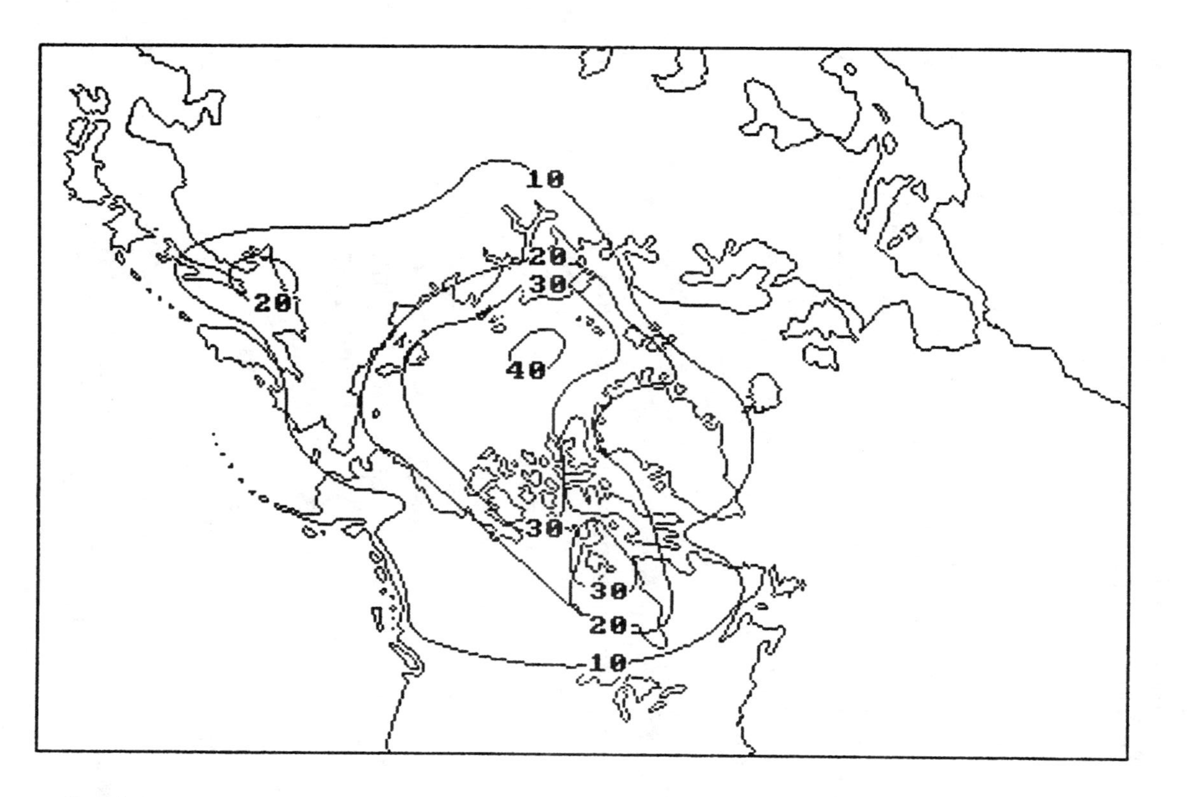

Figure 4.3 Surface temperature warming (° C) during winter due to an ice-free Arctic ocean, which was set at the freezing point of sea water (redrawn from Newson, 1973).

Expansion of Snow and Ice

The point of the above discussion is that the pattern favoring initial glaciation would be maintained, and only gradually change, as the oceans cooled. Based on the amount of heat given off by the warm ocean, a post-Flood ice age would be mild—that is, characterized by "warm" winters and cool summers. The ice sheets would be temperate, wet-based, and move rapidly (see Chapter 7). They would grow and spread into areas that were too warm for a perennial snow cover at the beginning of the ice age.

Figure 4.4 estimates the area covered by ice in the Northern Hemisphere, and the storm tracks characteristic of the mid point of the ice age. Most of Hudson Bay probably would be frozen over with ice sheets converging on it from the east and west. Mountain glaciers in western North America would descend to lower altitudes, and glaciation would spread farther south into the Sierra Nevada Mountains. The north-central United States, which would have been initially glaciated, would be vulnerable to melting, during volcanic lulls, because of its southerly latitude.

With respect to Europe, as the higher latitude ocean surface cooled, more storms would assault Scandinavia. The Baltic Sea probably would be frozen over by this time, with the Scandinavian ice sheet plunging into it. The initially minor storm track south of the ice sheet would become major, due to an enhanced north-south temperature difference. The Scandinavian ice sheet, and the icecap over the Alps, would be expanding rapidly at this time. Ice in northern Germany and Poland probably developed during the middle of the ice age, eventually merging with the Scandinavian ice sheet. The British Isles would be very slow in forming an ice sheet, due to the warm ocean; but by the middle of the glacial buildup, highland icecaps would have been established in the northern portions.

The mountain icecaps on Greenland would grow rapidly, and descend to lower elevations, coalescing into the incipient Greenland ice sheet.

The storm track around Antarctica would be stable, with a very gradual northward expansion, as the ocean slowly cooled adjacent to the continent. The East Antarctica ice sheet would continue growing rapidly, and the mountain icecaps in West Antarctica would be descending and spreading out over the sea.

The northern North Pacific would cool more slowly than the northern North Atlantic, because of its larger size. Consequently, little change in the main storm track in the North Pacific is expected. The size of the warm Pacific, as well as the average position of the main storm track and the geography of eastern Asia (as discussed at the end of Chapter 3), may be the reason why 90% of the ice in the Northern Hemisphere accumulated around the North

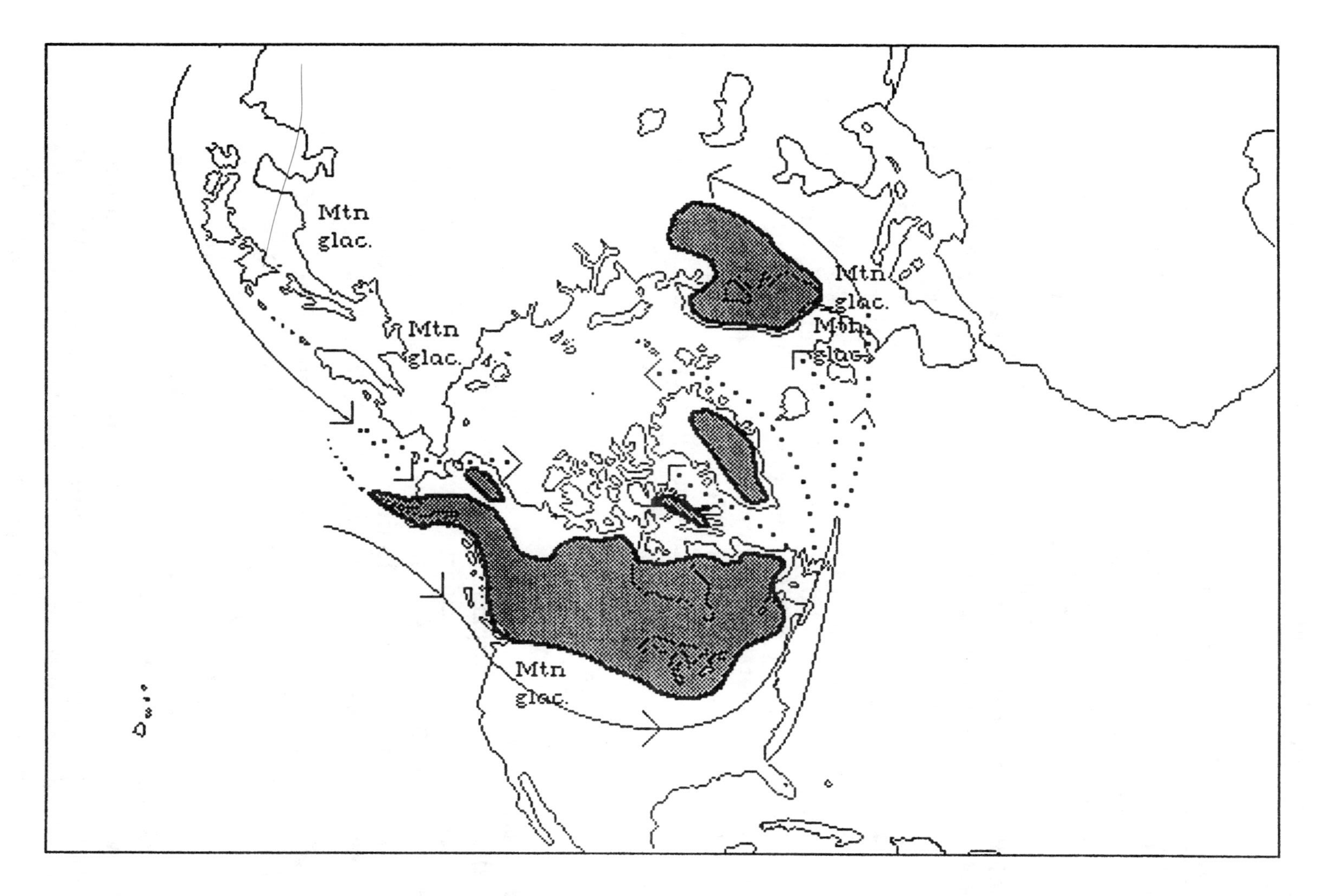

Figure 4.4 Distribution of snow and ice and storm tracks about midway towards glacial maximum. Notation same as in Figure 3.6.

Atlantic (Charlesworth, 1957, p. 1146). The lack of ice over the lowlands of eastern Asia and Alaska is difficult to explain within the uniformitarian framework.

Pluvial Lakes and Well-Watered Deserts

In the post-Flood climate, heavy precipitation would occur south of the ice sheets, in the Northern Hemisphere. Overwhelming scientific evidence is found for a wet climate, in regions that are now desert and semi-arid. Large lakes filled the basins of the arid southwestern United States (Figure 4.5). We know this from ancient shore lines found high on the hills and mountains surrounding the lakes. For instance, ancient Great Salt Lake, or Lake Bonneville, as it is called, was about 285 meters deeper and 17 times larger at maximum extent, during the ice age. Another lake covered large sections of western Nevada, and smaller lakes filled the currently hot basins of southeast California, such as Death Valley. The ice-age fauna and flora, from the southwestern United States, indicate a relatively recent cooler and wetter climate (Spaulding et al., 1983; Spaulding, 1985). This evidence is partially based on fossils and actual plant debris from preserved packrat middens (post-Flood), which indicate that pigmy conifers and woodland vegetation grew in the lower deserts—even in Northern Mexico, and subalpine conifers, including Douglas Fir, inhabited the higher deserts. The wetter climate is called the pluvial period by paleoclimatologists, and in the southwestern United States occurred during the ice age, since ancient shore lines in the Owens Valley of eastern California have been connected to end moraines of former Sierra Nevada glaciers (Flint, 1971, p. 444).

Pluvial lakes are also found in many other now dry areas of the world—specifically Mexico, the antiplano of South America, Australia, Africa, and western and central Asia. A particularly impressive example of a pluvial lake is ancient Lake Chad, in north Africa. "Lake Chad was formerly nearly 1,000 km long, requiring a water intake 16 times greater than at present, in an area that is now mostly desert ..." (Sutcliffe, 1985, p. 22).

The eastern Sahara Desert is now known to have been well-watered not very long ago. New technology allows radio-wave observation through the dry, featureless sand of the desert (McCauley et al., 1982). Scientists were amazed to find an old drainage network, with some channels as large as the Nile River Valley. Most amazing of all, the eastern Sahara Desert now receives rain at any one locality only once every 30 to 50 years! Fossils of many animals have been discovered, including the elephant, hippopotamus, buffalo, crocodile, giraffe, antelope, and rhinoceros (Kerr, 1984; Pachur and Kröpelin, 1987). Some of these animals are aquatic, implying very wet conditions. This wet climate occurred rather recently, as suggested by degenerate crocodiles that still survive in isolated western Sahara lakes (Charlesworth, 1957, p. 1113).

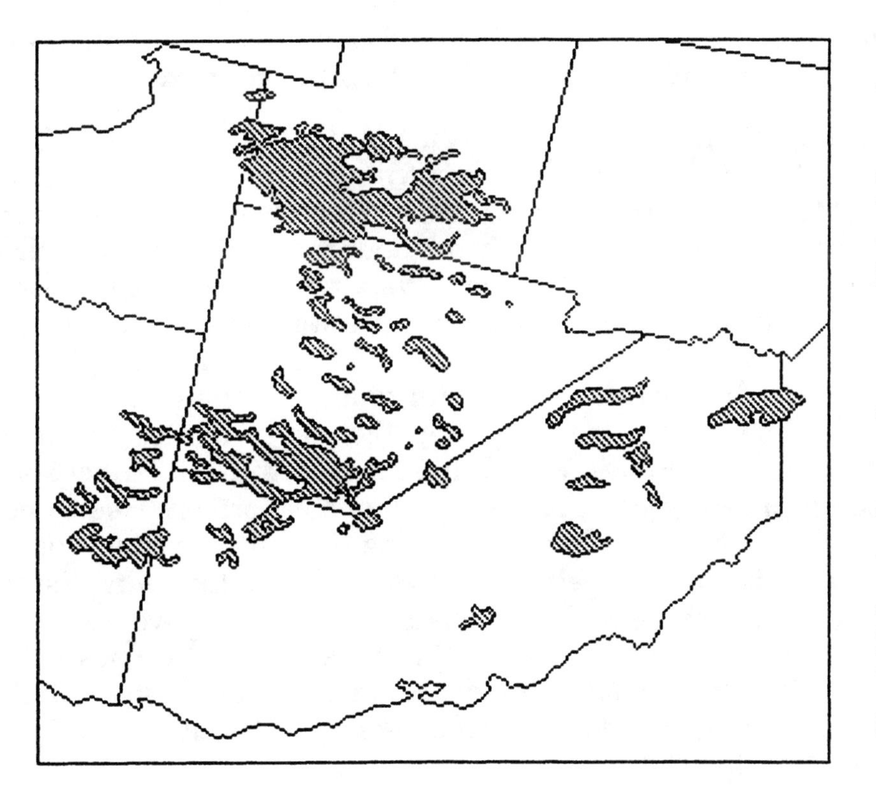

Figure 4.5 Pluvial lakes in the southwestern United States during the ice age.

Rock pictures and carvings depicting these animals are well-preserved, and so cannot be very old (Nilsson, 1983, p. 342). These pictures not only show that man once lived in the Sahara Desert, but also that the pluvial period is mainly a post-Flood phenomenon.

Needless to say, pluvial lakes and well-watered deserts are difficult to explain, on uniformitarian principles. Flint admits the serious problem of explaining the quantity of rain needed to satisfy the geological observations (Flint, 1971, pp. 444,445). Hydrologic calculations for the amount of rain necessary to fill and maintain pluvial lakes in the American Southwest are very complicated, and range from double to ten times the current rainfall (Smith and Street-Perrott, 1983, pp. 191,192). More refined calculations, based on 10°C cooler temperatures and reduced evaporation typical of the ice age climate, indicated that about six times more runoff from the surrounding drainage basin of Great Salt Lake was required (Smith and Street-Perrott, 1983, p. 195). No climate simulation has ever shown such a large increase in rainfall for ice age conditions. Practically all of them indicate dry, cold conditions for the mid latitudes at maximum glaciation, and even before maximum.

The initial filling of pluvial lakes, and some of the ancient large drainage features in currently dry regions, can be attributed to the Genesis Flood (Whitcomb and Morris, 1961, pp. 313-317). As the Flood waters drained, water would naturally remain in depressions throughout the world. Many of these lakes in currently arid regions would slowly evaporate, but not as fast as the modern climate would indicate. Higher, ice-age precipitation would maintain high lake levels and large river runoff. Calculations in the next chapter will show that the amount of moisture available for rainfall in non-glaciated areas was at least three times higher than today. At the end of the ice age, much colder winters, at higher latitudes, would drive the storm track farther south than in the modern climate (see Chapter 6). Many of the Northern Hemisphere deserts, that were recently well-watered, are along the southern fringe, or just south of the modern, winter-rain belt. A southward shift of the average storm track after glacial maximum—say five or ten degrees latitude—would greatly increase rainfall in these now dry locations. The above features of a post-Flood ice age would explain the abundant evidence, in the southwestern United States, of "... an environment and ecology remarkably different from today's" (Spaulding et al., 1983, p. 259).

Disharmonious Associations

One of the more puzzling problems for uniformitarian theories of the ice age is disharmonious associations of fossils, in which species from different climatic regimes are juxtaposed. For example, a hippopotamus fossil found together with a reindeer fossil. Reindeer prefer cold climates, and hippopotamuses love warmth. South of the former ice sheets in North America and Europe, fossils display a unique climatic mix. Reindeer, musk oxen, and woolly mammoths are found in this zone, which is understandable, since ice sheets covered the north. But fossils of warmth-loving animals are also found there. For example, hippopotamus fossils have been unearthed in England, France, and Germany (Nilsson, 1983, pp. 223-233; Sutcliffe, 1985, p. 24). Sutcliffe (1985, p. 120) writes:

> *Finding conditions so favourable the hippopotamus (today an inhabitant of the equatorial regions) had been able to spread northwards throughout most of England and Wales, up to an altitude of 400 meters on the now bleak Yorkshire moors ....*

These associations are highly unlikely in today's climate. There are no modern examples of this unique, ice-age biological distribution (Guthrie, 1984).

To account for hippopotamus fossils so far north, it has been postulated that they lived during a warm, interglacial period. We live in a "warm," interglacial period today, and today's interglacial climate is much too cold for hippopotamuses to live in northwest Europe. Furthermore, they are often found in the same sediment layer with animals that preferred the cold, although Sutcliffe (1985, p. 24) disputes this. But Grayson (1984a, p. 16) informs us:

> *In the valley of the Thames [southern England], for instance, woolly mammoth, woolly rhinoceros, musk ox, reindeer (Rangifer tarandus), hippopotamus (Hippopotamus amphibius), and cave lion (Felis leo spelaea) had all been found by 1855 in stratigraphic contexts that seemed to indicate contemporaneity ....*

Disharmonious associations are not rare, but are common, and include a wide variety of plants, animals, and insects. Graham and Lundelius (1984, p. 224) state:

> *Late Pleistocene communities were characterized by the coexistence of species that today are allopatric [not climatically associated] and presumably ecologically incompatible .... Disharmonious associations have been documented for late Pleistocene floras ..., terrestrial invertebrates ..., lower vertebrates ..., birds ..., and mammals ....*

It should be added, that this non-uniformity occurs **throughout** the Pleistocene, and not just in the Late Pleistocene. It should be noted that, in the uniformitarian time scale, the late Pleistocene contains most of the ice-age sediments (Sugden and John, 1976, p. 138), and, therefore, most of the ice-age fossils. The obvious climatic implication of disharmonious associations, assuming animals had similar climatic tolerances as today (in some cases this is a big assumption), is aptly stated by Grayson (1984a, p. 18):

> *If the musk ox required cold, and the hippopotamus required warmth, and the stratigraphic evidence implied that they had coexisted, then a*

straightforward reading of all this information could imply that glacial climates had not, as most felt, been marked by severe winters, but had instead been equable.

To explain the close association of animals from vastly different climatic regimes, some researchers postulate the mixing of fossils from glacial periods with those from interglacial periods (assuming the warmth-loving animals could migrate so far north). Nilsson states: "The occurrences of such taxa as hippopotamus that are closely adapted to warmth, may result from the reworking of older, interglacial deposits" (Nilsson, 1983, p. 227). This hypothsis is likely based on theory. Glacial animals do not live with interglacial animals, pure and simple. However, the postulated mixing is not a likely explanation for many disharmonious associations, because the associations are widespread, and disappear in post-ice age sediments. Graham and Lundelius (1984, p. 224) write:

Most of the presently available evidence suggests that individual stratigraphic units are deposited in too short a time in relation to the rate of environmental change for this [mixing of remains] to be a likely cause .... The widespread occurrence of disharmonious faunas in Pleistocene deposits also indicates that these associations were much too common to be spurious in all cases. In addition, if these associations are caused by sedimentary mixing, their frequency should be about the same for all time periods; but disharmonious associations are rare in Holocene [post-ice age] faunas, and in stratified faunas they usually disappear at the Pleistocene/Holocene contact.

Disharmonious associations during the ice age are not in conformity with uniformitarian expectations. An ice age, in the uniformitarian framework, is very cold. Computer simulations of the climate at ice-age maximum, indicate temperatures immediately south of the ice sheets on the order of 10°C colder than are characteristic of present conditions (Manabe and Broccoli, 1985b, p. 2180; Kutzbach and Wright, 1985, pp. 153,159). The climate was also drier, at maximum. A colder, drier climate is also theoretically expected well before maximum glaciation in the uniformitarian system. One would not expect warmth-loving, and even many cold-tolerant animals and plants, to survive relatively close to the ice sheets, under the above conditions. Severe climatic stress should have occurred during a uniformitarian ice age—much more than expected with a post-Flood model. However, great numbers of the animals existed—many of them large (McDonald, 1984). Moreover, as the ice sheets melted, presumably from a warming climate that was more favorable to survival, many species became extinct—the opposite of what one would expect. No wonder uniformitarian scientists are greatly perplexed!

A post-Flood ice age can explain the mid-latitude occurrence of warmth-loving animals and disharmonious associations. When the Genesis Flood ended, the plants and animals would spread and multiply rapidly, to repopulate the earth. The tremendous, unused space available would favor the highest possible multiplication rates. Plants would spring up from shoots and viable roots left by the Flood. The geometric progression that occurred can be shown easily on a hand calculater. Two of each "kind" of animal, except for the clean varieties, descended from the Ark at the end of the Flood. If every kind doubled each year, each kind would have 67 million individuals in just 25 years, and over two trillion in 30 years. Small animals, insects, fish, reptiles, and amphibians, would multiply at a much faster rate. Large mammals would increase more slowly (McDonald, 1984). Predation and disease would take their toll, but it would be low at the beginning, since the animals were spreading into uninhabited ecological niches. The rate of repopulation growth would have been determined, primarily, by the rate at which an adequate food supply became available. Thus, soon after the Flood, the world would have been teeming with life.

Since mammoths are of special interest, and will be discussed in the last section of this chapter, their rate of increase will be estimated. According to McDonald (1984, pp. 421,428), modern elephants usually have one baby per litter, but sometimes two, and give birth about every five years, although the time can be as short as four years. Elephants, theoretically, could give birth more frequently, since the gestation period is only 21 months. Elephants live about 60 years, and are not able to bear young until 15 years old. With the combination of these features, the doubling rate for modern elephants is probably somewhere near ten years. If mammoths reproduced at the slow rate of modern elephants, more than two million would have been born in 200 years, and about two billion in 300 years. Since the ice age did not reach maximum until about 500 years (see Chapter 5), mammoths had plenty of time to multiply and spread across the Northern Hemisphere after the Flood.

Since the ice age began immediately after the Flood, cold tolerant animals, like the musk ox and reindeer, could not migrate to the far north. They would be forced to live south of the ice sheets in Europe and North America, but could move into Siberia and Alaska, where only mountain glaciers developed. The most challenging problem is presented by the existence of warmth-loving animals, especially the hippopotamus, so close to the maximum ice sheet boundaries, and in association with cold-tolerant animals. The climate caused by the warm ocean at mid and high latitudes provides the solution.

The warm ocean would have been a large heat source for the atmosphere. Winter temperatures over the ice sheets would not be extremely cold, and areas south of the ice sheets would have been rather mild, mostly cloudy, and wet, in winter. Summers south of the ice sheets would be cooler due to volcanic dust, greater cloudiness, and the proximity of the ice sheets. In other words, winters would be warmer, and summers cooler, than at present. The seasonal difference in climate would have been less extreme, or, in other words, more equable.

England, France, and western Germany, where the hippopotamus fossils are found, would have been characterized by warm, onshore winds, for many years after the Flood. Only in the middle and latter years of glacial buildup would the ice have occupied the northern portions of England and Germany. Before this, the climate was probably wet and mild enough for the hippopotamus and other warmth-loving animals to find a good home. There they would live side-by-side with cold-loving animals who could not find a habitat more suitable to their liking.

Land Bridges

Land bridges, in some areas, would have facilitated dispersal of the animals after the Flood. One such land bridge is the Bering land bridge, which connected Asia with Alaska, by means of the currently shallow northern Bering Sea, Chukchi Sea, and East Siberian Sea (Figure 4.6). Even small mammals, like the shrew and meadow mouse, apparently traveled the long distance from Mount Ararat to North America over this land bridge. Although they could have been transported on a log raft, they more likely crossed over on land. Dispersal strictly over land is a potential problem for Biblical creationists (Lammerts, 1988), but can be explained with this post-Flood, ice-age model, since Siberia and Alaska would have been much warmer than at present, during the early part of the ice age.

Sea level, at the end of the Flood, would have been about 40 meters higher than at present, because water had not yet been locked up in the Greenland and Antarctic ice sheets. Sea level would have decreased slowly, as ice built up on the land. Since ice volume at maximum glaciation, according to this model, would have been significantly less than uniformitarian estimates, the maximum sea-level lowering would have been only about 50 to 60 meters. The Bering Strait would be partially dry land, but still mostly under water at -55 meters, assuming the present depth contours (Flint, 1971, p. 774). Thus, if the topography has remained the same, maximum exposure of the Bering land bridge may have occurred when the climate was too cold for migration.

This land bridge probably was initially at a higher elevation, and exposed, but sank towards the end, or after the close of the ice age. This scenario is the opposite to that envisioned by glacial geologists who postulate the Bering land bridge was exposed only during eustatic lowering of sea level as a result of a large ice volume, on land. However, they do admit that the Bering land bridge probably was significantly controlled by earth movements (Matthews, 1982, p. 150):

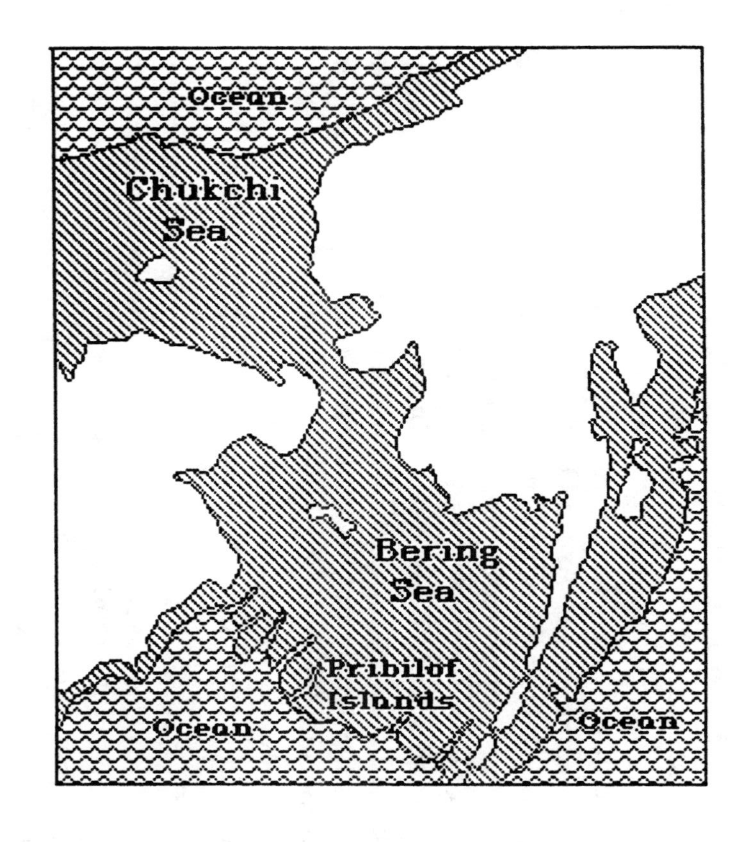

Figure 4.6 Map of the Bering land bridge drawn from the 200-meter depth contour. Note the large number of Submarine canyons along the continental slope in the Bering Sea. These Submarine canyons indicate that most of the continental shelf was most likely dry land.

Emergence of the Bering land bridge is often thought of as being "in phase" with the periods of coldest world climate, but in reality, because of the mediating effect of local tectonism, existence of the land bridge is only partly dependent on eustatic [sea level from ice and snow on land] fluctuations ....

In other words, the sea-shore line is mostly controlled by vertical land movements. Flint (1971, p. 773), although accepting eustatic control during the Pleistocene, allows for crustal movement to account for pre-Pleistocene migration across the Bering Strait. If tectonic factors are allowed, then the Bering land bridge could have existed at the beginning of the ice age.

There is a large body of evidence for the existence of this land bridge during the ice age. Figure 4.6 shows the Bering land bridge, which is commonly outlined by the 200 meter depth contour, according to uniformitarian estimates. The area may or may not correspond to the land exposed during a post-Flood ice age, but is probably closely similar. Remains of mammoths are found on the New Siberian Islands in the Arctic Ocean; on the Pribilof and Unalaska Islands, along the southwestern edge of the Bering Sea continental shelf; and on the shallow ocean bottom surrounding Alaska (Charlesworth, 1953, p. 1237; Dixon, 1983). It would be very difficult to account for these remains without the Bering land bridge. Furthermore, deep submarine canyons are found along the southwest edge of the continental shelf in the Bering Sea (Carlson and Karl, 1984). These submarine canyons are far from the mainland, and indicate that most of the continental shelf was likely exposed at the end of the Flood. Moreover, the sediments on the Arctic Ocean continental shelf contain permafrost, which can form only above sea level (Untersteiner, 1984, p. 137).

Land bridges likely existed in other areas, at the beginning of the ice age, or became exposed by sea level lowering during the ice age. Land bridges allowed migration across the English Channel (including portions of the North Sea), the Irish Channel, and the Sunda Shelf, connecting the Malay Peninsula to Borneo. At least, during maximum lowering of sea level to about -55 meters, these land bridges would have existed with the present topography.

Abundant fossil evidence has been discovered, which indicates that large portions of the North Sea floor and the English Channel bottom were above water during the ice age. Widespread peat has been found in the off-shore sediments (Charlesworth, 1953, p. 1229; Flint, 1971, p. 333). In situ, unweathered, and sometimes articulated bones of ice-age mammals abound on the bottom of the North Sea. In just ten years, 2,000 mammoth molars were dredged from the Dogger Bank in the North Sea (Charlesworth, 1953, p. 1230).

The Woolly Mammoth

The woolly mammoth has inspired legends and stories of ferocious beasts. It is one of several types of mammoths, each of which is not much different from modern elephants. The woolly mammoth was smaller than a modern elephant. A close cousin to the mammoth was the mastodon. This section will focus only on the question of why the woolly mammoth lived in Siberia and Alaska, where its bones and tusks are regularly found, occasionally accompanied by frozen flesh (Tolmachoff, 1929; Farrand, 1961).

What exactly is a woolly mammoth? It is distinguished from other mammoths by its long hair, short ears, and other anatomical features that seem adapted to the cold. In general, it is found in more northerly localities than the other types of mammoths (Agenbroad, 1984, pp. 92-99). This could easily be a simple adaptation by the elephant family to different environments. The classification, or taxonomy, of mammoths is a problem, especially when such unique features as long curved tusks are missing (Agenbroad, 1984, pp. 91,92). It is likely that similar problems exist for the mastodons and extinct elephants. Mammoths may provide another example of the usual tendency towards taxonomical splitting. Classification of elephants is based mainly on dentition (Farrand, 1961, p. 730), but, like the phylogeny of the horse, significant overlap exists between types. Some authorities point out that because of morphological gradation of dentition between species, dentition, alone, should not be the basis for identifying species (Agenbroad, 1984, p. 91). Churcher (1984, p. 412), referring to mammoth taxonomy based on teeth, and used to establish a time sequence, states: "Thus the dating of faunas or deposits by the relative compression of the teeth is unsure taxonomically. There are lots of pitfalls in palaeontology like this ...."

Of special concern to creationists is whether or not the remains of woolly mammoths, and other mammoths, are post-Flood. From the evidence at hand, it seems certain that they represent animals which lived in early post-Flood time—not Flood burials. Mammoths are found, together with other ice age animals, in surficial deposits throughout the mid and high latitudes. They are sometimes found in ice wedges within sediments of the far north. (This fact probably produced the belief that mammoths were buried in ice.) Ice wedges form only in permafrost, a post-Flood phenomenon. Woolly mammoths are depicted in cave-wall drawings made by prehistoric people who obviously lived after the Flood. Some mammoth remains have spear points embedded in them. The mammoths in Siberia, as far as anyone knows, are found only in the surface layer (Tolmachoff, 1929, p. 51):

> *Everywhere carcasses of the mammoth and rhinoceros were found, they had been buried within the frozen ground of tundra near its upper surface and usually on comparatively elevated points, on the top of bluffs, etc. This has long been known ....*

Although woolly mammoths are usually found on elevated points, or cliffs, the deposits in which they are found are predominantly river flood-plain, or river valley sediments (Farrand, 1961, p. 732). Tolmachoff (1929, p. 52) writes:

Also, on the mainland the mammoth was not always found in recent river valleys, or within deltas, but, just as on the islands, in the sediments deposited by former rivers the channels of which were obliterated later. Certainly some remnants of the mammoth were found outside of any river valleys ....

In other words, only a few mammoths have been found outside modern or ancient river valleys. The high elevation mentioned by several authors is usually a higher flood-plain terrace that was deposited when the rivers first laid down a vast blanket of alluvium, and before they proceeded to downcut into that sediment. The combination of all evidence indicates that the mammoth and its associated mammals, were deposited in post-Flood time. Some time would have been required for the mammoths to multiply and migrate from Mount Ararat to Siberia (see earlier section). By the time they reached Siberia, the ice age would have been fully developed in other parts of the world.

The mammoths were widespread during the ice age. They extended from Europe, through Asia, into North America, and as far south as Central America. Mammoths are nearly always found south of the ice sheets, but some have been recovered from within the periphery of both the Laurentide and Scandinavian ice sheets (Mangerud, 1983, p. 5; Agenbroad, 1984). The woolly mammoth lived side by side with many other types of mammals—animals such as the woolly rhinoceros, saber-toothed tiger, bison, horse, reindeer, musk ox, antelope, and cave lion. Most uniformitarian scientists try to downplay the large number of woolly mammoths (not to mention other animals) that lived in Siberia and Alaska (Farrand, 1961, p. 731). But woolly mammoth fossils were especially abundant in the wastelands of Siberia, according to Vereshchagin, of the Zoological Institute in Leningrad, who is considered the world's foremost authority on ice-age elephants (Stewart, 1977, p. 68):

Through such causes almost 50,000 mammoth tusks are said to have been found in Siberia between 1660 and 1915, serving an extensive mammoth ivory trade. But this is nothing compared to those still buried, according to Vereshchagin, who calculates that the heavy erosion of the Arctic coast spills thousands of tusks and tens of thousands of buried bones each year into the sea and that along the 600-mile coastal shallows between the Yana and Kolyma [rivers] lie more than half a million tons of mammoth tusks with another 150,000 tons in the bottom of the lakes of the coastal plain.

They are also found in abundance on Arctic Ocean islands north of Siberia, and on the Bering Sea Islands. These islands are on very shallow shelves, and indicate that, at one time, there was a vast land bridge connecting Siberia with Alaska (Figure 4.6). This land bridge, between eastern Siberia and western Alaska, is called Beringia. Consequently, a million or more woolly mammoths must have lived in Siberia and Alaska.

There are three questions to answer, with regard to the woolly mammoth's presence in Siberia and Alaska: 1) Why did they live in these areas? 2) What did they eat? and 3) How did they die? Many theories, which generally fall into two main categories—uniformitarian or non-uniformitarian—have been proposed to answer these questions. Early geologists, like Agassiz, Cuvier, and Buckland, were keen observers, and favored a warmer climate, or a non-uniformitarian explanation. On the other hand, Charles Lyell, consistent with his uniformitarian bent (Gould, 1987), favored gradual changes in a similar climate (Grayson, 1984a, pp. 11-16). Lyell's explanation, with generally small differences from today's climate, is preferred by modern scientists (Hopkins et al., 1982). From a climatological point of view, the first two of these three questions require a non-uniformitarian model. The demise of the woolly mammoth will be treated in Chapter 6.

Could millions of large mammals live in Siberia and Alaska today, if the climate were slightly warmer? Many scientists think so, but an examination of climatic considerations shows that this is nearly impossible.

Siberia, in winter, has been a frozen wasteland ever since the last mammoths lived there, as proven by the carcasses that have remained frozen to this day. Very few animals could survive Siberian winters. Vereshchagin and Baryshnikov (1984, p. 492) state: "There would be no place for mammoths in the present arctic tundra of Eurasia with its dense snow driven by the winds." In the uniformitarian view, an ice-age climate would be much colder than the present climate. It is, therefore, very doubtful that the woolly mammoth and the other large animals could survive a winter in Siberia, either today or during an ice age. Even if they could, why would they want to? Surely many favorable habitats existed elsewhere. Interestingly, the fossil remains increase towards the north, and are especially abundant on the Arctic coast and on the New Siberian Islands in the Arctic Ocean. This is the opposite pattern expected from the present climate.

Another possible, but doubtful, explanation proposes that the animals only migrated there in summer, and left before winter. The abundant remains makes this unlikely (Farrand, 1961, p. 731). Another problem with summer migration, as well as with living all year round in Siberia and Alaska, is that summers would have been just as tough on the mammoth and its companions, as winter. In summer, the land is a vast, almost impassable series of bogs (Vereshchagin and Baryshnikov, 1984, p. 492). These bogs are caused by the melting of the top few feet of permafrost, with the water unable to penetrate into deeper, frozen ground. The mud, from the topsoil, is extremely sticky. A few inches of this mud are practically impassable for a man, and a foot or more would probably trap a mammoth (Tolmachoff, 1929, p. 57). Farrand (1961, p. 734) agrees that the mammoth would have had trouble negotiating marshy ground due to its stiff-legged locomotion and pillar-like leg structure. The mammoth wouldn't have been able to pass over any trench that barely exceeded its maximum stride length. Consequently, the woolly mammoth could not have lived in Siberia or Alaska during either summer or winter, in a climate similar to that of the present "interglacial."

The most reasonable explanation for the extensive woolly-mammoth population at northern latitudes is a warmer climate—the explanation given by some of the early geologists who were not committed to uniformitarianism. This implication for climate presents a severe problem for a uniformitarian theory. But, in early post-Flood time, the climate of Siberia and Alaska, because of their proximity to the warm Arctic and North Pacific Oceans, would have been much warmer and wetter than it is today. There would have been no permafrost, and, therefore, no extensive summer bogs. The winters would have been cold, but probably with temperatures more like those in the central plains of the United States. The animals living there would need to adapt, somewhat, to a cold winter, but would face nothing comparable to a modern Siberian winter, or the colder winters proposed in most uniformitarian models of the ice age.

The existence of mammoths in Siberia and Alaska also implies only one unique ice age, because no reasonable glacial or interglacial climate could provide the necessary conditions for their survival. Elephants could not live there in the present "interglacial" climate. A non-uniformitarian climate is required—one which may be expected to occur only once.

The second question posed above concerns food for the mammoths and other animals, if they did migrate to Siberia under climatic conditions similar to those at present. From a comparison with modern elephants, a large woolly mammoth would have required 200 to 300 kilograms (440 to 660 pounds) of succulent food daily (Vereshchagin and Baryshnikov, 1982, p. 269). There obviously is not enough food in Siberia today for the ice-age animal population. Moreover, elephant activity would severely damage the marginal vegetation that currently grows in Siberia. The robust and healthy condition of most fossil carcasses indicates the animals were well fed. This is called the "productivity paradox." Schweger et al. (1982, p. 425) explain the problem this way:

> *Pleistocene Beringia attracts our attention in part because of the paradoxical former abundance and diversity of large, gregarious ungulates in a region that now supports very few large mammals—a paradox heightened by the apparent presence of this larger, more diverse ungulate fauna at a time when colder world climates would seem to have made for ecosystems less productive than those of the present time.*

The productivity paradox has caused considerable controversy among uniformitarian scientists, as expected, and is still unsolved (Schweger, 1982, p. 221).

Besides the problem of food, there is the equal difficulty in obtaining sufficient water during the winter. Animals that thrive in cold winter climates today, scarcely find enough water to meet their needs. However, the lakes, streams, and rivers of Siberia are so deeply frozen in winter that a large animal such as the woolly mammoth would likely be unable to find sufficient water.

In the post-Flood climate, as already mentioned, higher precipitation would accompany the warmer, unstable air caused by the ice-free Arctic Ocean. The climate would be able to support much more vegetation than it does now, whether grasses, trees, or both. Water would be abundant. The post-Flood habitats of Siberia and Alaska appear to have been a good environment for a large population of animals.

CHAPTER 5

GLACIAL MAXIMUM

Glacial maximum occurred when the largest volume of ice and snow covered the land (see Figure 6.3). At this time, some ice sheets would be melting, while others would be growing, but the net volume of ice would begin decreasing. Figure 5.1 presents the postulated areas of glaciation at maximum ice volume and the position of the storm tracks at that time. The time to reach glacial maximum, in this post-Flood model, probably seems like mere speculation. It is speculation, in that the many variables for the post-Flood climate cannot be precisely known. But ice age maximum depends on two principal controlling variables—the coolness of the summers and the annual snowfall. When one, or both, of these conditions ameliorated, the ice sheet would have begun melting. An estimate of the length of time from the Flood to glacial maximum, is, basically, an estimate of how long the controlling conditions favored an increase in ice volume.

Time to Reach Glacial Maximum

Volcanic eruptions during the ice age eventually dropped off, so that significantly more sunshine penetrated to the surface of the earth. But, as long as the other cooling mechanisms—higher cloudiness, highly reflective snow, and low atmospheric carbon dioxide remained effective, the volume of ice would continue to increase. The first two cooling mechanisms depend upon the available moisture at mid and high latitudes, while the third is of small consequence, as explained in Chapter 3. High atmospheric moisture would be maintained as long as the ocean surface was sufficiently warm. Once the moisture source dwindled enough, cloudiness and snowfall would decrease, and the solar radiation would become more effective in melting snow and ice. Therefore, the temperature of the ocean surface at mid and high latitude is the controlling variable for the length of glacial buildup.

The gradual cooling of the ocean surface would be controlled by the temperature of the water below the surface, since the temperature of the surface

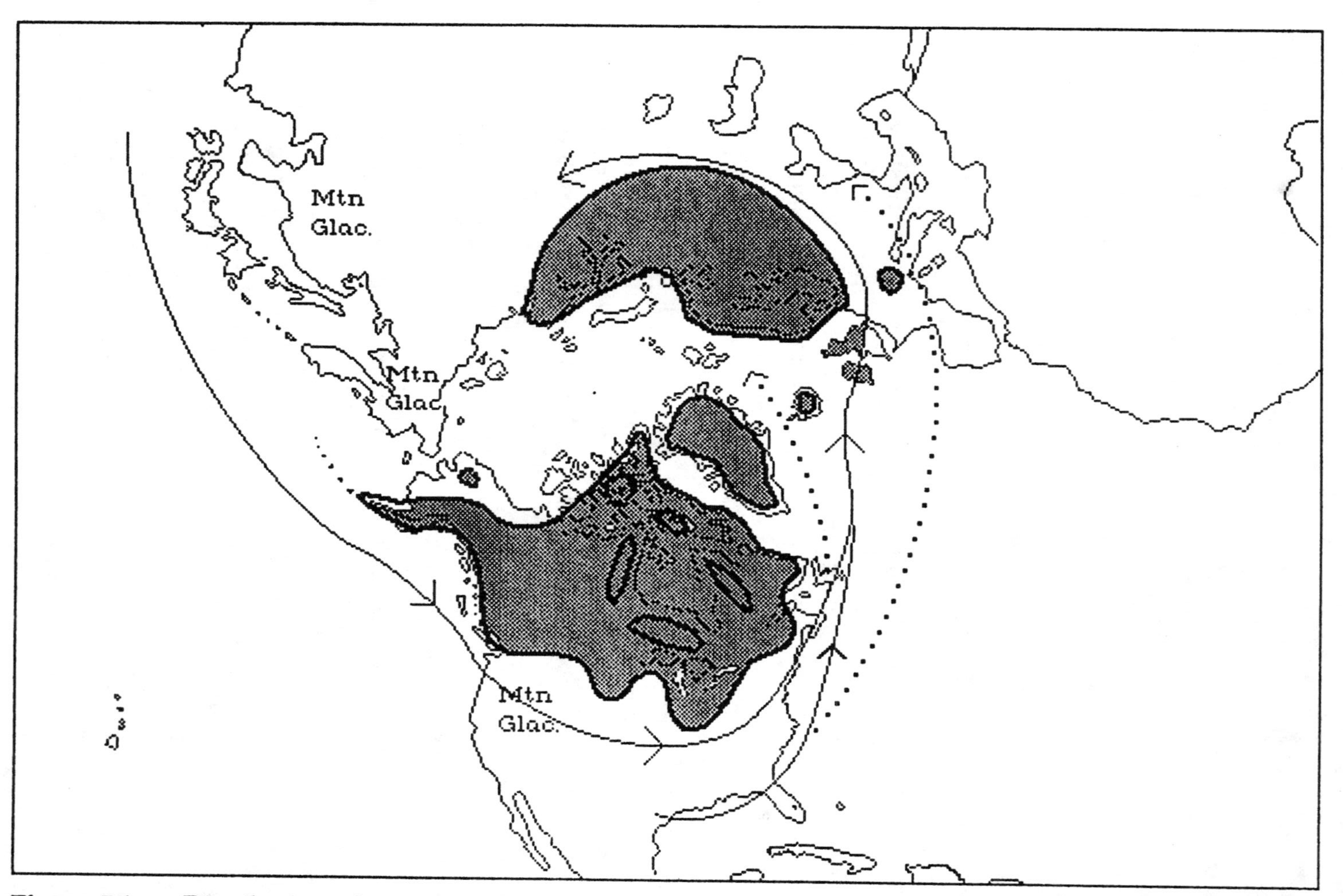

Figure 5.1 Distribution of snow and ice and storm tracks at maximum glaciation. Notation the same as in Figure 3.6. Circular areas within the North American ice sheet represent postulated ice domes. Little sea ice has formed as yet.

at mid and high latitudes is determined by the three-dimensional ocean circulation. At some threshold average temperature of the ocean, the warm surface would finally cool to a point at which the volume of global ice would begin to decrease. Consequently, the time for glacial maximum can be approximated by estimating the time to cool from an initial uniformly warm ocean, to an appropriate threshold temperature.

Now that we have established the key variable for determining the time until glacial maximum, how can we obtain a quantitative value for it? It is impossible to determine a precise value, because there are too many variables that are poorly known. Even the present values of these variables are only roughly known. But a "ballpark" figure can be found from reasonable estimates of post-Flood climatology and the heat balance equation for the ocean. Since the variables for the post-Flood climate cannot be precisely calculated, maximum and minimum estimates will mostly be used, thus bracketing the time to reach glacial maximum. As it turns out, both extremes involve very short time spans, compared to the standard ice-age chronology.

For an ocean that is cooling, the heat balance equation for the whole ocean, from the Flood to glacial maximum, is (Budyko, 1978, p. 86):

$$F_R - F_E - F_C = -Q/T \quad (5.1)$$

where F_R is the average surface radiation balance per unit of time between absorbed solar radiation and net outgoing infrared radiation; F_E and F_C are the average evaporative and conductive cooling, respectively, per unit of time; and Q is the total amount of heat that was lost by the ocean, from the Flood until the time of glacial maximum, T. The heat balance for the ocean is represented in Figure 5.2. Geothermal heat added at the bottom of the ocean is small, and will be neglected. The sign of the terms in this, and other balance equations, can cause a problem. In this chapter and in Appendix 1, variables that add heat to the system are positive, and those that subtract heat, are negative. For example, in Equation 5.1, the net radiation balance, F_R, adds heat to the ocean, and is positive; this is the only variable that heats the ocean. Evaporation and conduction at the surface, F_E and F_C, subtract heat from the ocean, and are negative. The net effect of the three terms on the left is to cool the post-Flood ocean. Hence, the term on the right is negative. Solving equation 5.1 for T is complicated, and the details are shown in Appendix 1. Only a brief summary of key points will be given in this section.

In order to solve the ocean heat-balance equation for T, the atmospheric heat balance must be included. The reason for including the atmospheric heat balance is because the heat subtracted from the ocean is added to the atmosphere, which, in turn, influences the rate of oceanic cooling. The atmosphere, therefore, acts like a thermostat, regulating oceanic cooling. By

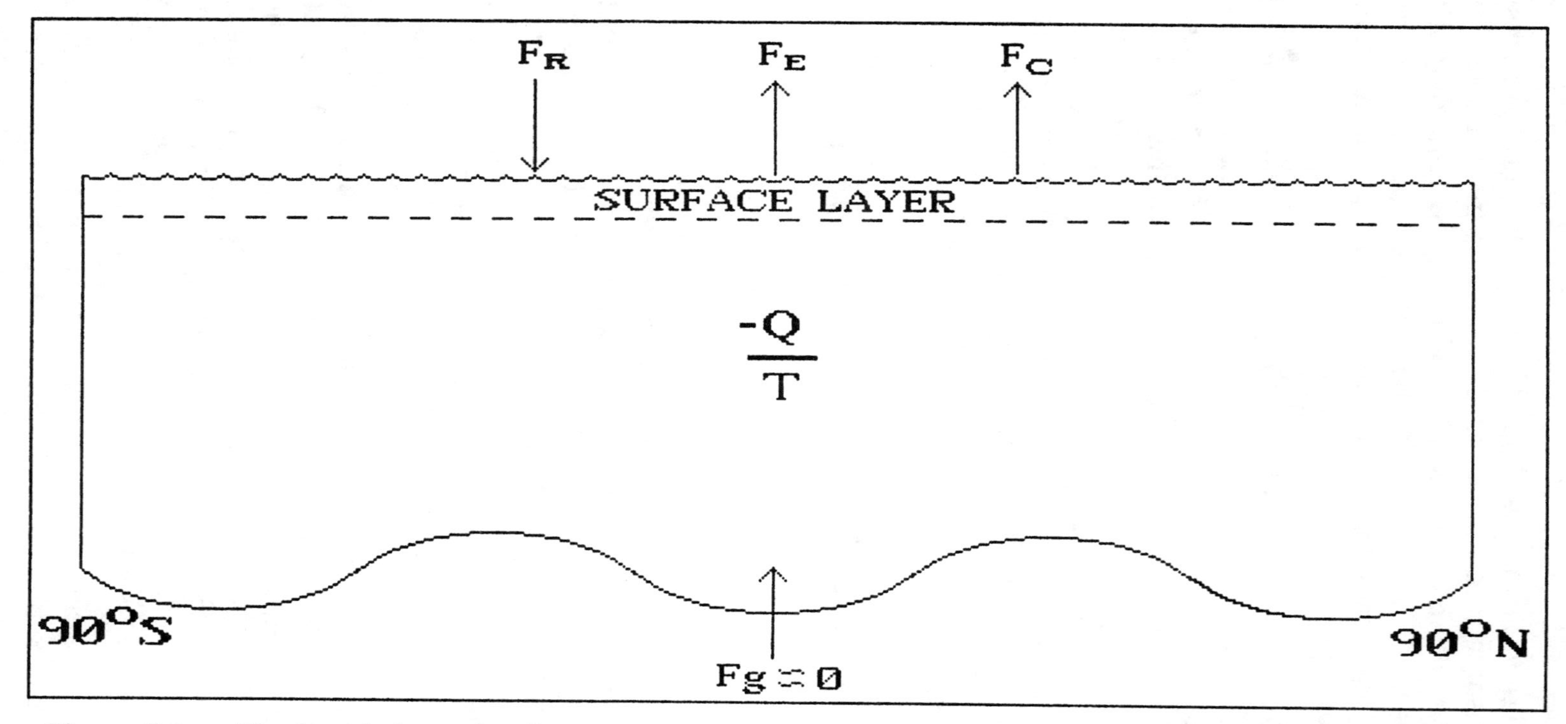

Figure 5.2 The heat balance for the ocean as a whole. F_g is the flux of geothermal heat, which is small, F_R is the flux of net solar and infrared radiation, F_E is the flux of heat from evaporation, F_C is the flux of heat from conduction, and Q/T is the change in the heat content of the ocean.

including the atmospheric heat balance, several terms in the ocean heat-balance equation are eliminated, and substitute terms are introduced which are easier to estimate in the post-Flood climate. Equation 5.1 then becomes:

$$T = -Q/(-F_{RE} + F_A + F_O) \tag{5.2}$$

where F_{RE} is the average radiation balance between absorbed solar radiation and the outgoing infrared radiation per unit time at the top of the atmosphere, and F_A and F_O are the average higher latitude heat transport by the atmosphere and ocean, respectively, per unit time (see Figure A1.1 and A1.2 in Appendix 1). To find Q, the initial ocean temperature at the end of the Flood was assumed to be 30°C, and the threshold temperature at glacial maximum was estimated at 10°C. A 20°C average cooling of the ocean temperature represents a total heat loss of 3.0×10^{25} calories.

The solar radiation absorbed by the earth and atmosphere depends upon the average amount of volcanism, cloudiness, and snow-covered area. These mostly reflect solar radiation, but they also absorb and re-radiate infrared radiation back to space. Since these effects are unknown, it was assumed that the amount of solar radiation lost to space would range from a minimum of 10% to a maximum of 75% of the present average. Infrared radiation loss at the top of the atmosphere was assumed greater in the post-Flood climate than at present, for latitudes higher than 60°. The reason for this assumption is the greater warmth at high latitudes compared with present circumstances, and the fact that infrared radiation loss is roughly proportional to the surface temperature (Budyko, 1978, pp. 93,94).

The values of F_A and F_O in the present atmosphere are not well known, individually, but their sum can be estimated indirectly. The corresponding values for the post-Flood climate would, very likely, be less than those for modern conditions. Maximum and minimum estimates of these variables are given in Appendix 1. The minimum estimate for the higher-latitude heat transport was set at zero—an extreme approximation. Nevertheless, the minimum value gives us an idea of the sensitivity of equation 5.2 to variable heat-transport values.

Inserting all the variables, with their extreme ranges, into equation 5.2, gives a time to reach glacial maximum of 174 years for a 75% loss of solar radiation with no heat transport to higher latitudes. With a 10% loss of solar radiation and a maximum heat transport, the corresponding time is 1,765 years. These extremes are unrealistic, but they demonstrate that no matter what estimates are used for the variables in the heat balance equation for the ocean, only a short time is required to cool the ocean. The best estimate is probably 500 years, based on a 25% depletion of solar radiation and a 12.5% decrease in the current values of the atmospheric and oceanic heat transports.

An estimate of 30°C for the initial ocean temperature may be too high. If this initial average temperature of the ocean after the Flood is lowered to 25°C or to 20°C, the estimated time for glacial maximum is even shorter. These calculations make it apparent that the post-Flood ice age was a rapid development.

The higher values for solar radiation loss (a 50% and a 75% decrease) give us insight into the rate of glaciation. As a consequence of initially high volcanism, such values were probably characteristic of the beginning of the ice age. Table A1.4, in Appendix 1, shows that at these values of solar radiation loss, glaciation would be the most rapid. In other words, during periods of strong volcanism and reflection of solar radiation back to space, the cooling, over land, would be more intense. This, in turn, would cause colder, drier air to blow out over the warm ocean. As a result, ocean cooling would be more rapid, and the amount of moisture evaporated into the air would be higher. Consequently, ice sheets would grow rapidly, with high volcanism. Conversely, they would develop more slowly, or even melt back at the margins, during volcanic lulls. Higher solar radiation loss at the beginning of the ice age is likely the reason glaciation extended into the central midwest of the United States early in the ice age, and then melted back when the solar radiation absorption at the earth's surface increased, before glacial maximum. Variable volcanism probably was responsible for ice margin oscillations, which would deposit multiple till layers, with non-glacial sediments sandwiched between (see Chapter 7).

Average Post-Flood Ice Depth

To find the average ice depth after 500 years of post-Flood glaciation, the available moisture must be estimated. Since the geography of the Northern and Southern Hemispheres is so different, separate estimates of the moisture for the higher latitudes of each hemisphere must be made. In addition, an estimate must be made for the proportion of this moisture that precipitates on the ice sheets.

The two sources of moisture for ice-sheet growth are represented in Figure A1.2, in Appendix 1. The first is oceanic evaporation at mid and high latitudes, F_E; the second is atmospheric transport from lower latitudes, F_A. In Figure A1.2, these sources are represented by the latent heat carried by the water when in vapor form. F_E, the latent heat from evaporation at mid and high latitude, was much greater in the early post-Flood climate, than it is at present. As has been explained before, evaporation at mid and high latitudes was the principal source of moisture for the ice sheets. F_E and the latent heat portion of F_A (F_A also includes some energy due to temperature difference) are averages in calories per year from the Flood to ice-age maximum. The estimate of the total latent heat transfer is obtained on multiplication by 500 years. Latent heat is transformed into the mass of moisture by dividing the total latent heat transfer by about 600 calories/gm—the latent heat of condensation.

The details of the calculations and the probable amounts of snow falling over the ice sheets are given in Appendix 2. The calculation begins with the solution of F_E from the heat-balance equation for the ocean (equation A1.8, in Appendix 1). Estimating from the present values of F_R and F_O, a range of probable values during the post-Flood period is plugged into equation A1.8, together with an average cooling for the ocean of 20°C in 500 years. Ranges in the values of latent heat transport to higher latitudes are found by assuming that the present transport in each hemisphere is the maximum post-Flood value. The minimum post-Flood value is assumed to have been 50%, and the best average post-Flood value is assumed to have been 75% of the present average. To determine the total amount of moisture available over a 500 year period for the regions north of 40°N latitude and south of 60°S latitude, the areas of the ocean from which the two major sources of moisture originated must be estimated. In making this calculation, it has been assumed that the size and configuration of the oceans were the same during the ice age as they are today.

Precipitation does not fall evenly over a large area. Areas close to major or minor storm tracks are especially favored. Also, the colder portion of a storm usually receives more precipitation (see Chapter 3). The ice sheets and non-glaciated land close to a storm track would receive much more precipitation than the mid-ocean areas. Based on these general meteorological considerations, estimates were made for the precipitation that fell on the ice sheets in both hemispheres. For a minimum estimate, a uniform distribution of precipitation over land and ocean was chosen. For the maximum, precipitation over land three times as great as over the ocean was selected. A median-estimated precipitation, twice as great over land as over the ocean, is probably the best post-Flood value. These estimates must be recognized as having a high degree of uncertainty.

Considering the extremes of all the variables discussed in this section, the average ice depth over the Northern Hemisphere was found to range from a minimum of 515 meters to a maximum of 906 meters. A depth of about 700 meters is considered the best estimate. The average ice age accumulation rate for the land north of 40°N was estimated to be 1.4 meters/year, which is at least three times the present average (Trewartha and Horn, 1980, back cover). For Antarctica, the estimated ice depth varied from a minimum of 726 meters to a maximum of 1,673 meters. The best estimate is about 1,200 meters, with an average annual accumulation of 2.4 meters/year, which is about an order of magnitude greater than the modern average.

The spread in the minimum and maximum ice depths for each hemisphere is not too high, considering the uncertainties in the estimates. The assumptions used in the estimates of available moisture and of the precipitation distribution between land and ocean are not crucial to the main conclusion—that the ice sheets were relatively thin, on the average.

Ancient Ice Sheet Thickness

The uniformitarian estimates of ice thickness are significantly larger than the average depths calculated here. They are about 150% larger for the Northern Hemisphere, and 50% larger for Antarctica. Is there any objective basis for the uniformitarian estimates, and are the values estimated for the post-Flood ice age hopelessly in error? We shall examine the methods for estimating ice depth, to check whether the uniformitarian values have a firm basis, and whether there is evidence to support thinner values.

Four main methods have been used to estimate past ice-sheet thickness: 1) analogy and theory, 2) the height of nunataks and of lateral features, like moraines, 3) the maximum lowering of sea level, and 4) the amount of isostatic rebound. This section will focus mainly on the Laurentide ice sheet, which is the largest of the past ice sheets. We assume the same, or similar, arguments hold for the other ancient ice sheets in Europe and northwest North America.

The above methods utilize a limited amount of hard evidence, and circular reasoning is commonly employed. Paleoclimatologists Ericson and Wollin (1967, p. 136) admit that past ice-sheet thicknesses are really guesses: "The estimates vary, because one can only guess how thick the ice sheets were ...."

The first, and perhaps the most widely used method, is analogy and theory. Uniformitarian scientists have an overabundance of time for ice sheets to develop, and little factual data. In reference to the Laurentide ice sheet, Bloom (1971, p. 367) states: "Unfortunately, few facts about its thickness are known .... In the absence of direct measurements about the thickness of the Laurentide ice sheet, we must turn to analogy and theory." Andrews (1982, p. 12) corroborates Bloom:

> *There have been several reconstructions of various Pleistocene ice sheets based essentially on glaciological theory. These have relied implicitly or explicitly on the analog premise that the appearance of the former ice sheets was not unlike that of the Greenland or Antarctic ice sheets today. This premise may not be valid.*

Consequently, most ice age investigators assume the ice sheets grew to the size of the Antarctic and Greenland ice sheets. Using the Antarctic ice sheet for analogy, investigators theorize the depth, basal shear stress, movement, surface slope, and other properties for the Laurentide ice sheet. This is, essentially, how Denton and Hughes (1981) arrived at their reconstruction of the past ice sheets at maximum glaciation (Andrews, 1982). In the Denton and Hughes reconstruction, the Laurentide ice sheet had one huge center over Hudson Bay, from which ice flowed outward in all directions, all the way to the margins. From an atmospheric science viewpoint, this seems theoretically impossible (see Chapter 1).

Although field evidence is used to support the Denton and Hughes reconstruction, a large body of field evidence from the Arctic contradicts the single ice-dome model. The Denton and Hughes reconstruction "... is radically different from the interpretation of most field workers ..." (Andrews and Funder, 1985, p. 2). Andrews and Miller (1985, p. 361) write:

> *Of course we can get into an argument about the interpretation of "firm stratigraphic evidence" because in our reading of this paper it is interesting how much of the field evidence from arctic areas is discounted in favor of a hypothesis developed largely on the basis of a reasonable model as to how the Antarctica Ice Sheet functions.*

What is the field evidence against the single-dome model? The field evidence consists of the direction of striae, drumlins, flutes, and roches moutonnées, and the provenance of distinctive erratics (Andrews, 1982). These data mediate against the former existence of one large ice center, but implies two or more smaller centers, or ice domes, within the ice sheet. The first dome was over Labrador-Ungava, and the second over Keewatin. Other postulated domes are located south of Hudson Bay, over the Baffin Island-Foxe Basin area, and over the Queen Elizabeth Islands (Figure 5.1). However, this evidence has been dismissed as the result of late glacial thinning of the ice sheet, after the single dome melted down to multiple domes (Andrews, 1982, p. 10).

Although much of this evidence does represent late glacial ice movement, one component, especially, represents long-term glacial motion. From an analysis of distinctive glacial erratics on the surface, and, most significantly, below the surface in Keewatin, Shilts et al. (1979) state that the Keewatin ice divide has always existed, and that ice never flowed westward from a large ice center in Hudson Bay into Keewatin (see Figure 1.3 for locations). In addition, Hillaire-Marcel et al. (1980) and Shilts (1980) contend that the ice-flow direction, on the east side of Hudson Bay, was always from the east. This evidence is strongly against the single-domed theory.

The above is not the only evidence favoring a multi-domed Laurentide ice sheet. In models based on an Antarctic ice sheet analog, the ice sheet in eastern Canada would have been buttressed on the continental shelf, and would have partially drained by fast-moving ice streams, through Hudson Strait, the Gulf of St. Lawrence, and other large geographic troughs . Much evidence can be brought against this hypothesis. Andrews (1982, p. 16) states that the ice sheet was drained by a series of fjords, and did not terminate on the continental shelf, but farther inland. (This statement was made in the context of the last ice age in the multiple glaciation system, but, since practically all the glacial debris is attributed to the last ice age, Andrews' statement likely applies to the entire multiple ice-age scenario. Besides, evidence will be presented, in Chapter 7 which strongly indicates that there was only one ice age.) Moreover, Hudson Strait does not provide evidence for parallel ice flow in the past, but, rather, for convergent flow from ice domes on Baffin Island, to the north, and on Labrador, to the south (Andrews et al., 1985). Hudson Strait and other large troughs, in the Canadian north, show very little evidence of deep, glacial erosion, as expected, from the single-domed theory, because these valleys are floored by "soft" pre-Quaternary sediments (Andrews, 1982, p. 25). In addition, large sections of Baffin Island and portions of the Ungava Peninsula exhibit little signs of glacial erosion (Andrews et al., 1985). Slight glacial erosion is a common observation, over most of Canada (Flint, 1971, p. 115; Eyles, 1983, p. 4). All this evidence favors the multi-domed, thinner, ice-sheet model, for eastern Canada.

To add further support to the multi-domed model, Andrews et al. (1983) have published evidence that Hudson Bay was deglaciated, at times, during the last ice age. Although dated by amino acid ratios, the basis of their claim comes from water-laid sediments containing marine shells, and interlayered with glacial till (Andrews et al., 1984). This result, if correct, fully contradicts the single-domed-ice-sheet reconstruction model.

The evidence for the multi-domed model implies that the Laurentide ice sheet was substantially thinner than required by the single-domed model (Andrews, 1982, p. 1). Occhietti (1983, p. 13) states: "These results change the concept of the Laurentide ice sheet radically. They imply, notably, a much smaller ice volume, and complex margins." Field data from the interior area of the Laurentide ice sheet **do** support the thin post-Flood ice sheet model. Not only that, these data also indicate that the "reconstructions" of global ice volume, based on oxygen isotopes from deep-sea cores, have serious problems (Andrews, 1982, pp. 1,2; Occhietti, 1983, pp. 14-16).

The second method for deducing the thickness of ancient ice sheets is the height of nunataks, which are mountains or hills that protruded above the ice, and the height of lateral features, like moraines left from previous marginal ice lobes. As with the first method, problems and misinterpretations abound. Conclusions are often based on an assumed thick ice sheet, which, naturally, should have overridden the mountains of New England, and elsewhere. Recent research on most marginal areas, where lateral features and nunataks are found, mostly indicates that the periphery of the Laurentide ice sheet was thin. The periphery is defined as a rather narrow strip, about 300 or 400 kilometers wide, around the edge of the ice sheet.

It has been known for some time that the southwest margin of the Laurentide ice sheet was thin. This conclusion is based on nunataks and driftless areas in Montana, Alberta, and Saskatchewan (Lemke et al., 1965; Mathews, 1974, p. 39). The north-south ice sheet profile, at the margin, was about one-fifth as steep as would be expected, based on analogy with the Antarctic ice sheet. Ice flow indicators also show that the ice sheet was strongly influenced by topography (Clayton et al., 1985, p. 235). The marginal evidence does not apply only to deglaciation, when the ice sheets were thinning, it also covers the entire period of glaciation.

In the north-central United States, the margin of the ice sheet repeatedly surged. These surges have left behind lateral moraines and other glacial features along previous ice lobes. The gentle slope of these lateral features indicates that the ice sheet must have been notably thin (Mathews, 1974; Clayton et al., 1985; Beget, 1986). The thin surges occurred during late glacial time, since they are on the surface, and mostly would have erased previous surface features. This surge pattern could have existed throughout the ice age; there is no evidence to the contrary. The driftless area, in Wisconsin, suggests that the ice sheet was thin throughout glaciation. Not only was the southwestern and south-central periphery thin, but recently evidence has been obtained which indicates that the northwest margin also was thin (Beget, 1987).

The only marginal area showing evidence for a thick ice sheet is the southeast periphery. Several mountain ranges, or peaks, over 1,500 meters elevation, exist in this area. Most glaciologists believe the Laurentide ice sheet swept down from the north and completely covered these mountains. Evidence from glacial-flow indicators and distinctive erratics high up on the mountains are cited as proof.

On the other hand, without dismissing the evidence of an earlier inundation of the mountains by an ice sheet, other investigators claim late glacial icecaps—not a glacial advance from the northwest—covered the mountains of New England and southeast Quebec. It is difficult to tell whether glacial features were produced by local icecaps, or by advance of the Laurentide ice sheet (Wagner, 1970, p. 2467). The evidence favoring the various hypotheses seems equivocal. For instance, Waitt and Davis (1988, p. 513) claim that far-traveled erratics, from the north, have been found within 45 meters of the summit of 1,605-meter-high Mount Katahdin, in central Maine. But Caldwell et al. (1985, p. 55), in referring to the Laurentide ice sheet, which is presumed to have covered the mountain, state: "No deposits were left by the thinning ice sheet on Mt. Katahdin until the ice surface lowered to the 760-m elevation .... Deposits related to the 760-m level occur in many places on the mountain ...." Furthermore, erratics are scarce. Caldwell et al. (1985) believe in local mountain glaciation on Mount Katahdin, after general deglaciation. They base their conclusion on the sharp features of cirques that would have been planed down by an overriding ice sheet.

Some of the presumed glacial features, in the mountains, actually can be due to debris flows and avalanches—probably a more common situation than most workers are willing to admit (Gerath et al., 1985, p. 27; Waitt and Davis, 1988). Debris-flows can mimic most glacial features. Even grooves and striations on stones and bedrock can be carved by debris flows (Schermerhorn, 1974, pp. 679-682). For example, the striations and grooves in a cirque in the northern White Mountains of New Hampshire, previously cited as proof of southward ice flow from the Laurentide ice sheet, have been determined to be formed by recent creep (Bradley, 1981, p. 323). Creep is the very slow, downslope movement of rocks and soil under the force of gravity.

Evidence that the Laurentide ice sheet may have been thin along the southeast periphery, is accumulating. Caldwell and Hansen (1986) conclude that, at maximum glaciation, the ice was only about 800 meters above sea level on Mt. Katahdin and other mountains in the same area. The nongranitic rocks on Mt. Katahdin, which have been assumed to be erratic, are claimed, by Caldwell and Hanson (1986), to be left-over, weathered country rock that the granite pluton intruded. Similar to Caldwell and Hanson (1986) and Caldwell et al. (1985), Wagner (1970,1971), claims abundant evidence for low-level, valley glaciation in the Green Mountains of northern Vermont. Although he is not clear whether he believes the Green Mountains were previously overrun by the Laurentide ice sheet, he clearly rejects the local icecap concept on the higher mountains. The evidence he cites may be deposits left over from a thin Laurentide ice sheet that filled the valleys of the Green Mountains. To add to the confusion, illustrating the difficulty of interpreting glacial evidence in New England, Waitt and Davis (1988, pp. 501-513) dispute Wagner's evidence for even low-altitude glaciation.

The possibility of ice-advances, from local mountain icecaps, or from a thin general ice sheet in New England, is additionally supported by the abundant evidence for northward flow of ice into the St. Lawrence Valley (Lamarche, 1971; Borns et al., 1985). This evidence indicates that there was an ice divide in northern Maine. Some of the early geologists noticed the indicators of northward glacial movement, but, for many years, this evidence was overlooked, showing the strong psychological influence of models. Detailed surveys in the 1960s and 1970s even reported no indication of northward ice flow. Chauvin et al. (1985, p. 112) report:

> *By the early 1960s the idea of Appalachian glaciers in Quebec was almost completely abandoned. Extensive mapping work in southern Quebec carried out by the Geological Survey of Canada firmly establishes that the last glacial*

flow in southern Quebec was toward the southeast and does not provide any evidence supporting the existence of Appalachian glaciers ....

The now-abundant evidence for northward glacial movement is attributed to late glacial motion, which was opposite to the general trend. However, the late glacial motion could indicate the general trend, and give support to the thin, ice-sheet model.

It is supposed that a thinner ice sheet is more likely, because it is also supported by the evidence from other areas of the Laurentide ice sheet. Why should only the southeast periphery be thick? This area probably would have a relatively thick ice sheet in the post-Flood ice age, since it was close to a main storm track most of the time, and, also, close to the moisture source of the warm ocean. Regardless of whether the southeast periphery was thick or thin, sufficient evidence from the remainder of the Laurentide ice sheet supports the contention that this ice sheet was significantly thinner than specified by most uniformitarian estimates.

The thin peripheral ice with a low slope—as much as one-fifth the surface slope of the Antarctica ice sheet—presents theoretical problems for models of past glacial flow. The investigators, actively working on this problem, have developed several possible solutions. Boulton and Jones (1979), and Boulton (1986), propose that the ice sheets mostly flowed on soft, easily deformable, pre-Quaternary sediments. These sediments, and the till from these sediments, were water-saturated, in many areas. Consequently, most of the basal movement of the ice sheets is presumed to have been by till deformation. Support for this view comes from the rapid motion of ice stream B, on the edge of the East Antarctic ice sheet. This ice stream has a low slope, and flows over water-saturated till (Blankenship et al., 1986; Alley et al., 1986).

Further evidence of fast ice movement comes from Northern Hemisphere ice cores that come from drilling, which probably has penetrated ice that was formed during the ice age. Ice-age ice apparently is different from later ice. Ice-age ice possesses smaller ice crystals, and more microparticles from wind-blown dust (Reeh, 1985; Fisher and Koerner, 1986). Because of these properties, ice-age ice is estimated to have flowed three to four times faster than recently formed ice.

The third method of inferring ancient ice thickness, is the reduction of sea level at maximum glaciation. The water held in the ice sheets is water lost from the ocean. But past sea levels are not known, and are mainly estimated from theory and analogy. The sea-level lowering is usually estimated from presumed ice-sheet volume. Flint (1971, pp. 317,318), while discussing the problem of estimating past sea levels from the volume of glacial ice on land, candidly admits:

A greater potential error lies in the estimation of average thicknesses and volumes of glaciers, particularly ice sheets that no longer exist. Thus far the profiles of such glaciers have been reconstructed by analogy with those of existing ice sheets, which for one reason or another may not be truly analogous.

Circular reasoning is obvious, when relating sea level lowering to ice sheet thickness, since each has been used to support the other, and each is just as unknown.

The raw, sea-level data are equivocal. Blackwelder et al. (1979) claim that the sea level data near the maximum of the last ice age, are faulty. New measurements on "non-movable" ancient sea-level indicators revealed that the difference between modern sea level, and sea level at glacial maximum, was only about half that given by previous estimates. This implies "... that substantially less ice was present from 17,000 to 10,000 years B.P. [before present]" (Blackwelder et al., 1979, p. 620). Consequently, the high uniformitarian estimates of thickness based on sea level data are not reliable, and there is support for a thinner ice sheet. Sea-level data will be discussed further in Chapter 8.

The fourth and last method of estimating past ice-sheet thickness is by glacial isostasy, which is also discussed in more detail in Chapter 8. Glacial isostasy is the depression, or rebounding of the earth's crust, due to the addition or subtraction, respectively, of an ice sheet. The amount of crustal rebound that has occurred over previously glaciated terrain, plus the rebound remaining, could be used to calculate an ice-sheet thickness. Some authors have postulated a rebound of over 800 meters at the center of the Scandinavian ice sheet, probably based on models of presumed ice-sheet thickness (Mörner, 1980a). However, the highest shore line observed in Scandinavia is 290 meters above sea level (Eronen, 1983, p. 188), and around Hudson Bay, is 315 meters above sea level (Fairbridge, 1983, p. 7). The average rebound for the whole area covered by the Laurentide and Scandinavian ice sheets, is much less. If the ratio of uplift-to-thickness of the ice is one-to-three for a 3:1-density ratio of rock-to-ice, the uplift of Scandinavia and the Hudson Bay region suggests that the ice sheets were thin.

Or course, the above conclusion depends upon the amount of isostatic rebound remaining. Some scientists believe they have found an index of the unrecovered isostatic rebound from gravity anomalies. The surface of the earth is characterized by slight positive and negative anomalies in the average force of gravity. This is mainly due to differences in crustal densities, but, also, is partially a result of distortion from the weight of ancient glaciers. Negative gravity anomalies that have been measured in the areas occupied by the former ice sheets, strongly indicate that mantle rock is flowing horizontally, towards these areas. Tide-gauge readings show that the formerly glaciated area is currently rising. For instance, the northern Gulf of Bothnia, in the Baltic Sea, near the presumed center of the Scandinavian ice sheet, is rising at 1 cm/yr. This figure is for only a small area; the average for all of Scandinavia is much less.

Based on gravity anomalies, values of 100 to 200 meters of potential, remaining crustal rebound are commonly stated. Unfortunately, gravity anomalies are difficult to measure, and the uplift, when not averaged over a large area, is rather chaotic, especially over Scandinavia (Mörner, 1980b). It is not certain that the gravity anomalies are due to unrecovered glacial rebound, either totally or partially (Walcott, 1980, p. 6). There are areas of positive gravity anomaly which should be subsiding, but actually are rising (Walcott, 1973, p. 20). Although the gravity anomalies probably do reflect unrecovered isostatic rebound, especially in view of current observations and indications of past changes, the magnitude of glacial uplift cannot be specified. The negative gravity anomalies, and the uplift that has occurred in Scandinavia and the Hudson Bay region, can be accounted for by a thin ice-sheet model, just as well as by thick models.

CHAPTER 6

DEGLACIATION

According to the model presented in this book, when the average ocean temperature cooled to 10°C, less oceanic evaporation occurred, fewer clouds were present at higher latitudes, more radiation penetrated to the surface, and most ice sheets began to melt. The mid and high-latitude winter climate would continue to cool, until it became colder than it is today. Summers would become warmer, but still cooler than at present. Storms would become drier and windier, while rivers would be gorged with meltwater and sediment. Drastic ecological changes would stress plants and animals. Some animals would become extinct, while others would be forced equatorward. At this time, the woolly mammoth most likely became trapped in Siberia and Alaska, where it was unable to survive.

In this chapter, we will discuss, in more detail, the changes that took place during deglaciation. We will first examine the climate to see what would cause further mid-latitude cooling. Then, we will calculate the time required to melt the ice sheets in the Northern Hemisphere. The water from the melting ice sheets would produce significant changes in the river valleys. We will conclude with reasons for the extinction of many ice age megafauna, with special focus on the woolly mammoth in Siberia and Alaska.

The Big Chill

What would cause the winters to cool during deglaciation? At glacial maximum, the relatively warm ocean (10°C) would still cause a somewhat mild climate. Although volcanism was probably very low, and sunshine more intense than during ice buildup, the presence of the ice sheets would continue generating cold continental air. This air, spreading out over the higher latitude ocean, would cause further cooling of the deep ocean. Eventually, the deep-ocean temperature would reach the current average of 4°C. At the same time, the mid and high-latitude atmosphere, during winter, would gradually cool, because of the presence of the ice sheets and because of diminishing heat and moisture added to the air due to the cooling ocean. The ocean and atmosphere would likely cool below today's average, as long as a substantial proportion of the ice sheets remained.

Climate simulations, initialized for maximum ice-age conditions, have regularly demonstrated a drastically colder climate. Kutzbach and Wright (1985) found at least a 10°C drop in winter temperature, and about a 30°C cooling in summer over the ice sheets, compared with the present. The drop in temperature south of the ice sheets in summer was less than 10°C, the difference decreasing with distance from the ice sheets. Their model has major deficiencies and large differences from the model presented in this book. Kutzbach and Wright used the assumed one-to-three kilometer high elevation of past ice sheets, and a yearly albedo of 0.8. Each of these values is much too high. Manabe and Broccoli (1985b), using uniformitarian ice-age boundary conditions—except for the sea-surface temperature which their model predicted, rather than assumed—found much the same summer temperature distribution as Kutzbach and Wright had. However, summer temperatures warmed more rapidly with distance south of the ice sheets in Manabe and Broccoli's simulation than they did in Kutzbach and Wright's treatment. These models generate too much cool air, but they nevertheless indicate the chilling effect of an ice sheet.

As the post-Flood climate cooled, the Arctic Ocean would eventually freeze over. Sea ice would spread over the northern North Atlantic and North Pacific Oceans, becoming more extensive than in modern winters. These changes would occur hand in hand with the atmospheric cooling, reinforcing each other. This strong cooling may explain why the Arctic Ocean is frozen today. Some investigators believe that if the Arctic Ocean suddenly became ice free, it would not refreeze (Fletcher, 1968, pp. 98,99). Evidently, a significantly colder climate than we experience at present must have caused the Arctic Ocean to freeze over for the first time.

There are two reasons why the present climate would have difficulty freezing the surface of the Arctic Ocean. First, an ice-free Arctic Ocean warms the air substantially (Newson, 1973). A much warmer atmosphere would cause more heat absorption by the water, making it more difficult to cool, in winter. Second, it is difficult to freeze sea water. When the salinity is higher than 24.8 parts per 1,000, the density of the water continues to increase as the temperature falls below 4°C. This is just the opposite of fresh water. The salinity of sea water is around 36 parts per 1,000, and does not vary significantly in the ocean surface layer. Consequently, when the surface cools in winter, the water will continually sink and be replaced by slightly warmer water from below. The surface would freeze only when the surface salinity is sufficiently lowered, by the addition of less-dense, fresh water, and/or cold surface temperatures extend by mixing to considerable depths (Stewart, 1978). Once sea ice forms, it will cool the air above and reinforce the conditions for its survival. Although their climate simulations are exaggerated, both Kutzbach and Wright (1985), and Manabe and Broccoli (1985b), show that sea ice, in the North Atlantic, would cool the winter atmosphere above the ice, 30 to 40°C below current values.

Since the atmosphere late in the ice age would be significantly colder than it is at present, the average ocean temperature probably would cool a little below the present average of 4°C, before the ice sheets completely melted. The change in the average temperature of the ocean, following the Flood, is depicted in Figure 6.1.

While the ocean and atmosphere cooled, the atmosphere eventually would become even drier than it is now. The drying trend would be mostly a result of the reduced ability of colder air to hold moisture (Figure 1.2), together with less evaporation from the cooler ocean. Models have consistently indicated less precipitation over the continents under such circumstances (Kutzbach and Wright, 1985, p. 147). Sunshine probably would be greater, although non-precipitating low clouds may have increased, due to the chill from the ice sheets.

A strong anticyclone (high pressure) with katabatic winds (outflowing downglacier winds) would frequently blow off the ice sheet margins (Kutzbach and Wright, 1985, pp. 154-156). The air above the ice sheets would be replaced, from high levels in the atmosphere. This process would further dry the air, over and near the ice sheets.

Although the tropics would cool slightly during the ice age, once ice-age volcanism diminished, the lower latitudes would recover more rapidly than mid and high latitudes. This would make the hemispheric north-south temperature difference during deglaciation greater than it is today, with the greatest gradient near the periphery of the ice sheets. Consequently, the jet stream would be more intense, and the storm tracks would average further south (see the discussion of the thermal wind equation in Chapter 3). The average major and minor storm tracks, as well as areas covered by ice sheets and sea ice midway through deglaciation, are illustrated in Figure 6.2. These changes in the storm tracks and the jet stream have been modeled on a theoretically consistent basis (Kutzbach and Wright, 1985; Manabe and Broccoli, 1985b, pp. 2174-2178).

Although the climate at mid and high latitudes would be drier, on the average—especially over and south of the Northern Hemisphere ice sheets—some areas close to the southern main storm tracks likely would be wetter than they are now. So, during deglaciation, some regions between about 20 and 40°N would have been favored with more precipitation than they are in the current climate. But this would not prevent the pluvial lakes in this

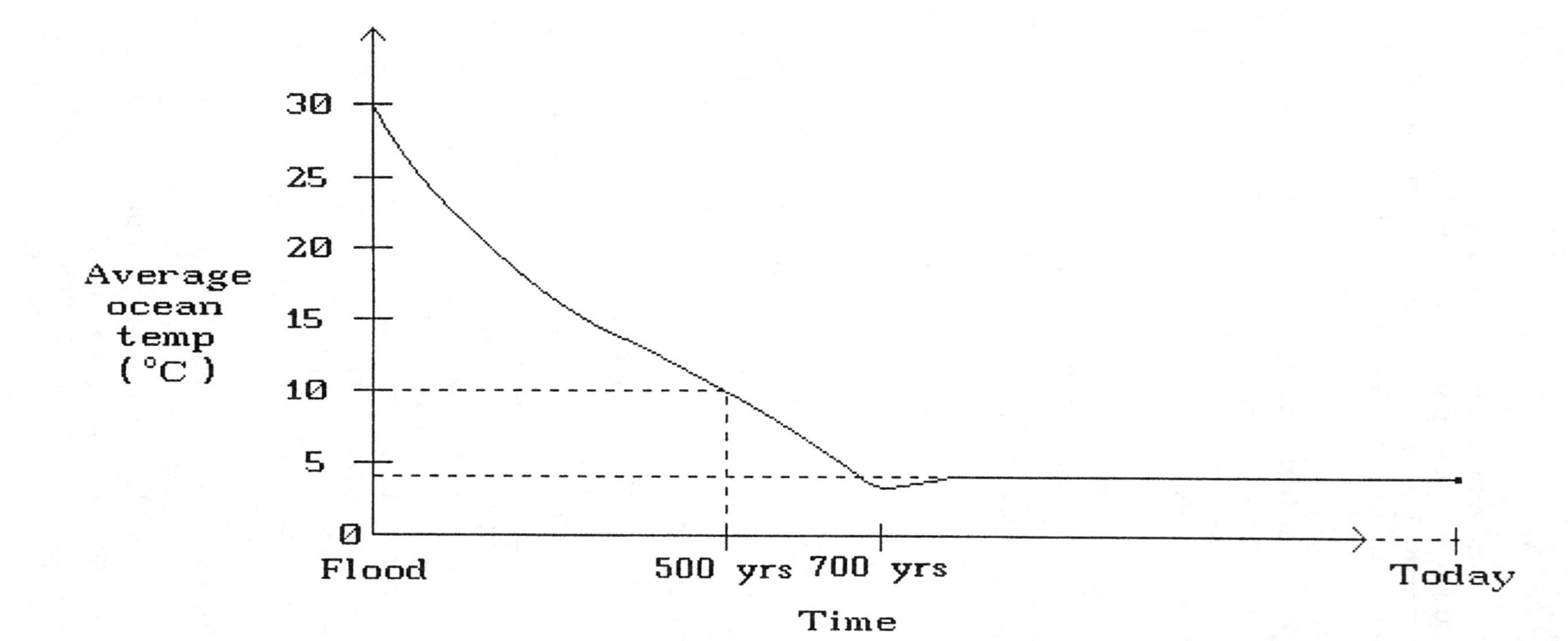

Figure 6.1 Graph of the average temperature of the ocean following the Flood. The average ocean temperature cools below today's average as the ice age glaciers melted because the atmospheric temperature at higher latitudes is much below the present.

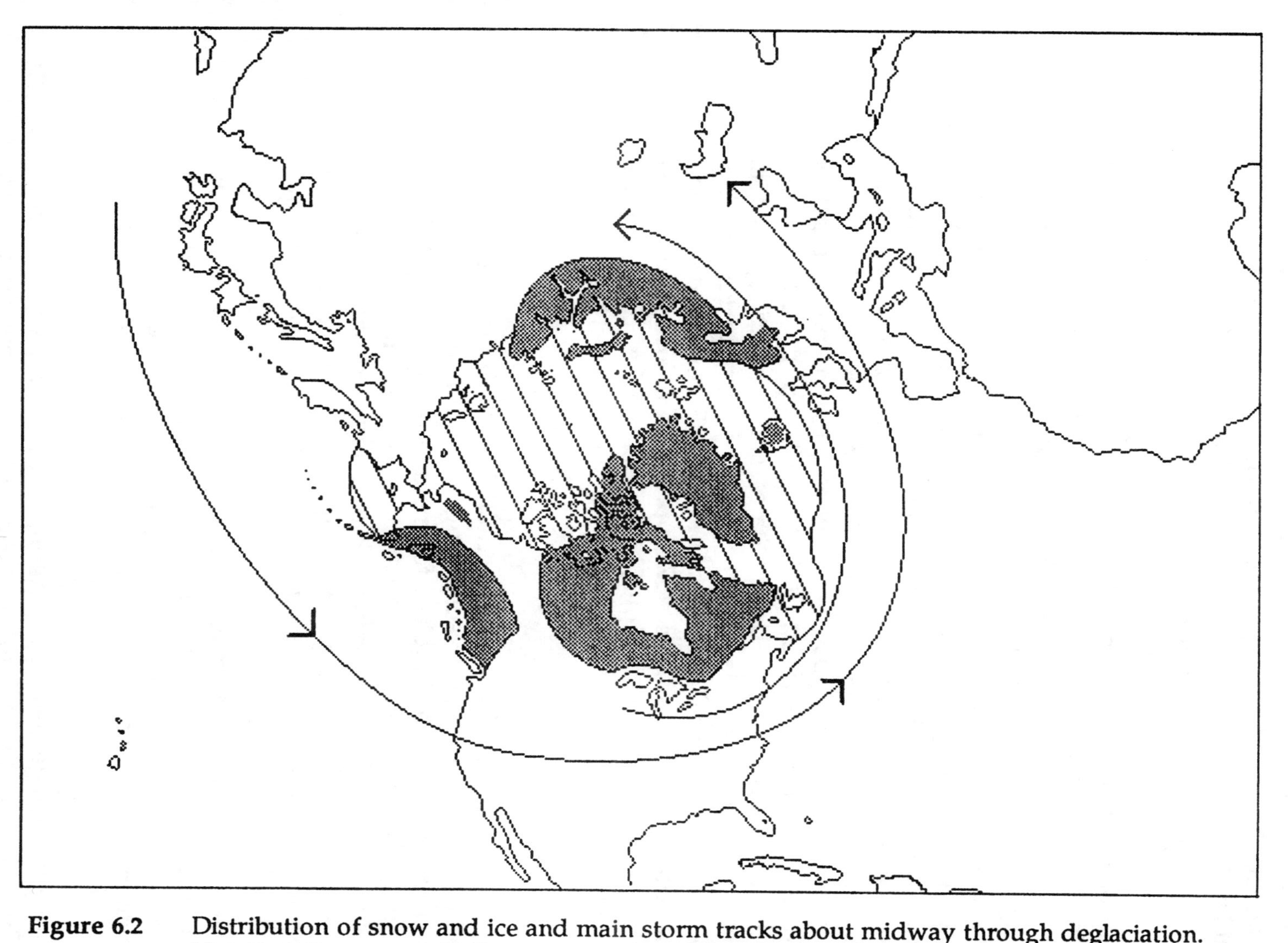

Figure 6.2 Distribution of snow and ice and main storm tracks about midway through deglaciation. Notation the same as in Figure 3.6. Sea ice coverage represented by slanting lines. Southerly main storm track caused by colder climate than at present.

latitude belt from drying. According to recent calculations, Lake Bonneville would have needed six times the precipitation in its drainage basin, to maintain its maximum level. Even if precipitation was twice the present value and the temperature was significantly cooler, Lake Bonneville would shrink during deglaciation.

As a result of the storm track located just south of the ice sheets in the Northern Hemisphere (Figure 6.2), stronger storms than those which develop today would tend to track parallel to the southern periphery. The storms over continental areas south of the ice sheets would be characterized by strong winds and relatively low precipitation. Blowing sand and dust would be a frequent occurrence, especially in the dry season. This feature is likely the reason for the extensive ice-age sand dunes, like the Nebraska sand dunes, and the loess sheets found south of the former ice sheets and sometimes intermingled with glacial till near the periphery. At one time, there was uncertainty as to whether or not loess was a wind-blown deposit. It is now considered to be wind blown (Smalley, 1975; Pye, 1987, pp. 199-265). Loess is found over much of the midwestern United States, and is especially thick in, and eastward of, major river valleys, such as the Mississippi River valley (Ruhe, 1983). Loess is also found over much of central Europe, and eastward into the Soviet Union and China (Flint, 1971, pp. 251-266). Wind-blown dust is also extensive in the lower sections of Greenland ice cores, which, presumably, represent late glacial time (Bradley, 1985, pp. 165-166).

Rapid Melting of Ice Sheets

Would the ice sheets melt during the big chill? The answer is a resounding yes; and the required time is surprisingly short. The most scientific approach, to determine the time required for melting of the ice sheets, is by use of the energy balance equation to estimate ablation rates (Hay and Fitzharris, 1988, p. 145). This approach has been attempted only within the past decade or two (Pollard, 1980, p. 384). Lack of acquaintance with it is probably the principal reason why long-age estimates for deglaciation continue to be proposed.

The big chill would produce much colder temperatures in winter, but summers would be warmer than during the buildup of the ice sheets, although cooler than in the modern climate. Winter snowfall would be light, so that most of the summer sunshine and heat would be available to melt the ice sheets.

In calculating an average melting rate during deglaciation, we may assume no ablation by icebergs calving into the ocean or into extensive proglacial lakes. We may also assume no sublimation, which is evaporation, without passing through the liquid state. These can be significant effects in local areas of the ice sheet. Neglecting the above effects will result in a conservatively low ablation rate. Disregarding geothermal heat and the transfer of heat from the air to the snow by molecular conduction, each of which is a relatively small contribution, the energy balance equation is (Paterson, 1981, pp. 299-320):

$$Q_I + Q_M = F_R + F_E + F_C + F_P \quad (6.1)$$

in which Q_I is the heat gain in a vertical column of ice from the surface to a depth at which vertical conduction is negligible; Q_M is the heat used for melting; F_R is the difference between solar and net infrared radiation; F_E is the heat gained by condensation onto the snow surface; F_C is the heat added to the surface due to warmer turbulent air; and F_P is the heat added by rain. All quantities in Equation 6.1 are expressed in amount of energy per unit area, per unit time, i.e., as rates per unit area. F_P is significant and positive, if the rain can freeze, but generally is small, and will be neglected in the dry post-maximum climate (Paterson, 1981, p. 301). The first three terms on the right are the same terms that enter into the heat-balance equations for the ocean and atmosphere. But over a snowcover, F_E and F_C are practically always positive during the melt season when the air temperature just above the snow is warmer than 0°C and the water vapor pressure is greater than the saturation vapor pressure at 0°C. Q_I is the heat needed to raise the temperature to 0°C, so that the ice can melt. Since the specific heat of ice is about one-half that of water, the temperature of the ice can be raised rather quickly, up to freezing, early in the melt season. Q_M can be negative, if meltwater refreezes, but this will mainly occur only at the beginning of the melt season, and will greatly aid the warming, or "priming," of the ice sheet. This is because the freezing of one gram of meltwater will raise 160 grams of snow or ice one degree Celsius (Paterson, 1981, p. 311).

According to these considerations, during the remainder of the melt season after the ice sheet has been primed, Equation 6.1 becomes:

$$Q_M = F_R + F_E + F_C \quad (6.2)$$

The details of the solution for Q_M, during deglaciation, are given in Appendix 3. From a comparison with modern glaciers, F_R normally accounts for 60% of the ablation, and F_E and F_C, about 40%. Therefore, the latter two terms can be eliminated by adding $.67F_R$, so that ablation is simply expressed in terms of the radiation balance.

Central Michigan was chosen as the location at which to calculate the melting rate for the periphery of the ice sheet. Although the ice sheet would have begun melting when oceanic and atmospheric temperatures were relatively mild, the average deglaciation temperature for central Michigan was assumed to be 10°C colder than the current warm season average. The ablation season was assumed to begin May 1, after the winter snow melted, and the ice sheet primed, and to end September 30. Since the melting of one cubic centimeter of ice requires a specific amount of heat energy (80 calories), the terms in Equation 6.2 can be expressed as meters of ice melted per year, rather than energy units per square centimeter per year.

The radiation balance depends, partially, on the average cloudiness and albedo. For these effects, maximum and minimum values were determined. From a range in cloudiness and albedo, Q_M varied from 7.2 to 17.7 meters/year. The best average melting rate is estimated to be 10.4 meters/year. From the range of ice depths calculated in Chapter 5, the periphery of the ice sheet would melt in 50 to 87 years—surprisingly short, compared to uniformitarian estimates. The interior of the ice sheets would melt more slowly, but probably within 200 years. Thus, the total length of time for a post-Flood ice age from beginning to end, is about 700 years. Figure 6.3 graphs the projected change in ice volume with time. After the ice sheets melted, ice volume would be less than today, because Antarctica and Greenland ice sheets would not have built yet to their current size.

The melting rate for a post-Flood ice age is considerably greater than given by uniformitarian estimates. The uniformitarian estimates are based on an expanded time scale, and not on physical principles. Up to the present, only one climate simulation (to this author's knowledge), has attempted to physically calculate ice sheet ablation. In this model, ice-sheet topography was held constant, but a subprogram calculated the annual ice balance (Manabe and Broccoli, 1985b, pp. 2179-2181). According to Manabe and Broccoli's Figure 20, the ice in a 400-kilometer-wide strip along the southern periphery of the Laurentide ice sheet, melts at about 3.5 meters/year. This is in spite of the huge size of the ice sheet, and an unrealistically high constant albedo of 0.7 for the melt season. Manabe and Broccoli (1985b, p. 2180) state: "An extremely rapid depletion of ice occurs in a relatively narrow belt along the southern margin of both ice sheets." Referring to this result at a conference on the astronomical theory of the ice age, Birchfield (1984, p. 857) states: "A new mass budget calculation for the Laurentide ice sheet by Manabe, produced very large melt rates, implying a long-term, ice-sheet retreat, far in excess of that observed."

"Observed" in the above quotation means, "inferred according to the geological time scale," in which one glaciation lasts 100,000 years. During this time, glaciation is rather slow, with very large retreats and advances, called interstadials and stadials, respectively, followed by a complete termination that occurs relatively fast in about 10,000 years (Broecker and Van Donk, 1970). An attitude, in which physical calculations, although crude, but, nevertheless, qualitatively sound, are rigidly subordinated to a geological time scale based on many assumptions, is unfortunate, but common. This is but one example of the reinforcement syndrome that keeps a model, or paradigm, intact,

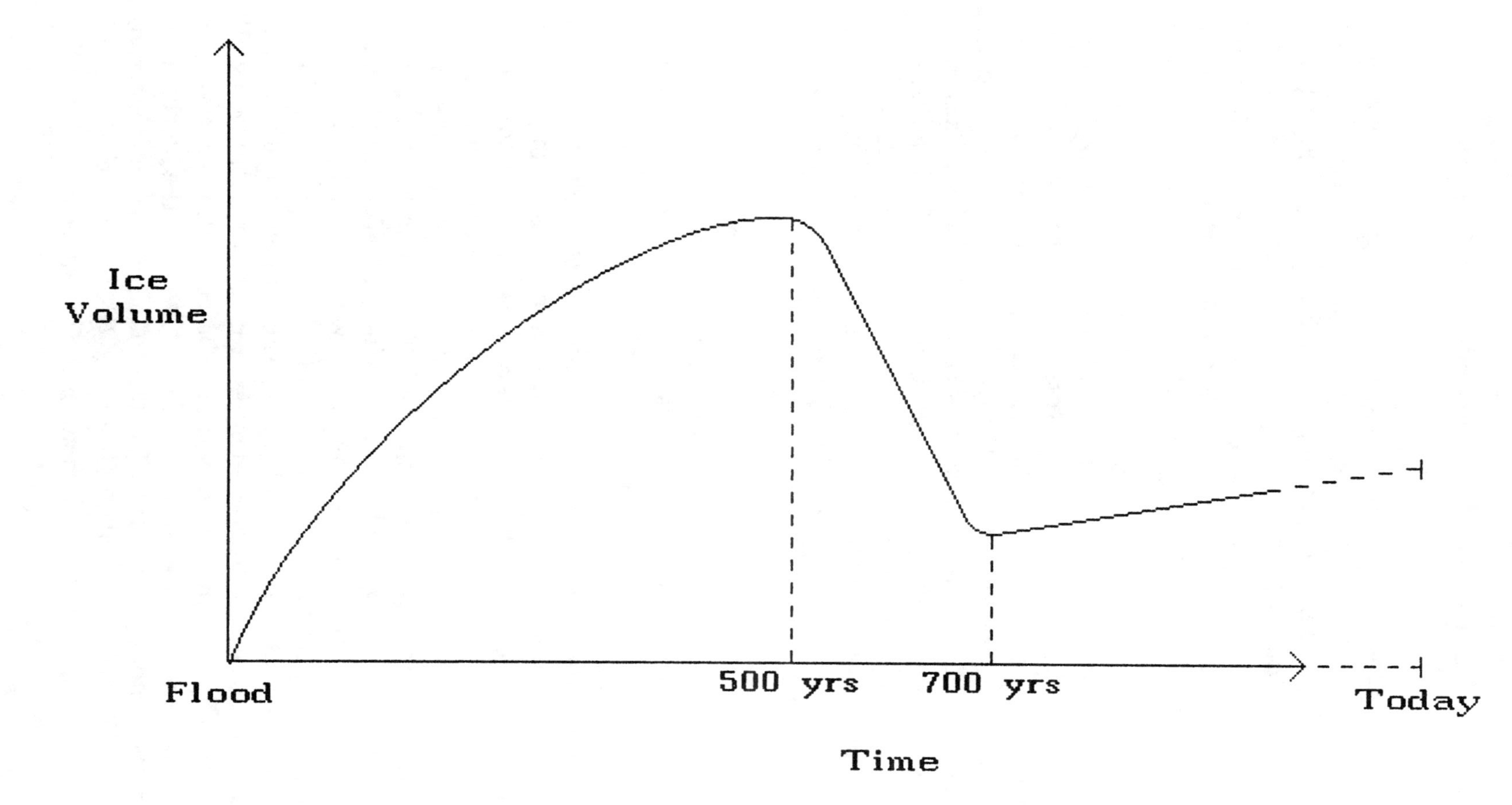

Figure 6.3 Graph of world ice volume following the Flood. The volume of ice gradually increases after the ice age glaciers melted because Greenland and Antarctica ice sheets still were growing.

internally consistent, and impressive to laymen and scientists alike (Oard, 1985, pp. 178,179).

The results reported in this chapter are consistent with modern observations of temperate glaciers. Ancient glaciers, especially along the southern terminus, probably were similar to modern temperate glaciers. Sugden and John (1976, p. 39) state that glacier-melting can be rapid as indicated by "... many mountaineers whose tents in the ablation areas of glaciers may rest precariously on pedestals of ice after only a few days." 12 meters/year is the average melting rate at the snout of some Norwegian, Icelandic, and Alaskan glaciers (Sugden and John, 1976, p. 39).

Even high-latitude glaciers have large ablation rates. As mentioned previously, the fastest moving glacier in the world, the Jakobshanvs Glacier, at about 70°N, has been measured to melt at 55 meters/year (Hughes, 1986). This is due to several positive-feedback mechanisms, and is unusual, but these positive feedbacks would be operative in some areas of the melting ice sheets. Beget (1987, p. 85) has found that current glaciers, about 70°N latitude in northeast Canada, melt at 5-7 meters/year at low elevations, and 1 1/2-3 meters/year at elevations of a kilometer. These modern observations indicate that the values estimated in this chapter and in Appendix 3 for ice-age glaciers, are indeed reasonable and conservative.

Not all of the ice sheets would melt during the deglaciation epoch. The Antarctic and Greenland ice sheets would continue growing, even after the other continental ice sheets disappeared. This is because of the high latitude, relatively high altitude, and usually fresh snow surface of these ice sheets.

At glacial maximum, the depth of ice on Antarctica averaged about 1,200 meters. East Antarctica would have received more than this amount, since it would have started the ice age mostly above sea level. West Antarctica, on the other hand, would have consisted of only mountain glaciers, during the early phase of the ice age. Since the ocean between mountain ice caps is rather deep in places—even considering glacial rebound—some time would be required before these mountain glaciers would be coalesced into the West Antarctic ice sheet. During early deglaciation, the ocean water would still be relatively warm. As the ocean temperature fell from 10°C to 4°C, snowfall would be significantly heavier than at present, and the ice sheet likely would grow a few hundred more meters. When the water temperature became cold, snowfall would have tapered off to the present slow rate. The current, average-water equivalent precipitation for Antarctica is 17 cm/yr. At the periphery, precipitation is higher, and in the interior, it is less than five cm/yr (Paterson, 1981, p. 56). At the 17 cm/yr rate, at least another 600 meters of ice would have accumulated on Antarctica since the end of the ice age, especially at the margins. These considerations indicate that a rapid ice age and the modern climate can account for the present depth of ice on Antarctica.

A scenario, analogous to the one for West Antarctica, would have occurred on Greenland. Due to the proximity of the warm ocean, only mountain glaciers would have developed, at the beginning. During the later stages of the ice age, the mountain ice caps would merge into the Greenland ice sheet. Interior areas of Greenland may have accumulated more than the Northern Hemisphere ice-age average of 700 meters. A few hundred more meters of ice could have been added, during deglaciation. Currently, Greenland accumulates a yearly average of 15 cm of ice in the north, and more than 90 cm of ice in the south, with a yearly average of 30 cm of ice (Fristrup, 1966, p. 234). Since the end of the ice age, an additional 1,050 meters of ice could have accumulated on Greenland, in the present climate.

From a uniformitarian point of view, it is difficult to account for these ice sheets (Loewe, 1971, p. 331; Anonymous, 1978, p. 25). Conditions may have been unfavorable for their beginning. Sugden and John (1976, p. 97) write: "It is often argued, for example, that if the ice were suddenly removed from Greenland and Antarctica, the climate would, perhaps, be too mild to nourish new ice sheets." The high East Antarctica ice sheet is now a polar desert, receiving less than five centimeters of precipitation a year. How it grew to over three kilometers deep is a uniformitarian puzzle: "Exactly why ... the Antarctic Ice Sheet grew to the dimensions it has today, is not yet known, however" (Anonymous, 1978, p. 25).

Alluvial Terraces and Underfit Streams

River valleys around the world are usually deeply filled with river sediment, or alluvium. Within these valleys, terraces, or steplike features, are cut in the alluvium, along each bank. Some terraces are high above the present-day river (Figure 6.4). Practically all river valleys show signs they were once filled by much larger rivers. The current rivers are, therefore, underfit. This is shown especially by the size of ancient river-meanders, but can also be deduced by the width of the valleys compared with the width of the present rivers. Both creationists and evolutionists have explanations for these observations (Whitcomb and Morris, 1961, pp. 318-324; Strahler, 1987, pp. 284-292). This section will supplement the creationist explanation with a post-Flood, ice-age model, and will address Strahlers' criticisms.

Before discussing terraces and underfit streams, we must back up a bit, to the end of the Genesis Flood. As the land was rising to drain the Flood waters, tremendous erosion of soft, or loosely consolidated continental sediments occurred. This eroded material flowed towards and into the sea, through the river valleys. Where the river slope became fairly flat in its lower reaches, like the lower Mississippi River Valley, much of this sediment would be deposited

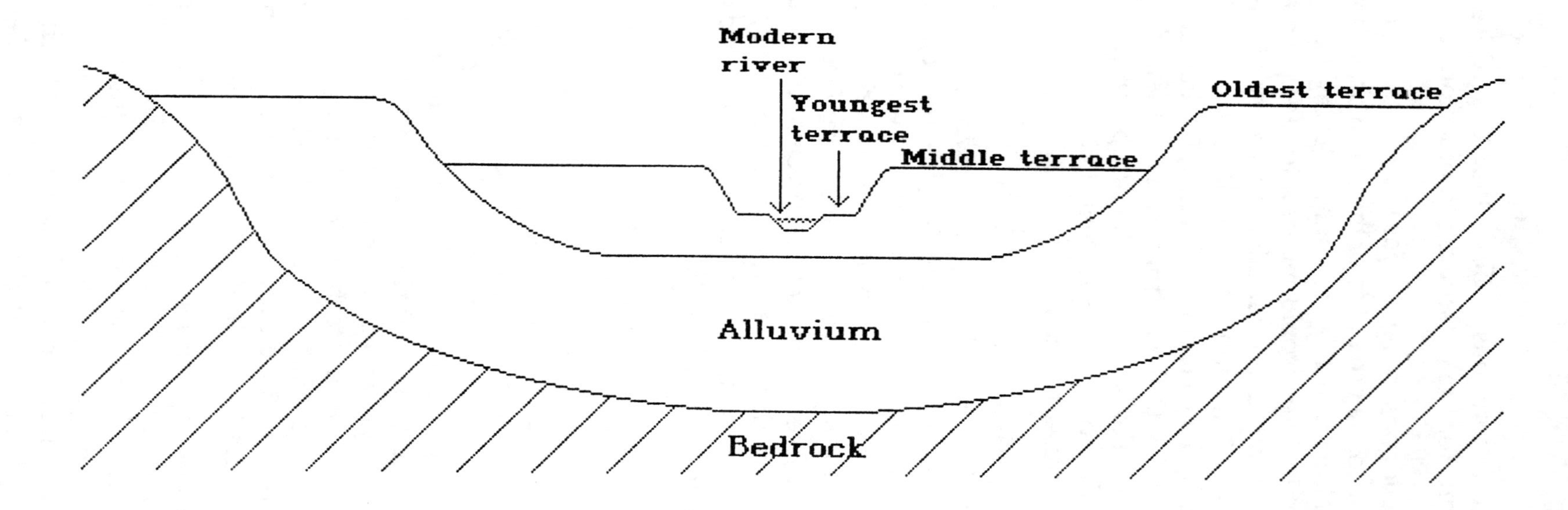

Figure 6.4 River valley showing three cycles of valley filling and cutting.

in vast alluvial plains. At this time, large river deltas would have developed at the seacoast. As the ice age began, vast blankets of alluvium would already be in place, as observed in most river plains today. In other areas of the river courses, mainly in the central and upper reaches, wide valleys and large meanders would have been cut by the retreating flood waters.

As the ice age developed, precipitation would have been at least three times greater than it is today. Over non-glaciated lands, this precipitation would have reinforced flood geomorphological features, and probably caused multiple terraces in the river valleys. Significant downcutting of the lower reaches of alluvial valleys may also have occurred. In glaciated areas, valleys cut by the draining waters of the Genesis Flood would be filled with glacial till, since these valleys would be natural traps for glacial debris.

While the ice sheets were melting rapidly, tremendous volumes of water would have been added to the rivers each summer. The amount of water would be very difficult to estimate, but 10 to 20 or more times the present flow would be likely. Immediately south of the melting ice sheets, the cold climate would have caused permafrost, which has left signs of its former existence. Water could not percolate below the permafrost in summer, and would run off, further adding to the volume of water carried by rivers.

Large fluctuations in river volume, mainly between winter and summer, would cause a complex pattern of terraces south of, and within, the glacial boundary. Sometimes the rivers would deposit sediments, while at other times, the rivers would cut through these sediments.

Schumm (1977, pp. 214-221) describes how variable numbers of terraces can form rapidly, due to episodic erosion and sedimentation in a stream that drains terrain of high relief. Douglas Creek, in Colorado, has formed one to seven discontinuous stream terraces, since 1882. The total downcutting has been about nine meters. The discontinuous nature of the terraces indicates a different erosional-depositional history at various points in the channel. Although Douglas Creek is not an exact analogy for rivers during the melting of the ice sheets, it does have implications for other streams and rivers with episodic high stream flow. Schumm (1977, p. 220) extends the observations to other areas, and summarizes:

> *This suggests that perhaps the flight of terraces that form where large quantities of stored glacial and alluvial sediments are being removed from a valley are also the result of the complex response or episodic erosion mechanism ... rather than a response to climatic fluctuations ....*

In other words, terraces can be formed by episodic erosion, and not just from climatic fluctuations. Within the context of the ice age, terraces could just as easily form by episodic flooding and erosion from the melting of the ice sheet, as from the long-period glacial/interglacial oscillations that are used by uniformitarian scientists to explain them. For instance, Gage (1970, p. 621) states:

> *Vertically spaced by tens of feet and underlain by tens of feet of gravel, such terraces in many parts of the world have been attributed to glacial-deglaciation cycles spanning thousands of years; yet similar features of the same magnitude are known to form, basically by the same processes, within a minute fraction of the time. A striking example was provided by the Waiho River, which drains the Franz Josef Glacier in New Zealand. During a single high-intensity rainstorm in December 1965, the riverbed was aggraded from 10 feet to about 80 feet over several miles, and in the succeeding few weeks rapid downcutting and channel shifting produced a flight of 10-foot terraces .... Colonized rapidly by plants in this moist temperate region, they soon acquire a false aspect of antiquity and in another environment might be mistaken for late Pleistocene degradational terraces.*

River terraces can form rapidly by the rapid melting of the post-Flood ice sheets; and they may lay exposed for sufficient time to form a soil, and then be buried by another depositional event. Thus, paleosols, which are ancient soils, can sometimes be found associated with the top of terraces. Paleosol formation need not take a long period of time, as we will discuss in the next chapter. Glacial/interglacial oscillations may seem reasonable within the uniformitarian framework, but Baker (1983, pp. 118,119) states that, because of the problems of separating climatic controls from other factors, terraces likely are unreliable for Quaternary chronology. Strahler (1987, p. 289) does recognize that creationists can explain river terraces by just the mechanism proposed above: "One possibility would be enormously increased precipitation; another would be extremely rapid melting of the glacial ice during deglaciations." Because of his neo-uniformitarian presuppositions, he does not accept this explanation. However, given the initial conditions of a post-Flood ice age, with a warmer ocean, and the physics of snow and ice ablation, what Strahler believes impossible is very probable.

River valleys over most of the world show obvious signs of much larger runoff rates than occur today. This heavy runoff could be due to draining floodwater, higher post-Flood precipitation, or rapid melting of ice. Dury (1976, p. 220) describes most rivers as "manifestly underfit," meaning very large differences between present and past flow. Many properties of present rivers, such as bankfull width, depth, slope, and meander geometry, are correlated to each other, and to river discharge. Equations relating these properties have been derived by many investigators (Dury, 1976; Williams, 1986, 1988). Unfortunately, most of these properties are difficult to extrapolate to paleorivers (Dury, 1976, pp. 221,222). However, the wavelength of incised meanders has a high degree of significance, and can give a reasonable estimate of river discharge.

Dury has worked, for years, on relating meander wavelength to river discharge for both present and past rivers. In general, discharge rate increases with the square of the average meander wavelength (Dury, 1976, pp. 222-224; Williams, 1988, pp. 328-330). Dury has found that the average paleomeander in the United States is five times the meander of the current underfit stream or river (Baker, 1983, p. 120). Near the ice front in Wisconsin, the meanders are ten times larger. This implies an average discharge 25 times greater than the present value, and discharge values near the face of the melting ice sheets 100 times greater than present stream-flow in the area. Dury (1976) later modified these estimates with more data, and a better meander geometry-discharge relationship. The revised values came out to 18 and 66 times, in place of 25 and 100 times. He (Dury, 1976) also found consistent relationships between meander wavelength, bed width, drainage area, and several other variables. Dury attributes the much higher discharges of paleorivers to higher precipitation during the ice age, and to melting of the ice sheets.

The above figures for past river discharge are difficult for most uniformitarian scientists to accept. They may be able to explain terraces due to glacial/interglacial oscillations, but the lack of greatly increased rainfall during the ice age, and the slow presumed melting of ice sheets, taxes the uniformitarian model. Strahler (1987, p. 291) states the problem very well:

> *Nevertheless, the requirement of former stream discharges as great as 20 to 60 times those occuring [sic] today presents a difficult problem for mainstream science, which insists that principles of atmospheric science and hydrology be applied in a reasonable manner.*

Consequently, various aspects of Dury's data have been questioned—specifically, the validity of extrapolating the present meander geometry-discharge relationship to the past, whether discharge refers to bankfull river flow or to floods—and the influence of additional variables that have been neglected. Perhaps the most favored additional variable is the type of sediment transported by the river. Schumm (1967, 1977, pp. 113-119) claims that a coarser bed load will cause significantly larger meanders, and will reduce the scatter in Dury's meander-wavelength-discharge data. According to Strahler (1987, p. 291):

> *Given two streams of equal mean annual discharge (or equal mean annual flood discharge), the one transporting a high proportion of its load as bedload of mixed sand and gravel will have a meander size (wavelength) larger by a factor of approximately 10 than the stream carrying mostly clay, silt, and fine sand held in suspension.*

Does a difference of ten times, due to the type of bedload, seem reasonable? The effect of bedload character is controversial. Undoubtedly, bedload has some effect on meander wavelength, but several investigators have found that it is a small and relatively unimportant factor (Williams, 1988, pp. 328,329). Bedload is not significant enough to be included as a second independent variable in a multiple-regression equation. A number of investigators, over the years, have demonstrated an excellent correlation between only meander wavelength and discharge. For instance, Williams (1988, p. 329) lists one report in 1965, which contained an equation that closely describes 31 rivers—mostly in the central United States. This equation showed even higher discharge for a given meander wavelength than given by Dury's wavelength-discharge equation.

A restudy of Dury's original graph of meander wavelength versus discharge (Schumm, 1977, p. 116) revealed that the order of magnitude of scatter, which Strahler claimed could be explained by the type of sediment carried by the river, was mainly a characteristic for lower discharge rates. The fit of the data was very good at higher discharges rates, which are of more interest for paleorivers. Furthermore, Dury (1976, p. 222) has refined and updated his graph. His newer data fit closely a regression line that accounts for 87% of the variance. There is adequate evidence that Dury's relationship between meander wavelength and discharge rate, and his conclusions about past river flow, are sound.

What about Schumm's data and claim that bedload is a significant variable? One of his most significant items of data, from Australia, is disputed by Dury (1977, p. 71), and also by others. Moreover, the type and quantity of sediment discharged through former channels, is mostly unknown (Dury, 1976, p. 228; Williams, 1988, p. 324). Only rarely can bedload characteristics be specified for a paleoriver. Williams (1988, p. 324) adds that Schumm's bedload parameter "... may not apply to environments other than that for which it was deduced...."

In summary, Schumm's additional variable of sediment load does not invalidate the good correlation between meander wavelength and river-discharge rate that has been established by Dury and other investigators. An extrapolation of this relationship to paleorivers indicates that past river discharge estimates of over 60 times current values in some areas, are justifiable. This consideration supports the Flood model better than a uniformitarian model for the ice age.

Massive Extinction of Megafauna

If the association of animals from diverse climates during the ice age is mysterious, the extinction of many of these large animals, as well as birds, at the end, is just as mysterious. At this time, the climate was supposedly warming, according to most uniformitarian theories. A related mystery is the massive extermination of the woolly mammoth, in Siberia and Alaska. Since the woolly-mammoth problem is a special case and has a long history of controversy, it will be treated in the next section. This section will offer a post-Flood explanation for the demise of much of the ice age megafauna, and will introduce the climatic background for treatment of the woolly-mammoth extinction problem.

According to the uniformitarian model, the megafauna species, and/or genera, survived each previous glacial and interglacial period. But at the end of only the last ice age, many large mammals became extinct, or disappeared from entire continents. These mammals include mammoths, mastodons, saber-toothed tigers, and ground sloths. North America was especially hard-hit, with about 34 genera of large mammals becoming extinct, compared to only 7 to 15 (depending on the investigator) in all the previous Pleistocene "ice ages" (McDonald, 1984, p. 415). Moreover, the largest species were preferentially decimated; and, in contrast to other extinctions in the geological record, the mammals were not replaced, in their habitats, by other animals (Lewin, 1987, p. 1509). To compound the mystery, these mammals ranged over North America, Europe, and Asia, and had broad climatic tolerances.

The mystery of their extinction remains unsolved after 200 years of effort. Bruce Bower (1987, p. 284) states the problem well:

> *What caused the virtually simultaneous demise of mammoths, mastodons and saber-toothed cats, not to mention native horses, ground sloths, native camels, armadillo-like glyptodonts, giant peccaries, mountain deer, giant beavers, four-pronged antelopes, dire wolves, native lions and giant short-faced bears? Scientists have grappled with this question for nearly two centuries, and, as evidenced by a recent symposium at the Smithsonian Institution in Washington, D.C., the debate is not about to cool down.*

Grayson (1984b, p. 807) expresses the mystery as follows:

> *We have accumulated facts on the nature of ancient floras and faunas, on past climates, on human prehistory, and on the chronology of it all. These are precisely the kinds of facts that scientists have assumed all along are needed to provide an adequate explanation of late Pleistocene extinctions. Nonetheless, from an historical perspective one of the most interesting lessons to be learned from this volume is that we are apparently no closer to that adequate explanation, or at least to agreement as to what that adequate explanation is ....*

In other words, scientists are no closer to agreement, after 200 years of gathering data, which should have brought greater understanding. The problem, likely, is in their uniformitarian assumption. A few scientists involved in the investigation of the mystery, have admitted the inadequacy of this rigid constraint. Guthrie (1984, p. 292) candidly writes:

> *Looking at the extinction problem through the eyes of a young paleontologist in the early 1960s, I encountered my first important lesson—that the present can be used to understand the past only with sensitive discretion. In fact, much of the past may have no modern analogue.*

Guthrie is essentially saying that the uniformitarian assumption is almost useless. It will be argued here that the environment following the post-Flood glacial maximum provides a probable cause for the extinctions.

Before discussing this solution, a summary of the main uniformitarian arguments for these extinctions will be given. These arguments are instructive, and have a bearing on a post-Flood ice-age explanation, since the treatment given by uniformitarian scientists is partially correct.

Two main theories of Late Pleistocene extinctions are currently debated (Martin and Klein, 1984). One theory states that climate change at the end of the ice age killed the animals, and the other theory claims man killed them, in a great slaughter. Those who believe climate change is the culprit, point to the harsher climate at the end of the ice age, but "overkill" theorists ask why the last glaciation should be any different from the previous 20 to 30 postulated Pleistocene glaciations.

Overkill enthusiasts claim the extinctions in North America coincided with man's conquest of the New World, at about 11,000 years ago, in their dating scheme. Climate theorists counter by questioning the exact date. Krishtalka (1984, p. 226) points out:

> *Their selective acceptance of only the "good" dates —those that fit the model (for example dates for human beings in North America no older than 12,000 yr BP, and those for mammoths no younger than 10,000 yr BP)—may play fast and loose with the evidence that doesn't fit.*

Grayson reinforces the above comment with this eye-opening quotation: "The timing of Ice Age extinctions is really very poorly understood .... Radiocarbon chronologies are bad in North America and worse in Europe" (Bower, 1987, p. 285).

Those who support climate change as the principal factor, doubt whether man could have killed all those animals, especially since some of them ranged over most of the Northern Hemisphere. Animals that were not obvious prey to human hunters also became extinct (Lewin, 1987, p. 1509). Even ten classes of birds, mostly scavengers, became extinct in North America (Bower, 1987, p. 285). It is significant that primitive man did not kill off many large animals in Africa. If man was responsible for the mass slaughter, why did he not wipe out large, edible mammals like moose, elk, deer, and bison, in North America and Europe?

Overkill theorists charge that large mammals can easily migrate as the climate changes, and can better survive the cold (McDonald, 1984). Furthermore, the climate must have warmed, in order to melt the ice, and less ice should have provided more land for grass to grow. Proponents of the opposing view counter that, although the average climate was warming, the climate was also more continental, with colder winters and warmer summers. Fewer species of animals live in modern continental climates (Guthrie, 1984, pp. 287,288). A drier climate, while the ice sheets melted, would also favor smaller animals who needed less food.

So on and on the debate goes, each side making strong points. The reader can appreciate the quandry the experts are in. Most scientists have adopted some sort of compromise position (Anderson, 1984, p. 41).

Can a post-Flood ice age account for the extinction of many large mammals? The answer is yes. First, the animals thrived **during** the ice age because the climate was wetter, with milder winters, in contrast to uniformitarian expectations. Although large animals can survive the cold better than small animals, they can do so only if enough food is available. A wetter climate would provide adequate food. During the development of the ice sheets, the climate wasn't cold enough to cause animal extinction. As the ice sheets melted, winters became colder and drier—not warmer, as some authorities believe. Consequently, the largest animals would be the most stressed, due to lack of food. Many could have migrated, but, if the change was relatively sudden over a large area, they would have starved to death, by the time they found a suitable habitat.

Here is where man, the hunter, enters the picture, to finish the job. Man, who by this time had spread over most of the world, would also have been stressed by the harsher climate. Fruits, vegetables, and grains would have been scarce. He would have found these large mammals to be good hunting prey, and, possibly, the only food available. The fact that man did hunt the large animals, especially mammoths and mastodons, is shown by Neanderthal and Cro-Magnon cave paintings of these animals (Sutcliffe, 1985, pp. 82-104). In North America, 14 mammoths, with spear or arrow points embedded into the bone, have been found (Marshall, 1984, p. 790). Arrow points have also been found in mastodons in North America, and in a toxodon in South America (Nilsson, 1983, pp. 415,428). Burned bones of several other animals have been found with presumed human cultural remains.

We may conclude that man probably took part in the extinction of many large mammals; but, as the survival of other large animals attests, man was not completely responsible for the extinctions. Climate change is the other culprit. The reason for very few extinctions after other uniformitarian ice ages, is that there weren't any other ice ages.

While on the topic of extinction, something should be said about fossilization during the ice age. Fossilization is a rare event in the present world, but was common in the ice age. How did so many animals become buried and fossilized at that time?

Before glacial maximum, high volcanism could have trapped and buried some animals in ash, similar to when the eruption of Mt. Vesuvius buried the Roman city of Pompeii. In addition, heavy precipitation in non-glaciated regions would at times have caused severe flooding, which would have rapidly buried some animals.

During deglaciation, the cold, dry climate severely stressed the animals. Caves would have been good shelters. Many animals would have died of the cold, or starved in these caves. Caves are rich sources of ice-age mammals: "The quantity of mammalian remains found in caves and their fine state of preservation is sometimes astonishing" (Sutcliffe, 1985, p. 74). Rapid melting of the ice sheets caused large seasonal floods, rapidly trapping and entombing animals. Some animals became caught in violent dust storms south of the ice sheets. They would die of suffocation, and the dust would rapidly bury and preserve them. Fossil mammals are occasionally found in loess (Sutcliffe, 1985, p. 43). In areas close to the ice sheets, permafrost developed. When the top layer of permafrost melts in the summer, the mud is very sticky, and can flow down a gentle slope. This is called a gelifluction flow, and can sometimes bury an animal before it decomposes. Sutcliffe (1985, p. 41) relates about how 25 reindeer became trapped in a gelifluction mud flow in the Northwest Territories of Canada, in 1947. Local herders managed to pull 18 out, but the other seven were buried within a short time. It is evident that, during the ice age, the climate and environment provided many opportunities to trap, bury, and fossilize an abundant representation of the animal population.

Woolly Mammoth Extinction in Siberia and Alaska

The bones and carcasses of woolly mammoths unearthed in Siberia and Alaska, have taxed the imagination of scientist and layman alike. Explanatory theories are numerous. Most scientists adhere to the uniformitarian assumption, while some laymen have suggested strange catastrophes. For example, Charles Hapgood (1970, pp. 249-279) postulates a large, northward shift of the Siberian crust of the earth after the ice age. This shift, along with extensive volcanism and strong winds, presumably cooled Siberia, and killed the mammals.

The woolly mammoth cannot be isolated from the other late Pleistocene megafaunal extinctions discussed in the previous section. Mammoths completely died out all over the Northern Hemisphere during deglaciation. Hundreds of thousands, or perhaps millions of them died in Siberia and Alaska. The woolly mammoth, and the other mammals that were associated with it, are found, most abundantly, close to the Arctic Ocean, and on the islands off the coast (Stewart, 1977, p. 68).

The frozen carcasses have especially attracted attention, as indeed they should. They are only found in the area of permafrost which has preserved them to this day. Most of the mammoth carcasses are of animals that, apparently, were healthy and robust before they died. Some had eaten just before their death. The cause of death in at least some cases was by suffocation, or asphyxia. Farrand (1961, p. 734), reiterating the standard uniformitarian opinion, states:

> *The only direct evidence of the mode of death indicates that at least some of the frozen mammoths (and frozen woolly rhinoceroses as well) died of asphyxia, either by drowning or by being buried alive by a cave-in or mudflow. As stated above, sudden death is indicated by the robust condition of the animals and their full stomachs.*

Evidently at least some of the mammoths died suddenly, by suffocation, and were buried before major decomposition occurred.

The number of frozen carcasses must be kept in perspective. As of 1929, there were only 39 known carcasses of woolly mammoths and rhinoceroses (Tolmachoff, 1929, p. 20). Only about a half-dozen of these were actually complete; most were only a few small remnants of soft tissue attached to bones (Tolmachoff, 1929, p. 41). Since 1929, several more carcasses have been unearthed, including a baby mammoth discovered in 1977 (Stewart, 1977, 1979; Dubrovo et al., 1982).

Many more carcasses than are known must have existed, and must still exist in the frozen ground, because a carcass may completely rot before the sparse, superstitious, and fearful population of Siberia notice and report it. Often the carcass can decompose before a scientific expedition is organized to retrieve and find it in the barren, almost impassable terrain (Dillow, 1981, pp. 328-334). Most carcasses that have become exposed have completely decayed, without leaving a record. Tolmachoff (1929, p. 41) estimated that the number of carcasses, with some remaining soft parts, probably is hundreds or thousands of times more than known. This would bring the number of carcasses, or partial carcasses, up to about 50,000, which is still small, compared to the million or more that likely have been entombed. Consequently, most mammoths must have decayed completely, before, or while becoming interred in the permafrost. And the carcasses that are found show signs of partial decay before final freezing and burial in the permafrost.

Besides the small number of known carcasses, there are several other reasons for the conclusion that remains with flesh are rare. First, the mammoths are usually discovered while being eroded, and are practically always limited to bones and tusks (Tolmachoff, 1929, pp. 11-20; Stewart, 1977). Second, many bones and tusks were discovered by ivory hunters, who would be more willing than the few inhabitants to report a carcass. Third, a carcass can remain, at least partially intact, upon exposure, for several years before complete decay (Tolmachoff, 1929, pp. 24,31,60), increasing the odds that it would be discovered and reported.

The stomach contents of a few mammoth carcasses have heightened the mystery. Surprisingly, the stomach contents were only half digested—a condition believed to occur only if the mammoth cooled very quickly. Specialists from Birds Eye Frozen Foods Company concluded that the state of preservation of the stomach contents suggested an atmospheric temperature drop of below -150°F (Dillow, 1981, pp. 383-396).

Many of the plants in these stomach contents could still be identified. Some scientists have claimed that these plants indicate a much warmer climate, while others have claimed that they represent types found in the current Arctic tundra. The stomach contents have also led to the conclusion that the time of death was late summer or early fall. Since beans and other vegetation were found in the teeth of one carcass, the mammoth must have died while eating its last meal. Thus, a catastrophe seems to be the logical conclusion. But what kind of catastrophe? This depends upon the "facts" in the case, and the possible explanation of those facts. A close examination of what is known about the death of the woolly mammoth is needed.

A million or more mammoths that apparently were killed and buried in the permafrost suggest a climatic catastrophe. The climate must have been wetter and winters milder while they lived there. The permafrost must not have existed at the beginning of the catastrophe. Since the flesh has remained frozen to this day, the animals were buried while the permafrost developed. The catastrophe brought a permanent cooling of the climate. The rate at which the change in climate developed is an important consideration.

Since practically all the mammoth flesh decayed before, or during burial, the climate change could not have been a quick freeze. The small number of frozen carcasses is about what one would expect, by chance. In other words, the frozen carcasses are the result of rather rare conditions, involving rapid burial. It is clear that the mammoths were not quick frozen at -150°F and abruptly buried. Theories attempting to explain the frozen carcasses focus on the rare find, which could be due to rare, local conditions of preservation, and not to an instantaneous catastrophe of regional scale. The great number of animals that underwent normal decay and burial should be the actual basis for a theory of their demise.

Further evidence against a quick freeze is shown by the famished condition of the baby mammoth found in 1977, as proven by its lack of fat, and its ribs pathetically showing under the skin. If this mammoth was healthy before the catastrophe (as other carcasses were), its poor physical condition would take time to develop during the catastrophe. In addition, the contents of the skull were a putrified, structureless mass, which would not be the case in a quick freeze. The decay did not occur after becoming unearthed, because the carcass was actually bulldozed from below six feet of sediments, after being spotted in an ice wedge.

A third piece of evidence against a quick freeze, is that most of the remains are mammoths. Many other types of animals that were more fleet, lived with the woolly mammoth, and practically all escaped the catastrophe, probably by migrating out of the area. This would take time. A sudden drop in the temperature to below -150°F would stop all animals in their tracks.

Then how can the condition of the stomach contents be explained without a quick freeze? We may never know the answer. Dillow (1981, pp. 380,381) reasons that the state of stomach-preservation would have occurred, if the stomach temperature was reduced to 40°F in ten hours. This figure seems reasonable, but should be further evaluated. The reason for suggesting a quick freeze below -150°F is to produce a ten-hour cooling of the stomach to 40°F. There is a need to check into other possibilities that could account for the state of preservation of the stomach contents. Is there any other mechanism that can stop, or slow down the digestive processes immediately after death? This author has thought of several possibilities, but, so far, they are only speculation, without much knowledge of the mechanisms involved. The suggestion that other possibilities do exist is supported by preserved wood fragments from the stomach of a mastodon excavated in the warm country of Venezuela (Sutcliffe, 1985, p. 37).

What is the evidence, so far? First, a million or more well-fed mammoths, along with many other types of mammals, lived in a climate much warmer than at present, and with no permafrost. Second, the climate became much colder, resulting in the death of the mammoths, and the preserving of their remains in permafrost, which developed at the same time. The cooling was relatively rapid (otherwise, the mammoths would have been able to migrate out of Siberia) but not so rapid as to prevent most of the other animals from escaping. Third, since there are so few frozen carcasses, the catastrophe was not a regional quick freeze, as some popular accounts suggest. Most mammoth carcasses decomposed before burial, allowing enough time for normal decay. Fourth, after burial, the soil remained frozen to this day. The climate change to colder conditions was permanent. Taken together, the evidence indicates that the climate change was a relatively rapid and permanent shift from mild weather to a very cold climate.

Such a climate shift would occur at the end of a post-Flood, rapid ice age. Siberia and Alaska would have been much different during the ice age than today, with warmer temperatures and more moisture for plant growth (Chapter 5). As the ice age progressed and the Arctic Ocean cooled, these areas would also gradually cool. The animals living there would have been able to adapt, somewhat, to cold. The winter temperatures would still have been significantly warmer than they are now, as indicated by atmospheric simulations with an ice-free Arctic Ocean (Newson, 1973).

During deglaciation, the climate of Siberia and Alaska would turn colder, and drier, than it is at present. The melting ice sheets would provide fresh water for the Arctic Ocean. This fresh water would float on the denser salt water, and cause the rapid formation of sea ice, reinforcing the colder temperatures. Consequently, Siberia and Alaska, previously kept warm by an ice-free Arctic Ocean, would rapidly turn much colder.

Many animals had enough time to migrate to a less severe climate during deglaciation. The slower-moving mammals would, more likely, become trapped. The natural tendency for the mammoth, likely would have been to migrate to where the climate was always warmer in winter—towards the Arctic Ocean and away from the continental interior. But under the new climatic regime, north was the wrong way to go; and they died of the cold, in droves. The carcasses found with partially digested food in their stomachs may have suffocated after passage of a strong late summer or early-autumn cold front, accompanied by strong wind. The wind-chill factor can greatly enhance the cooling efficiency of the cold temperatures. For instance, at a temperature of -20°F and a wind of 30 miles per hour, the air can cool an animal as if the temperature was -78°F, and the wind calm. Cold wind has been known to suffocate and freeze cattle every year on the high plains of the United States (their nasal passages become blocked with ice).

Practically all the woolly mammoths decayed before final burial and freezing of the soil. Some, however, happened to be buried quickly enough to partially preserve their flesh. As the icecaps in the Asian mountains rapidly melted, the rivers of Siberia would be swollen with water and sediment. As the permafrost developed, the water could not soak into the ground. Gigantic floods would have occurred during rapid deglaciation, producing vast flood plains, especially close to the Arctic Ocean. In fact, Siberian rivers today swell to very large volumes in early summer because of snowmelt from huge drainage basins, and because the permafrost causes ground water to run off, instead of being absorbed into the soil (Untersteiner, 1984, pp. 137-139). The dead animals would be buried in this sediment at the beginning of deglaciation. Much of northern Siberia is one vast flood plain today, which is the result of the melting mountain icecaps. After depositing an alluvial flood plain, the rivers would eventually erode the alluvium, forming valleys and terraces. Thus, the mammoth remains would be left on the highest terraces, or bluffs, of modern or ancient rivers. This is where they are mostly found today.

The climate at the end of a post-Flood, rapid ice age answers most of the questions surrounding the death of the woolly mammoth in Siberia and Alaska.

CHAPTER 7

ONE ICE AGE, OR MANY?

Glacial geologists believe that ice ages occurred about once every 100,000 years. There is no agreement concerning the exact number of ice ages, but the usual estimate is in the neighborhood of 20, with complete deglaciations between them. Kennett (1982, p. 747) believes there may have been as many as 30 glacial episodes during the late Cenozoic, which includes the late Pliocene and the Pleistocene. In addition, several large oscillations, called stadials and interstadials, are presumed interspersed within each cycle. The Genesis Flood, on the other hand, was a unique event, and, consequently, the initial conditions for a post-Flood ice age occurred only once. The concept of multiple ice ages is directly contradictory to the model presented in this book. Is there actual evidence for just one ice age, as opposed to many? The purpose of this chapter is to investigate this question.

One could attempt to analyze all the detailed descriptions of glacial deposits on earth, but instead, let us examine the general, large-scale evidence that is more-or-less accepted by a majority of glacial geologists. Because of their attachment to the multiple glaciation hypothesis, they do not see the implication of this evidence. Glacial sediments, laid down by the ice sheets, are complicated and confused, on the local as well as the regional scale. Because of the many difficulties involved, it is probably impossible to sort out some of this data, in any model.

This chapter will focus only on the continental glacial deposits, which are the direct physical evidence of glaciation. Multiple glaciation, in relation to ocean sediments, was briefly discussed in Chapter 1, under the topic of the astronomical theory of the ice age, and has been treated elsewhere (Oard, 1984a,b, 1985). The continental glacial debris shows much fewer "glaciations" than the ocean sediments. Investigators are actively engaged in an effort to reconcile the two records.

The continental deposits are difficult to interpret, and the data are automatically fitted into the multiple glaciation model. In this chapter, a brief history of the multiple glaciation concept, with special focus on the alpine model, which held sway over the interpretation of geological data for over half a century will be presented. A discussion of the large-scale evidence for one ice age, as contrasted with multiple glaciations and their intervening interglacials follows. We will examine the basis for postulating interglacial periods, with special emphasis on soil stratigraphy. The chapter will end with an alternate explanation for the data used to support interglacial periods.

Early Debate on the Number of Glaciations

Glaciation, as an explanation for the surface deposits in the Alps and northern Europe, did not become popular until after 1840. It was not until Louis Agassiz published his *Studies on Glaciers*, that opinion switched from the Genesis Flood to glaciation, as the cause of the "drift," although a few men had previously held such a view (Imbrie and Imbrie, 1979, pp. 19-46). Unfortunately, there was a resultant erosion of belief that the Genesis Flood was a historic reality.

> *The catastrophist idea of the Noachian debacle was finally laid to rest when Louis Agassiz showed that his glacial theory could explain erratics, striations, till, fluvioglacial features, and so on. Old ideas die hard, however, and catastrophist absurdities still appeared in the literature of the early 1900's (as they do even today) (Baker, 1978, p. 1255).*

Early glacial theorists believed in only one ice age, but slowly, opinion changed to multiple ice ages. The reasons for this change are many. Some of them are: 1) the glacial deposits are complex, 2) till layers, separated by non-glacial deposits, do occur, 3) the complex behavior of modern glaciers was not well known at that time, and 4) the uniformitarian principle was strictly held.

The earliest suggestion that more than one ice age had developed came in 1847, when Edouard Collomb reported two layers of till in the Vosges Mountains of France. These layers were separated by stream deposits, and could easily be interpreted as a minor retreat and readvance of the glacial terminus (Imbrie and Imbrie, 1979, p. 56). So the first suggestion of multiple glaciation was a likely misinterpretation. But the concept of multiple glaciations caught on. Two ice ages were soon claimed for other glaciated areas, although most geologists, at that time, preferred one glaciation, with minor oscillations (Bowen, 1978, pp. 1,2; Imbrie and Imbrie, 1979, p. 57). Due to the complexity of the glacial sediments, by the middle 1870s three or more glacial periods were being proposed: "In some places, only two tills were found, but in others it was possible to show that there had been at least six separate glacial ages, each followed by a warm interval" (Imbrie and Imbrie, 1979, p. 90). Due to the influence of the alpine model, four ice ages were finally agreed upon, in the early 20th century. The alpine model has a valuable lesson to teach us, so it will be discussed in a separate section.

The astronomical theory of the ice ages, although poorly developed at the time, influenced scientists to accept multiple ice ages. Charlesworth (1957, p. 911) states: "The sceptics in all countries include those who accept elevation as the cause of glaciation ..., just as believers in astronomical causes favour multiple glaciation." The sceptics he is referring to are those who believed in one glaciation.

Charlesworth (1957, pp. 920-924) lists all the areas that provide evidence for anywhere from one-to-six glaciations. Despite the influence of the alpine model (which was strong at that time), he believed the evidence mainly supported only two glacial epochs:

> *Bearing in mind the conscious or unconscious influence of the Alpine classification and the tendency to confuse minor variations or retreat phases with oscillations of interglacial magnitude, definite evidence cannot at present be said to exist for more than one long interglacial epoch (Charlesworth, 1957, pp. 923,924).*

In other words, he believed the glacial sediments supported only two glaciations, with minor oscillations at the margin, and that the alpine classification influenced Quaternary geologists to think in terms of more than two. Notice, also, that Charlesworth indicates that minor oscillations, at the margin, have been taken to represent complete ice ages.

As of 1957, a few mainstream scientists still believed in one glaciation (Lougee and Lougee, 1976), although the number had been steadily dwindling. Charlesworth (1957, pp. 911-914) devotes four pages of his massive 1,700-page tome, to refuting these monoglacialists. His criticism is valid within the uniformitarian framework, but the problems he presents can also be solved by a relatively mild climate, during a single ice age.

Glacial Sediments Complex

Why is there so much debate on the number of glaciations (which still continues today)? The reason is because the glacial sediments are indeed complex, and many processes, other than ice, have shaped them. Bowen (1978, pp. 173-180) states that glacial deposition is more complex than previously thought, and has received much erroneous interpretation. Modern glaciers show a great variety of depositional sequences, with special complexity near the margins. For instance, glacial till is acted on by rivers and streams, and also by currents in proglacial lakes, and it can flow downslope as a debris flow.

Different till layers have overlapping characteristics, and there are rapid lateral changes in facies or sediment type (Eyles, 1983). Consequently, it is difficult to distinguish between different till layers that were supposedly deposited by separate ice ages. The "type section" approach has normally been employed to classify and correlate glacial sediments, as well as pre-Pleistocene sediments. In this method, a "classical," or well-behaved vertical sequence is selected that represents a specific period of time, and is then given a name, such as the Kansan till. Several of these type sections are pieced together from different regions to form a supposed time series. Vertical sections, or well cores taken from the periphery of glaciation usually penetrate only one layer of till, which causes difficulty in correlating the sediments to the type section. But each local vertical profile is, nevertheless, "dated," by matching to one or more of these type sections.

The type-section approach is simplistic and subjective. Many glacial geologists are advocating that it be replaced by a three-dimensional, or depositional basin approach. Eyles (1983, p. 15) states: "Many studies show that applying generalized stratigraphic names, derived from a single or few 'type-sites,' obscures the real nature of regional and local sedimentary sequences." By applying the depositional basin or land-system approach, multiple till layers have often been found to be the product of only one ice sheet, rather than several.

A recent controversy shows how difficult glacial deposits are to interpret. A classical area for studying multiple glaciations is the Scarborough Bluffs, on the north shore of Lake Ontario. Previous geological work had divided the bluffs into various till sheets, attributed to several different glaciations. More recent investigators not only changed the boundaries of lithostratigraphic units on the bluffs, but also concluded that the sediments were deposited by one ice advance. Furthermore, the whole sequence was presumed to have been laid down in a proglacial lake below a floating ice sheet, not brought into place directly by an ice sheet (Eyles et al., 1983a; Eyles and Eyles, 1983; Karrow, 1984). It would seem that glacial geology is in real trouble, if experts have difficulty telling the difference between sediments laid down directly by a glacier, and sediments dropped into a lake by floating ice.

Kemmis and Hallberg (1984, p. 889) try to excuse previous interpretations by saying: "We feel that competent glacial geologists have always tried to evaluate glacigenic sequences based on the best available depositional models at the time of their study." What they are saying, is that the interpretation of field data is filtered by, and interpreted by, models. This influences the "data" that are seen, as well as those which are reported. The multiple glaciation model is one of those models, and the glacial evidence has been automatically fitted into it. This is one good reason to give little emphasis to local data, and to be skeptical concerning the number of presumed glaciations.

One would think that borehole data, especially in areas with no vertical exposures, would greatly aid a three-dimensional interpretation of glacial sediments and show distinct till layers over large areas. This has not been the case (Eyles, 1983, p. 11). Nilsson (1983, p. 167) says that details of classification schemes that depend upon borings should be viewed with skepticism, because coastal cliff exposures reveal it is often difficult "... to establish a reliable stratigraphy in formerly glaciated areas because of disturbances induced by post depositional ice action."

The Alpine Model and the Reinforcement Syndrome

The alpine model did more to cement multiple glaciations in the minds of scientists than any other development. If you ask most laymen—and even some scientists today—how many ice ages occurred in the recent past, they would tell you four. The four-ice-age concept is derived mainly from the alpine model which was developed in the Swiss Alps at the turn of the century. This model was replaced in the 1970s by another model, the astronomical model, according to which the alpine model is now entirely wrong. Looking back on the development of the alpine model, its scientific basis, and its acceptance, provides considerable insight into the methodology in this field, and the influence of a few prominent individuals on two generations of scientists.

How did the alpine model develop? By 1885, Albrecht Penck had developed a method that he thought determined the number of glaciations. He connected gravel terraces along river valleys north of the Alps with end moraines farther south in the foothills. By counting river terraces, he arrived at the number of glaciations. At first, he was able to identify only three gravel terraces and connect the two lower terraces to end moraines. Later, he managed to find another river terrace and connect all four to end moraines (Bowen, 1978, pp. 10,13; Imbrie and Imbrie, 1979, pp. 114,115). The publication, in 1909, by Penck, along with Eduard Brückner, of their classic results, solidified opinion on the concept of four ice ages. Others later added more substages to the four-ice-age scheme by claiming some terraces were compound. The purpose of this was to harmonize the alpine data with the astronomical model of ice ages, which claims many more than four glaciations (Bowen, 1978, p. 18).

The alpine model became so influential, that all data worldwide were interpreted according to it, whether it fit or not. This is called the reinforcement syndrome—the initial discovery of a phenomenon exerts a powerful influence on subsequent research. All published data were fitted into the alpine model so well that there appeared to be no contradictions (Oard, 1985, pp. 178,179). Watkins (1972, p. 563) writes:

> *Perhaps, the best known, or at least most significant, result of the "reinforcement syndrome" in the geological sciences is the very firmly*

established concept of four glacial periods during the last Ice Age. The initially defined system was confirmed by many different studies.

After stating some of the serious problems facing Quaternary investigators, and referring especially to the alpine classification, Bowen (1978, pp. 7,8) corroborates:

Indeed it could be said that force-fitting of the pieces into preconceived pigeon-holed classifications is what is almost a way of life for the Quaternary worker .... Tendencies to oversimplify in this way lead to new discoveries being forced into a pigeon-holed classification. Such arbitrary methods tend to perpetuate an illusion of security and precision in an apparently repeated confirmation of the original model. This tendency to confirm discoveries from limited amounts of data has been called The Reinforcement Syndrome ....

The reinforcement syndrome continues in ice age research today, but with a new model—the astronomical theory.

Looking back on the alpine classification, glacial geologists are more free to point out its errors. Many problems of interpretation can readily be seen. For instance, the gravel terraces are usually not continuous along the edge of the rivers, but are highly dissected due to erosion (Bowen, 1978, pp. 13-16). It is, indeed, surprising that this kind of evidence could support multiple glaciations. This view is supported by Flint (1971, pp. 643-645), who says that the Alps is a poor area for defining the number of glaciations in the first place, because of the steep slopes and erosion that has destroyed much of the sedimentary record.

Another problem is that the river terraces are poorly connected to the patchy glacial moraines upstream, and Penck and Brückner concentrated on only a few of the river valleys which do not represent the north slopes of the Alps as a whole (Flint, 1971, p. 644). Moreover, the two upper terraces in the four-fold scheme are only small remnants at different elevations. This is probably the reason for Penck's early results supposedly verifying first three, then four glaciations. The alpine ice ages were separated by morphological criteria applied to the gravel terraces, and not by time data. There was little or no evidence representing interglacial time (Bowen, 1978, p. 10). The later discovery of peat, warm climate mollusks, and soils within the "glacial" gravels caused much confusion. The river terraces are now claimed, by some, as due to uplift of the Alps: "Kukla (1977) demonstrated that the fourfold sequence in the Alps may be a result of repeated tectonic uplift cycles, not widespread climatic change *per se*" (Eyles et al., 1983b, p. 217).

Since the gravel terraces cannot be related to any time scale, they could have formed rapidly (as indicated in Chapter 6). Bowen (1978, p. 17) even states:

Moreover, from what is now known about glacial pulse [sic] during the Pleistocene it could be argued that each end-moraine and its associated outwash terrace only represents a few thousand years at most of one cold stage or glacial cycle.

Bowen is speaking about new ideas on glacial oscillations within one glaciation, while still interpreting the time of formation of the terraces mostly within the uniformitarian framework of long ages. If the terraces could have formed as quickly as Bowen proposes during one glaciation in the greatly stretched-out uniformitarian time scale, they could have formed very rapidly during one rapid ice age (see Chapter 6).

The main point to be learned from the debate on the number of glaciations, especially in the alpine model, is that the number of glaciations proposed in the past has always been arbitrary, and based on poor evidence. The glacial deposits are so complicated, the number of glaciations is difficult to determine. The available methods for analysis of the observations have serious problems, and misinterpretation is easy. There is physical evidence for fewer than four, as Charlesworth's more objective appraisal indicates. The number of glaciations recorded by continental deposits is still an open, scientific question.

Evidence for One Ice Age

Perhaps the strongest evidence against ice ages repeating every 100,000 years is the uniformitarian principle itself. As discussed in Chapter 1, Williams (1979) showed that a temperature drop of 10 to 12°C, and double the winter snowfall would be required just to glaciate northeast Canada (Figure 1.3). If one ice age is this difficult to account for, what are the odds against two, three, or 30 in succession?

In the standard explanation of glaciation, an ice sheet develops in the far north, grows large, and moves outward to the southern periphery. In its advance from the far north, the ice sheet picks up debris at its base, and transports this debris southward. How far this debris is transported before deposition, depends upon the distance upward in the ice the debris is entrained, the velocity of the ice sheet, and the amount of basal melting. Each successive ice sheet should continually transport the debris farther and farther south. Since most of the debris is from the last ice age (see below), each ice sheet must have been able to totally incorporate almost all this debris. (Almost complete reworking of deposits from previous glaciations is the reason many investigators claim that the continental sediments are unreliable for determining the number of glaciations, and hence urge reliance on the indirect record from ocean sediments.) Some investigators now believe that ice sheets moved relatively fast (Boulton, 1986). Thus, we would expect to find a large amount of glacial till that has been transported long distances from the north.

Is this what we observe? Other than a small number of "far-traveled" erratics, practically all the glacial deposits are local (Flint, 1971, pp. 110,152,190; Whillans, 1978). Flint (1971, p. 174) writes:

> *The average distance of travel of the components of till is not known. It was long ago established that much of the coarse fraction consists of material of fairly local lithology, and this led to the belief that till as a whole is of predominantly local origin.*

The fine fraction, of course, cannot be used to identify provenance, because it is mostly crushed quartz and feldspar, which is common to many rocks. Flint generally accepts the local nature of most tills, but seems confused, due to the presence of far-traveled erratics. Admittedly, far-traveled erratics are a problem for a one-ice-age model, but there are problems of interpretation, and some seemingly contradictory data on these exotic rocks, which will be discussed in Chapter 9.

Other workers substantiate Flint's comment on the local origin of most glacial till. In referring to the Canadian Arctic, Bird (1967, p. 107) declares: "The majority of tills are derived from bedrock in the immediate vicinity." Feininger (1971, p. C79) indicates that the evidence for the short transport of till is solid, by the following comment:

> *Earlier in this report, the nearness of most glacial boulders to their source was cited as evidence that glacial transport is generally short. Even stronger evidence to support this view can be read from the tills themselves. Where the direction of movement carried a continental ice sheet from one terrain to another of markedly different rock type, the tills derived from each terrain are predominantly restricted to the area of their corresponding source rocks.*

We have been discussing North America, but the same holds true for the Scandinavian ice sheet. Most of the till in Norway and Sweden is local—moved not much farther than about five kilometers (Haldorsen, 1983, p. 11; Lundqvist, 1983b, p. 83).

The local nature of most till is not what one would expect, even with a standard uniformitarian interpretation for only one ice age. Efforts are being made to explain this contradiction (Whillans, 1978), but the evidence favors one relatively thin ice sheet that did not travel far, but grew in situ and melted after a short time.

Further indication of only one ice age is provided by the fact that practically all the till was laid down during the last of the uniformitarian sequence of ice ages. Moreover, most of this till is from the **last advance** of the last ice age (Flint, 1971, p. 641; Sugden and John, 1976, p. 133). The main reason for this conclusion is the fresh appearance of most of the till. Intensive search has been focused to find till from previous ice ages. (In view of the strong desire to find till from previous ice ages, and in view of the complexity of glacial debris, it **is** surprising that so little success has been claimed. From the viewpoint of the post-Flood model, the limited success **is not** surprising.) The amount of such material "discovered" is very small. Sugden and John (1976, p. 138), in reference to glaciations other than the last, state: "We shall not, therefore, consider these glaciations in any detail—a task which would in any case be difficult because of the scarcity of supporting evidence." Uniformitarian scientists commonly appeal to extensive erosion to account for absence of till from earlier glaciations. A popular analogy, credited to Maurice Ewing, likened each continental glaciation to an eraser. Each successive ice sheet erases all, or most of the evidence for the previous ice sheet, making the evidence analogous to the ephemeral writing on a blackboard.

If this is the case, an enormous depth of till should have accumulated at the periphery, much of it indicating long-distance transport from the north, but there is little evidence for either deep accumulations or far-traveled debris. A straightforward reading of all the evidence, without resorting to added hypotheses, better indicates that the main volume of till is the result of just one ice age, which was not only the last, but also the first.

In addition to the till, most of the loess south of the ice sheets is also from the last glaciation, at least in North America (Flint, 1971, p. 258; Pye, 1987, p. 245). With loess, ice-age authorities cannot appeal to extensive erosion and reworking by an ice sheet to account for the lack of loess from previous glaciations.

The character of the till left in the interior regions, like Canada and Scandinavia, is especially revealing. Interior regions are areas where each successive ice sheet is believed to have built up to over 3,000 meters high. We would expect to see a moderate amount of till in these areas. Just the last thick ice sheet, slowly melting northward through Canada for thousands of years, should have left behind thick, fine-grained till. The opposite is observed. The till is only two to ten meters thick, on the Canadian shield, and is found mainly in depressions, and partly deposited by streams (Eyles et al., 1983b, p. 227). The till is also coarse-grained, suggesting little transport and reworking. A similar pattern characterizes Scandinavia. Haldorsen (1983, pp. 11-13) states that till, in Norway, is not extensive, and, where found, is coarse-grained, and averages less than five meters deep. Till depth averages five to 15 meters in Sweden, and two to three meters in Finland (Flint, 1971, p. 150). Moreover, this till is predominantly from the last ice age (Lundqvist, 1983a, p. 77; 1986, p. 251; Bjorlykke, 1985, p. 198).

This puzzling state of affairs is no longer explained by enhanced erosion with deposition further south, but by ineffective deposition on the shield (Eyles, 1983, p. 4). The new explanation does not fit the evidence any better than the old one did. Observations on modern glaciers show that even if only one thick ice sheet melted northward through Canada, great erosion and till deposition would result. Due to the thickness of the supposed ice sheets, which insulates the base from the cold atmosphere and allows geothermal heat to warm the base, some investigators now assume that, on the Canadian shield, the ice sheet was wet-based (Eyles et al., 1983b, p. 226). Motion would be more rapid and erosion more intense with a wet-based glacier than with a cold-based one.

Interior regions received very little erosion from all the presumed glacial activity. The crystalline bedrock of the Canadian shield is of moderate relief, and only slightly planed down by glacial abrasion. Whether the crystalline rocks are underneath a cover of sedimentary rocks, or exposed, as they are in most regions, the bedrock relief is similar. This demonstrates that there has been little erosion from glacial ice. Flint (1971, p. 115) has noticed the evidence of slight erosion of the Canadian shield, and further adds:

> *Local evidence of slight depth of glacial erosion has been reported from many different districts .... Indeed, the detailed adjustment of drainage to lithology, long antedating the glaciation and yet not destroyed by that event, is a feature that characterizes wide areas of the Canadian Shield.*

Flint (1971, pp. 114,115) believes that erosion of Scandinavia must have been tremendous. This is inconsistent with the evidence from Canada. Other more modern studies, however, indicate Scandinavia was also only slightly eroded (Haldorsen, 1983, p. 11). The explanation offered for this slight erosion is the dominance of resistant bedrock types in Scandinavia.

So we are asked to believe that the many presumed ice sheets that have developed and melted northward in interior regions, neither eroded nor deposited much debris! A better explanation is that the thinness and coarseness of the till, and the slight erosion in interior regions, was the result of only one slow-moving, thin ice sheet that developed in Canada and Scandinavia.

The main "proof" of multiple glaciation actually comes from the periphery of the ice sheets (Sugden and John, 1976, p. 139). Andrews (1979, p. 208) states that areas of thick glacial "... deposits are really restricted to a belt about 300km wide which extends inward from the ice limits." This area will be examined more closely. Though thicker than in most locations, the till in this area is not excessively thick. Flint (1971, pp. 149-151) gives the average till thickness for many localities. Iowa averages about 52 meters, Illinois 35 meters, Central Ohio 29 meters, central New York 18 meters, southwest Alberta 15 meters, the Great Lakes region 12 meters, and New Hampshire ten meters. In general, the thickest deposits are close to the edge of the Laurentide ice sheet south of the Great Lakes area, and thinner in all directions from there.

The thickness along the edge of the Scandinavian ice sheet is not much different. Flint lists glacial debris thickness in Denmark ranging from 20 to 40 meters. More recent figures are about ten meters higher, but about 65% of this is glaciofluvial sediments (Nielsen, 1983, p. 193), which usually have been considered as "till" by most glacial geologists. In fact, Eyles and Eyles (1983, p. 152) indicate that substantial amounts of continental till are actually glaciolacustrine sediments. Thus, the average till thickness for the whole periphery of both the Laurentide and Scandinavian ice sheets is not over 30 meters, and much of this till does not represent the glacially eroded debris of land-based ice sheets. This is exceedingly thin, for all the presumed glacial activity, especially in view of the likelihood of the ice sheets incorporating unconsolidated pre-glacial surface deposits (Feininger, 1971).

The till thickness is much greater in buried valleys and some end moraines. Flint's list includes several maximum thicknesses of till in the 150-to-400 meter range. These examples are predominantly in buried valleys, which would be natural traps for glacial debris. Flint (1971, p. 149) comments on these areas: "The largest values in Table 7-A occur in buried valleys, and represent ancient valley fills. Other areas of thick drift occur in massive end moraines ...." In an analysis of mechanisms for till deposition, the average is what counts.

How much time would be required for an average of 30 meters of till to accumulate, assuming none of it is glaciolacustrine or pre-glacial regolith? To answer this question, many variables must be considered, such as whether a glacier is cold-based or wet-based, moves rapidly, is subject to surges, etc. Glacial-till can be deposited rapidly, under the right circumstances. Flint (1971, p. 149) states:

> *Volume of deposited drift is determined by load, velocity of flow, and time. With high load and velocity values, the time can be short. For example the Sefström Glacier in Spitsbergen built a pile of till 30m thick in less than 10 years.*

Goldthwait (1974) summarizes 16 years of observations of ice wastage in Muir Inlet and outer Lituya Bay, of Glacier Bay, Alaska. Discounting the rates of formation deduced from C-14 dating of wood, directly observed rates of formation of many glacial features, which could be analogous to glacial features in North America, were rapid. Basal till accumulated at 0.5 to 2.5 cm/yr. Each till sheet of about one-to-five meters thickness represented about two centuries of erosion and deposition. Minor moraine ridges abound in the area. They are 0.5 to 2.5 meters high, and each was deposited in one to five years. Meltwater channels were observed to erode rapidly. Most impressive was one stream with a flow of only 200 cubic feet per second on many summer days, yet cut into bedrock at a rate of one to two meters a year. A seven-meter-high esker probably formed in just five years. Kame terraces developed in a year or two.

These observations from modern glaciers, although rapid according to assumed rates for a uniformitarian ice age, are still too slow for a 700-year ice age. But the post-Flood ice age cannot be compared directly with modern glacial features. Evidence that the flow velocity for the ice sheets was significantly greater than for the preponderance of modern glaciers will be presented later in this chapter. A higher erosion rate would be associated with a higher velocity. For a comparison, consider the erosion rate on Glacier d'Argentière in the Alps, as measured by a marble platten attached to bedrock beneath the ice (Drewry, 1986, p. 84). The observed erosion rate was 3.6 cm/yr at a glacier flow rate of 250 meters/year. Another wet-based glacier in Iceland, with a much slower flow velocity, eroded at a much smaller rate. Since a post-Flood ice age would most likely have higher erosion rates, a 5 cm/yr rate might be assumed. At this rate, 30 meters of till could be deposited along the periphery, in 600 years. This does not take into account the loose, pre-glacial surface material that must have been incorporated into the till, or the significant proportion of this till that would be lake or stream deposits. In view of these considerations, one wonders why the till along the periphery is so thin, if 20 to 30 ice sheets repeatedly deposited material in this zone for over two million years.

Besides the character of till over the interior and at the periphery, the areas within the periphery, where till is lacking, also point more towards one, than to multiple glaciations. We are speaking of the "driftless areas," the most famous of which is located in southwest Wisconsin, in small portions of southeast Minnesota, and in northeast Iowa. This area, apparently, was never overrun by a glacier at any time. Other driftless areas are found on the low relief plains of northeast Montana and extreme south central Saskatchewan (Lemke et al., 1965, p. 16; Mathews, 1974, p. 39). These driftless areas are depicted in Figure 7.1, along with the boundary of the four postulated ice ages in the central United States. These driftless areas should have been covered, at least once, by a thick ice sheet descending out of Canada, according to the uniformitarian model. Even one thin post-Flood ice sheet may have trouble explaining why these driftless areas were not glaciated. But how could many thick ice sheets all miss these areas, if, indeed, there were many thick ice sheets?

Not only does the character of the glacial till better support one ice age, but also, the animals and plants that lived at the time give similar support. The fossils are generally the same in each postulated interglacial period between each theoretical ice age (Charlesworth, 1957, p. 1025). Flint (1971, p. 376) states:

> *Nevertheless, in Quaternary strata correlation by means of fossils encounters special difficulties. Rates of change of Quaternary environments were generally more rapid than rates of evolution in Quaternary organisms. The*

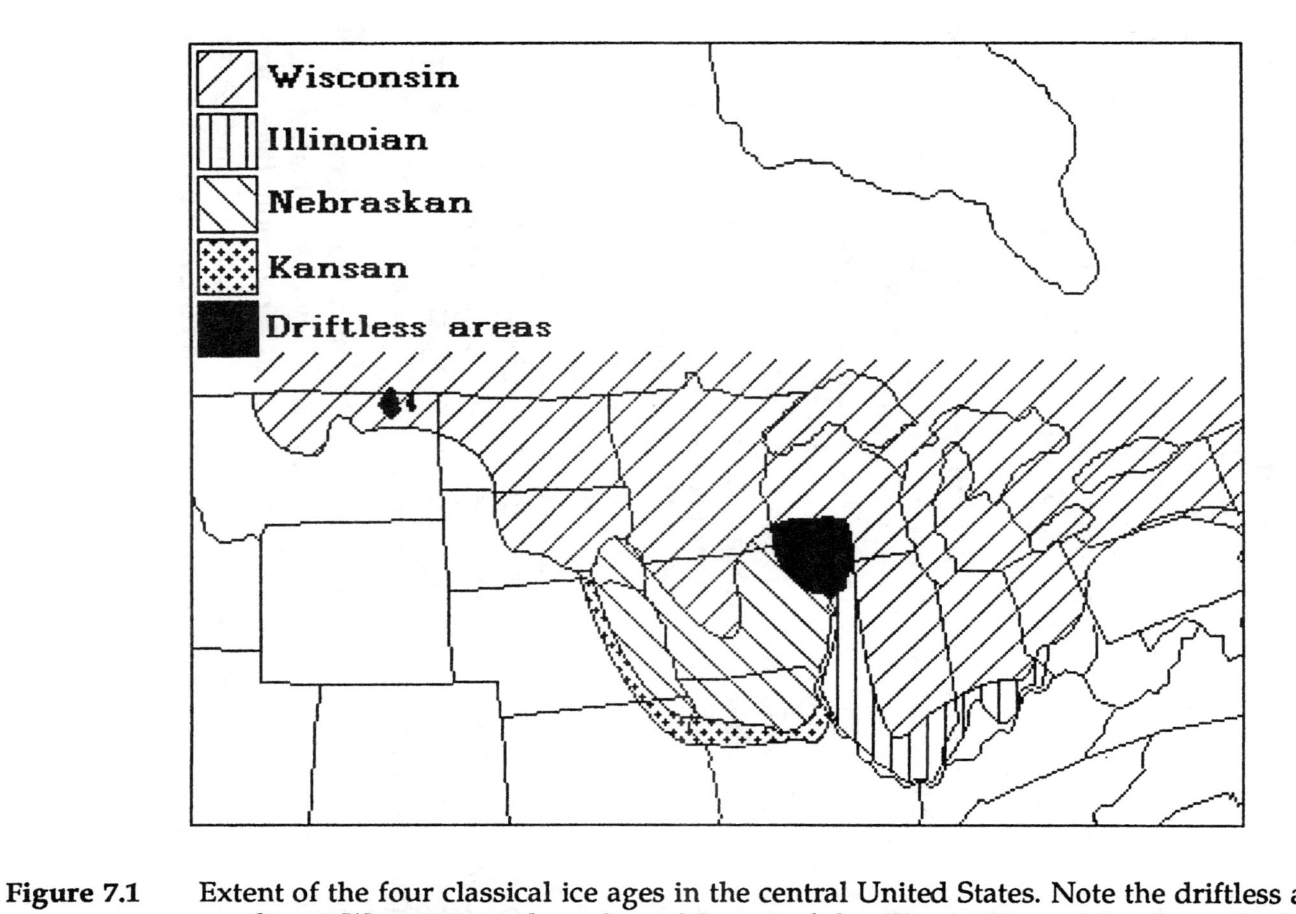

Figure 7.1 Extent of the four classical ice ages in the central United States. Note the driftless areas in southwest Wisconsin and northeast Montana (after Flint, 1971, and Lemke and others, 1965).

same faunas may appear repeatedly in successive strata, and their transgression of time is commonly evident.

With respect to the flora, Bowen (1978, p. 38) acknowledges: "The fact is that similar constellations of species were repeated several times in the Pleistocene, though not perhaps in the same relative abundance." Sutcliffe (1985, p. 52) also concurs. In other words, few fossil criteria are available to distinguish between each particular interglacial. We would expect sizeable flora and fauna differences between each interglacial, because the severe stress of the ice ages should have caused significant evolutionary changes (assuming the theory of evolution is true), and because of the many variables that should influence animal distributions over long stretches of time. Although the standard explanation is to simply postulate slight evolutionary changes, the data fits a single ice-age model more reasonably.

Secondly, practically all the fossils are found in nonglaciated areas. Animals and plants should have repopulated interior areas, after each ice sheet melted. The musk ox and reindeer would surely migrate back to the northland, after each glaciation. During the long interglacials, abundant bones, or fossils of cold-tolerant animals should have been deposited. Their absence is, indeed, mysterious within the multiple glaciation hypothesis. The claim may be made that animals simply did not become fossilized during interglacials. This contention is hollow, because the numerous fossils found in the muck of Alaska are attributed to an interglacial period. With respect to the fleet mammals, Flint (1971, p. 771) states: "The general rarity of fossil mammals in glaciated as compared with nonglaciated North America suggests that the rich Alaskan faunas are probably interglacial." The climate south of the ice sheets during each presumed glacial epoch, probably would have been similar to the climate over interior areas during interglacials. Many fossils are found in the former areas. Their lack in glaciated areas strongly suggests that there were no interglacial periods, which means there was only one ice age.

Thirdly, nearly all of the extinctions of large mammals occurred after the last glaciation. Very few occurred after postulated, previous glaciations. Each ice age would have been very stressful to the animals. How could they survive 20-to-30 ice ages, over a two-or-three-million year period, and then go extinct only after the last? The record of extinctions is more consistent with just one ice age.

Table 7.1. Summary of evidence supporting only one ice age

1)	One ice age meteorologically difficult
2)	Most till local
3)	Most till predominantly from the "last"
4)	Most North American loess from the "last"
5)	Interior till thin and coarse-grained
6)	Bedrock slightly eroded in interior areas
7)	Inadequate thickness of periphery till
8)	Driftless areas within periphery
9)	Little change in flora and fauna
10)	Fossils rare in glaciated regions
11)	Most extinctions after the "last"

The evidence supporting only one ice age is summarized in Table 7.1. As stated previously, this evidence is mostly general, and large-scale. The meteorological difficulties of accounting for just one uniformitarian ice age (see Chapter 1), the character of the till over interior areas as well as along the periphery, the lack of loess from previous glaciations in North America, and the character of the ice age fossils, all favor one ice age in preference to multiple ice ages.

The Basis for Interglacials

If there was only one ice age, why do uniformitarian scientists postulate interglacial periods between till sheets? What is this evidence for interglacials, and how valid is this evidence, as proof of multiple glaciation? Can a single ice age explain this evidence? This section will examine the evidence for interglacial periods. The last section of this chapter will explain the evidence from the viewpoint of a single ice age.

The evidence for interglacial periods is summarized by Charlesworth (1957, p. 900):

> *Interglacial or "warm" epochs are proved stratigraphically by sheets of till, fluvialglacial deposits or loess which are separated by zones of weathering and by fossiliferous beds, either fluviatile, lacustrine or marine, e.g. on Long Island, or by peat, forest or other vegetation layer, lignites, soils, tufas, iron-ores and diatomaceous earths (e.g. Jutland and the Lüneburger Heide).*

In other words, the evidence for interglacials consists of soils, zones of weathering, and fossils between layers of till, glaciofluvial sediments, and loess. Soils and zones of weathering include tufa ($CaCO_3$ layers), and iron-rich sediments, which are characterized by various shades of red color. Fossiliferous beds include peat, lignite, and diatomaceous earth. Lignite is a brownish-black, low-grade coal. Diatomaceous earths are beds of diatom remains, and are rare in glacial sediments.

How abundant are these interglacial deposits? Are we trying to explain widespread features, or rare occurrences? It makes a difference, since rare deposits can easily be due to local conditions during a complex ice age. The answer is that interglacial deposits are rare. They are almost nonexistent in interior regions of formerly glaciated areas. Even at the periphery, organic remains are not abundant. Charlesworth (1957, p. 1025) states:

> *Pleistocene correlations are difficult and uncertain; time divisions are short; glacial deposits are virtually unfossiliferous; interglacial accumulations, if fossiliferous, occur in isolated and discontinuous patches ....*

Elsewhere he writes: "Within the glaciated territory, interglacial horizons are rarely more than fragmentary" (Charlesworth, 1957, p. 903). As discussed in the previous section, practically all ice-age fossils are found in nonglaciated areas. The northern Alps, where the fourfold glacial classification became established, did not contain any interglacial deposits between the river terraces, although warmth-indicating fossils were found in the "glacial" gravels. Most of the fossils in interglacial layers are vegetable material: pieces of wood, peat, or lignite. This material is often found in small depressions, that provided protection from erosion (Ehlers, 1983, p. 234; Felix-Henningsen, 1983). It is possible that the vegetation layers were washed into the depressions during periods of high rainfall, instead of having been formed from plant growth, in place, over an extended period of time. The rare organic deposits at least indicate that in some areas there was sufficient time between glacial advances for vegetation to grow.

Before discussing soils, which is the main evidence for multiple glaciation, mention should be made of the postulated interglacial features in loess, and fluvioglacial sediments south of the ice sheet boundaries. This evidence consists mainly of an ancient soil, called a paleosol, between layers of loess, or on top of fluvioglacial terrace deposits. Since this evidence is found in nonglaciated areas, it is not directly linked to the glacial/interglacial stratigraphy of glaciated lands. Therefore, it provides uncertain support for multiple glaciations, at best.

Furthermore, there are just as many problems in deriving a stratigraphy in loess and fluvioglacial sediments, as there are in till. For instance, George Kukla (1975,1977) developed a loess/paleosol time scale from abandoned river terraces in eastern Europe. Figure 7.2 represents one of two key areas he studied near Brno, Czechoslovakia. He assumed that the higher terraces are much older than the lower terraces. After stating that miscorrelation has been common in past studies, he (Kukla, 1977) confidently correlates the loess/paleosol layers to the oxygen isotope record in deep-sea cores, mainly by simple curve-matching.

The depth of the sequence studied by Kukla, varies from ten to 30 meters (Figure 7.2), and was supposedly deposited in about one million years. The higher terraces are obviously older than those below them, but the time difference could be in years, rather than in the long time period Kukla presumes (see Chapter 6). Since the total depth of the deposits is rather thin, periodic strong winds during a dry period, could have laid these deposits in a very short time. The staircase structure of the terraces would have provided a natural trap for blowing dust. It is well known, that during the dust-bowl years in the midwestern United States during the 1930s, blowing sand and dust rapidly covered fences, and partially buried farm buildings (Landsberg, 1958, pp. 267,268). In the river valleys that Kukla studied, occasional strong winds are responsible for at least part of the sequence, as indicated by frequent sandy interlayers and wind-moved rock fragments on the slopes (Kukla, 1977, pp. 324,325). During periods of nondeposition, a soil, if they are really soils, could develop rapidly (see next section). Furthermore, the loess/soil transitions generally are sharp, indicating little erosion or time interval (Kukla, 1977, p. 335).

The best conclusion, from the evidence, is that loess/paleosol stratigraphy in non-glaciated areas does not represent a long period of time. This stratigraphy is not independent data, and is a poor basis for surmising glacial/interglacial oscillations.

Interglacial Soils

Since organic remains are rare in formerly glaciated areas, the most widely used method for distinguishing the various glacial periods has been paleosols between, or on top of, till layers at the periphery. Not only is a paleosol presumed to designate an interglacial period, but various properties of the paleosols are used to "date" each ice age. On this basis, a glacial/interglacial stratigraphy has been developed from ancient soils, especially in the north-central United States (Table 7.2 and Figure 7.1). Birkeland (1984, p. 325) states: "Soils are important to the subdivisions of Quaternary sediments, whether the soils are at the surface or buried." However, this method is now slowly being abandoned. The reason for this, is the replacement of soil stratigraphy with oxygen-isotope stratigraphy from the ocean. Soil stratigraphy is now claimed to have been always faulty. Since ancient soils are the main physical evidence for interglacials, paleosols will be

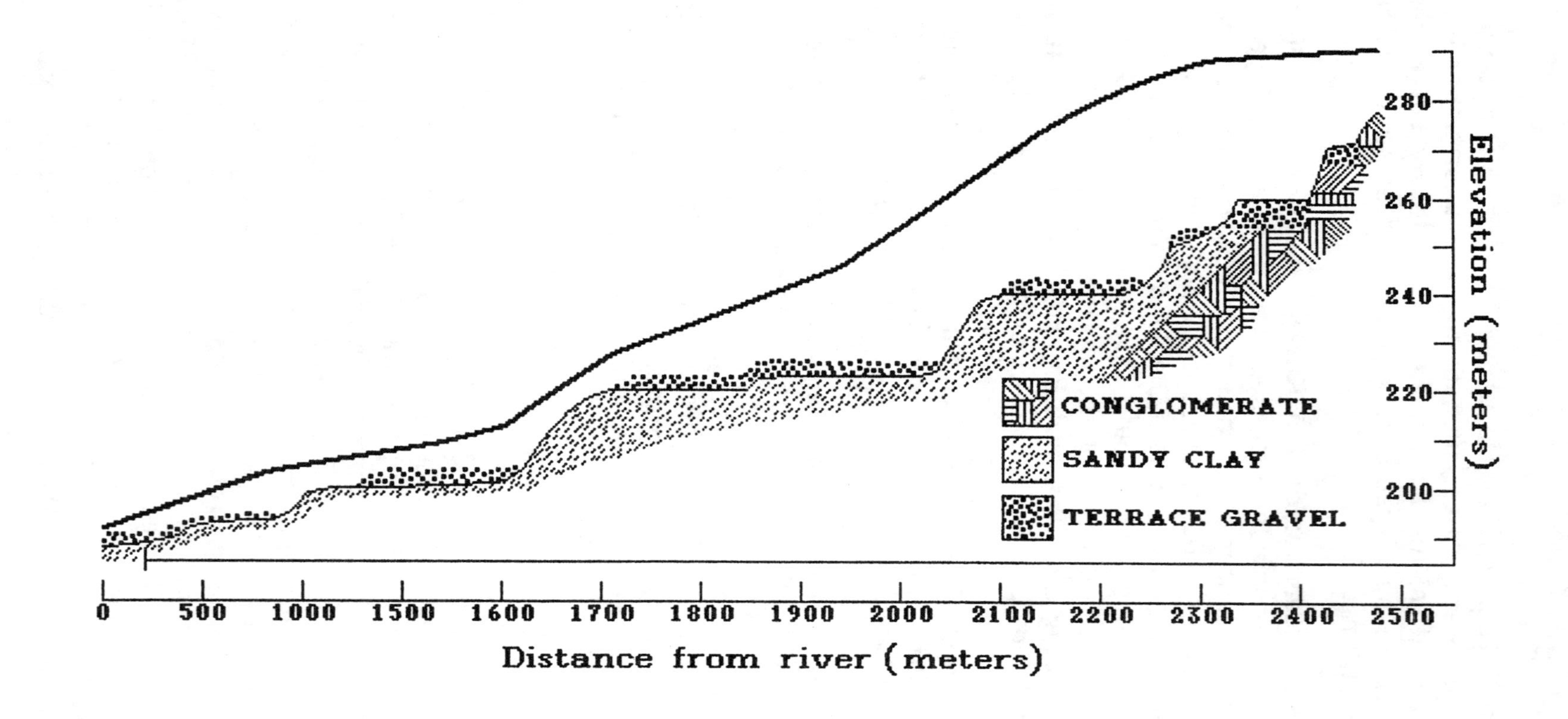

Figure 7.2 Cross section along the west bank of the Svratka River at Brno, Czechoslovakia. Loess, soil, and minor debris flow (not distinguished) are shown above abandoned terraces. Elevations and distances are in meters (Kukla, 1977).

discussed in detail. The method of using paleosols for a multiple ice-age stratigraphy will be examined in the next section.

Table 7.2. The classical glacial-interglacial sequence of the north-central United States.

Glacial	Interglacial
Wisconsin	Holocene or Recent
Illinoian	Sangamon
Kansan	Yarmouth
Nebraskan	Aftonian

What are the properties of a soil, or paleosol? A soil is simply the products of rock weathering, which have supported plant growth. A soil is divided into three main layers, called a soil profile. Figure 7.3 shows a general soil profile. This profile is composed of a top organic layer, called the A horizon; a middle layer of well-weathered material, called the B horizon, and a bottom layer of slightly weathered material, referred to as the C horizon. There are other minor horizons, and each major horizon can be further subdivided (Birkeland, 1984, pp. 3-37). The C horizon is very similar to the parent sediment, or rock, and has little use in soil stratigraphy. The B horizon is usually a clay layer, red-colored layer, iron or aluminum-rich layer, or $CaCO_3$ layer. This section will mainly examine clay soils—the predominant interglacial soil.

There are many problems with paleosols that should have made them unsuitable for use as evidence for multiple glaciations or relative time indicators. The most basic problem is that of defining and recognizing a paleosol in the field (Ruellan, 1971). Much confusion has occurred. Few unique properties of soils exist, as opposed to sediments. Soils are altered upon burial, and can look like sediments that have undergone diagenesis (Valentine and Dalrymple, 1976, pp. 209,210; Bowen, 1978, p. 182). Diagenesis includes the weathering of minerals by oxidation and reduction, hydrolosis and solution, biological action of bacteria, compaction, cementation, recrystallization, and lattice alternation of clay by the expulsion of water and ion exchange (Valentine and Dalrymple, 1976, p. 210). Thus, a buried soil and a sedimentary layer may be difficult to distinguish: "A review of the literature, then, confirms that the identification of a buried paleosol is 'rarely simple and irrefutable' ..." (Valentine and Dalrymple, 1976, p. 213).

Another problem with ancient soils is that they have been subject to erosion and redeposition, and can have large horizontal and vertical variations over short distances (Birkeland, 1984, pp. 234-259). Nilsson (1983, pp. 178,215) states that many paleosols in formerly glaciated areas of northern Europe have been destroyed by subsequent glaciation, and that fossil soils are subject to solifluction, causing them to flow into depressions and form extra thick "soils," or false paleosols.

It would seem that the most obvious tell-tale sign of a paleosol is the A, or organic horizon (Figure 7.3). However, the A horizon is usually missing in paleosols, making reliable identification of an ancient soil exceedingly difficult:

> *It is difficult to classify buried soils to the same degree of accuracy as surface soils. This is because during burial changes take place in properties critical to such classification. For example, A horizons are critical to classification, yet are rare in buried soils (Birkeland, 1984, p. 33).*

Flint (1971, p. 300) corroborates: "... indeed, in most buried soils the A horizon is lacking, because it is especially erodible."

Since the A horizon is rare, and the C horizon nondiagnostic, the only criterion left for soil identification and stratigraphy is the B horizon. In previously glaciated territory, especially in North America, the B horizon is most often a sticky clay, called gumbo, or gumbotil. But the origin of gumbotil has been controversial (Nilsson, 1983, pp. 378,379). Some investigators have considered gumbotil to be an actual ancient soil, while others have believed it to be only an accumulation, by lateral wash, into depressions (Valentine and Dalrymple, 1976, p. 215). If the latter is true, gumbotil is not a soil at all, and could not be used as evidence for interglacials, or as subdivisions of Quaternary time. Recently, experts have agreed that **both** origins are correct (Birkeland, 1984, pp. 246-248). Resedimented deposits by lateral wash were given the name accretion gley, while the original name, gumbotil, was retained as the remnants of an old soil which has been formed in "poorly drained" areas. This compromise only partly alleviates the problem of identifying the B horizon of a paleosol in a particular locality.

Several processes, other than time, can develop a thick B horizon. Besides the lateral accumulation of clays discussed above, clay, or other B horizon material, can develop by translocation of minerals upward from a high water table, or by the accumulation of fine material overlying coarse impermeable sediments (Birkeland, 1984, pp. 21,22,146-148). These conditions occur where there is poor drainage and a reducing environment, and can produce accretion gley or gumbotil, in a relatively short time. West (1969, p. 198) states:

> *The problems of interpreting fossil soils are several. The first is in the recognition of a fossil soil. An iron rich or ferrocrete or a calcrete layer, may be the result of post-depositional changes related to former or present water*

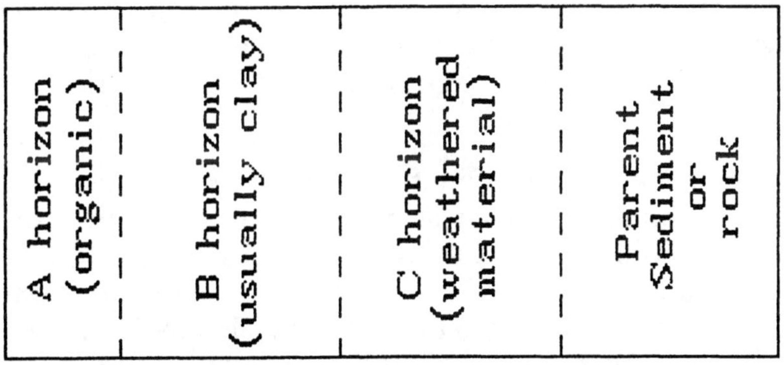

A horizon
(organic)

B horizon
(usually clay)

C horizon
(weathered
material)

Parent
Sediment
or
rock

Figure 7.3 General soil profile.

levels or to impermeable layers holding up drainage. A horizon rich in organic matter may be a result of primary sedimentation.

Flint (1971, pp. 299,300) agrees with this assessment. Although a thick B horizon of clay or other material may be a soil, again, it could have formed rapidly in a wet climate with poor drainage.

Soil Stratigraphy

It should be apparent to the reader that there is a basic problem of recognizing the B horizon of a paleosol which can support a postulated, interglacial period. But glacial geologists have taken paleosols even further, and have set up a dating scheme and a stratigraphy for multiple ice ages. Assuming that soils can be distinguished from sediments, how can they be used to date various till, or even loess layers, upon which the "soil" developed?

Vreeken (1984) gives a good description of the soil-dating procedure. First, one or more soil properties from several soils of different "known" ages, are given relative age values. These properties are usually the thickness of the B horizon (called its maturity), or its degree of redness for iron-rich layers (Birkeland, 1984, p. 24). The thicker, or redder the soil, the older it is assumed to be. Second, an estimate for an unknown age is obtained by matching to the "index of development."

The soils of "known" age are derived from the stratigraphy of the underlying, or overlying sediments, which is based on the geological time scale, and involves all the additional assumptions that have gone into its development. For the Quaternary period, the basis for soil stratigraphy, originally, was the four-ice-age alpine model (Table 7.2). This basis has been supplanted by the oxygen-isotope record in oceanic sediments, with resultant confusion, concerning previous correlations based on paleosols. Since the oceanic record has a longer time scale, the dates of the various soils and ice ages have been extended further into the past. For example, the last interglacial—the Sangamon, in the North American classification—is now dated at about 120,000 years ago. If the "maturity" of an unknown soil is similar to the Sangamon soil, the unknown soil is assumed to be about 120,000 years old.

To refine the soil-dating scale, soils assumed to be the most recent—Holocene and late Pleistocene—are sometimes dated by carbon-14. From the thickness of these dated soils, a typical soil formation rate is determined, and extrapolated into the Pleistocene, beyond the range of C-14 dating. Flint (1971, p. 291) states:

It has been possible to estimate the maximum time required for the development of some postglacial soils in glacial drift, in areas where deglaciation has been dated by C14 ... or by otherwise bracketing a soil between two relevant C14 dates.

Carbon-14 dating of Holocene soils has resulted in a length of time for soil formation to be tens of thousands of years. Consequently, soil formation is believed to be a very slow process.

For soils presumed too old for C-14 dating, which is practically all the Pleistocene, there is rarely any other method for absolute dating. Efforts are being made to develop techniques that will supplement and extend the range of C-14 dating (Mahaney, 1984). Kemp (1986, pp. 243,245) writes:

Many Quaternary sediments cannot be dated absolutely, primarily because their ages lie outside the range afforded to radiocarbon dating. Although new techniques such as thermoluminscence [sic] and amino acid racemization may in the future assist in the dating of deposits and soils, most sediments can still only be dated relative to others using lateral correlations based on lithological criteria and fossil assemblages determined by environmental conditions. These approaches, however, are liable to introduce errors in correlation, which could lead to incorrect dating of soils .... Particular doubts have been expressed over the differentiation of tills of successive cold stages ....

Such is the methodology of soil stratigraphy. Extensive problems with this simple scheme have been pointed out by a number of authorities. Many of these problems have been alluded to already in this section. Bowen (1978, p. 183), in reference to the four-ice-age scheme in the north-central United States, points out:

In retrospect it would seem that the earlier use of paleosols for subdividing the classical sequence of central North America outran the state of soil science at the time. Currently increasing knowledge of present soil forming processes serves to emphasize the inadequate basis of many such early correlations.

Richmond and Fullerton (1986, p. 184) add: "However, they [paleosols] have no definite chronologic significance and they cannot be correlated reliably from one region to another on the basis of their physical properties."

Vreeken (1984) essentially says there are too many variables in soil stratigraphy that cannot be treated adequately. The character of soils depends upon parent material, climate, topography, vegetation, and time, and each of these is related to a host of other variables, as well as with each other (Birkeland, 1984). Many environmental factors may cause a soil to form rapidly. Moisture and temperature are highly significant factors in soil development (Boardman, 1985, pp. 62-65). These variables control the rate of physical, chemical, and biochemical processes that occur within a soil. Higher moisture and temperature can greatly increase the weathering rate and soil formation (Birkeland, 1984, pp. 275-324).

The "type" soils of presumed known age have been taken from areas with little regard to lateral variations, or to the influence of other variables besides those on which the type classification of the soil is based (Valentine and Dalrymple, 1976, p. 215). Soils of the same age can vary in their "maturity," due to the different soil-forming factors (Birkeland, 1984, p. 24).

Some of these problems are illustrated in the north-central United States, where various tills have been subdivided by soils. Table 7.2 presents the old four-fold classification for this area, and Figure 7.1 shows the surface location of each of the four putative glaciations. From this classification, one would think that a vertical profile through the Wisconsin till would often reveal several soils, each separated by a till layer, one set for each glaciation. This is rare; most often, a single till layer and overlying paleosol is found. Flint (1971, p. 299), in referring to soils that developed on till, says: "... at rare localities two interglacial soils occur." (This is probably why Charlesworth felt the field evidence favored only two glaciations.) In other words, each till layer and its associated interglacial soil are found predominantly in the periphery area represented by each supposed glaciation in Figure 7.1. The four-ice-age model for the north-central United States, like models for other periods of the geological time scale, is built up from these "interglacial" soils. The important point is that these "type" soils are selected from **different** locations. The patches are then pieced together into a vertical sequence that is suppose to represent a universal time sequence.

The Sangamon soil of the last presumed interglacial illustrates some of the pitfalls (Boardman, 1985, pp. 67,68). This soil is widespread, but mostly is found south of the margin of the last glaciation—the Wisconsin ice age (Follmer, 1983, pp. 138,139). In other words, the Sangamon soil is rarely covered by till, and in its "type area," in central Illinois, the Sangamon soil is covered by loess. The Sangamon soil varies considerably from one location to another. As a result, the method of distinguishing this soil is questionable. The Sangamon soil is usually just assumed to be the youngest strongly developed clay layer in any locality (Birkeland, 1984, p. 338). Bowen (1978, p. 53) believes this practice is ill-advised. Furthermore, the Sangamon soil resembles the soils from the presumed previous two interglacials (Flint, 1971, p. 299), differing from them largely in the thickness of the B horizon. But thickness differences can be due to factors other than time, making the whole subdivision into four ice ages subjective.

Coupled with the poor methodology of soil stratigraphy is a lack of knowledge concerning modern soil-formation rates. Very few quantitative studies on soil formation have been undertaken (Birkeland, 1984, pp. 118,119). Boardman (1985, p. 65) states:

> *Formidable problems concerning dating, correlation, and a lack of knowledge of rates of contemporary soil-forming processes, frequently preclude more precise evaluation of the effects of time versus environmental factors.*

A modern-day example of rapid soil development is a 14-inch-thick soil that formed in 45 years on the volcanic ash deposited from the Krakatoa volcanic eruption (Leet and Judson, 1965, pp. 83,84). Ash below the soil, while not yet classified as soil, has already been significantly altered.

The red color of the B horizon has been used as a relative guide to soil development and age. The redder the deposit, the older it is assumed to be. However, redness may not develop at the same rate for all deposits, and there are processes that can cause a soil to be red which do not involve extensive time (Boardman, 1985, pp. 65,66; Pawluk, 1978, pp. 63,64). Valentine and Dalrymple (1976, p. 212) write: "It [color] may be inherited from the parent material, or color variations may be produced by deep subsurface weathering, associated with ground-water movement in layered sediments."

Considering all the difficulties involved, paleosols should not be used to date glaciations, or to separate them into multiple events. A strict application of the principle of uniformitarianism would require that soil stratigraphy be disqualified as a relative dating method. Due to all the problems in trying to find evidence for 20 or 30 glaciations in the continental deposits, most glacial geologists have abandoned soil stratigraphy, and now feel free to comment on the significance of the method. This section will end with one such comment. Ericson and Wollin (1968, p. 1227) state: "Furthermore, the long interglacial stages are often represented by nothing more than a weathered, or chemically altered zone on the surface of glacial detritus left by a preceding ice sheet." They are not impressed with the evidence for multiple glaciation based on continental deposits.

One Dynamic Ice Age

The character of the till, with interbedded clay and organic remains in some areas along the periphery, can be explained by one ice age. The explanation is basically the same as that advocated years ago by the monoglacialists. They postulated an ice sheet that oscillated at its margin, sometimes widely. These oscillations are no different, except for scale, than those observed for modern glaciers. Glaciers, at present, advance, retreat, readvance, and in some instances, surge. Ice motion is governed by many variables, most of which are related to climate. A recent example is provided by glaciers in the Swiss Alps. These glaciers reached a recent maximum about 1820, and remained relatively stable, with only minor oscillations, for about 50 years. Around 1870, they retreated rapidly, and then readvanced until shortly before 1900 (Paterson, 1981, p. 241). These glaciers, as well as most other glaciers in the Northern Hemisphere, have been retreating during the 20th century.

How can an ice sheet in the post-Flood climate, although rather thin, oscillate widely? Before this is answered, we need to examine the variables that determine the speed at which a glacier moves. We will then take a look at these variables in the post-Flood climate. We will conclude by showing that some glacial geologists recognize that one glaciation can, indeed, form multiple tills, with nonglacial deposits between.

Glaciers move over relatively flat terrain by three mechanisms: 1) internal deformation of the ice crystals, 2) basal slip, and 3) the deformation of the basal till.

The force for ice deformation has been correlated to two large-scale ice-sheet variables. These are ice thickness and surface slope. The relationship between these factors and deformation is highly non-linear. When the surface slope is small and the flow is smooth, ice deformation is generally proportional to the fourth power of the thickness and the third power of the surface slope (Paterson, 1981, p. 87). Therefore, a thick ice sheet with a relatively steep surface slope will deform quickly. But, if the surface slope exceeds a modest value, the power relationships become invalid. The ice can still deform rapidly, scientists just have difficulty formulating the glacier response.

A given force can cause a large range of motion in a glacier, depending on several variable characteristics within the ice. Internal deformation of the ice crystals depends upon their orientation, the number of crystal lattice dislocations, and the amount of impurities. As a result, internal deformation is a highly complex and non-linear phenomenon that no model can represent adequately (Paterson, 1981). In general, a glacier will deform faster for a given stress, if the crystals, after recrystallization, are orientated in the direction of the stress, and if the number of dislocations and impurities is relatively high. Ice crystals tend to slip more easily along dislocations and over areas of impurities. These variables illustrate some of the problems inherent in modeling glacial motion.

Basal slip depends upon such variables as bed roughness and basal shear stress. It is potentially much faster than ice deformation. Modern sliding velocities range from zero for cold-based glaciers, to several kilometers per year for large outlet glaciers of the Greenland and Antarctic ice sheets, and for glacial surges (Paterson, 1981, pp. 112,113). There are many problems in developing a model for basal slip, and observations below the ice are, of course, difficult. One feature, in particular, is highly correlated to rapid motion. That is reduction of sliding friction by a layer of water at the base (Paterson, 1981, p. 128). Sugden and John (1976, p. 30) state:

Furthermore, it has long been known that there is a relationship between high summer rates of glacier flow and the existence of basal meltwater, at least in the ablation area of glaciers.

Surges are poorly understood, but most likely are related to basal water buildup in the ablation zone (Paterson, 1981, pp. 275-298). A surge is a sudden increase in glacial flow, from normal to perhaps 100 times faster, over a period of a few months, to as long as three years. Surges can rapidly advance a glacier. The greatest known surge advance is 21 kilometers for a glacier in Spitsbergen.

The temperature of the ice sheet, which depends on the climate, is an important variable that controls both the rate of ice deformation and the rate of basal slip. A temperate ice sheet will deform faster than a cold ice sheet. Sugden and John (1976, pp. 25,26) state: "The warmer the ice, the more easily it deforms. For example, the strain rate [deformation rate] at a temperature of -22°C is one-tenth of its value at 0°C ...." A temperate glacier will slip faster along its base, due to more water from melting ice and snow.

Another mechanism for rapid sliding of a glacier has been discovered recently in Antarctica. Using radar to penetrate through an ice stream with low surface slope, it was discovered that the deformation of a thin layer of basal till under high pore water pressure was likely causing unusually rapid motion of the ice (Blankenship et al., 1986; Alley et al., 1986). Boulton (1986) suggests that this new information may cause a paradigm shift in glaciology, especially for concepts of ancient Quaternary glacier velocity. He notes that Quaternary glaciers flowed over strongly deformed and predominantly soft-sediment beds, and probably, as a result, moved rapidly under low-driving stresses:

It has been further argued that such a mechanism controlled the behaviour of mid-latitude Quaternary ice sheets, with a soft, easily deforming sedimentary substratum permitting high glacier velocities for relatively low driving stresses; rapid responses to changing climate; and fast volumetric growth and decay facilitated by rapid changes in the extent of the ice sheets (Boulton, 1986).

Now that we have discussed the variables that influence glacial motion, we can ask, would the post-Flood ice sheets have moved rapidly? The answer is yes. Most of the factors discussed above would favor rapid motion at the periphery, but not in the interior of ice sheets.

As stated by Boulton, the substratum was easily deformable and favorable for rapid ice motion, with low driving stress. This applies mainly along the periphery, where the substratum is composed of soft sedimentary rocks. In the mild, post-Flood winters, the ice sheets would have been relatively warm at the periphery, favoring rapid deformation. Also, volcanic dust would have added impurities, which would give the ice a greater rate of internal deformation. Ice, presumably from the ice age, in Greenland and Devon Island ice cores contains sufficient mircoparticle content to deform about three-to-four times faster than pure ice (Reeh, 1985; Fisher and Koerner, 1986).

The Laurentide ice sheet did not build in northeast Canada and flow south into the United States. It more-or-less developed in place, and moved according to the complex dynamics of ice-sheet flow. Generally, this direction would have been south, at the southern periphery, but there is no reason for it to not move in a different direction in some areas. Since the storm tracks paralleled the southern and eastern edge of the ice sheet, the margin, in this area, would become thicker, with a relatively greater surface slope. Consequently, the outward-flow rate would have been greater along this portion of the periphery.

Another factor that would have contributed to rapid glacier movement is the large amount of basal water expected in a mild ice age. Geothermal heat will melt an average of about six millimeters of ice annually. Frictional heat melts another six millimeters if the ice sheet moves at only 20 meters/year (Paterson, 1981, p. 142). Since the evidence indicates the ice sheets moved much more rapidly than that, significant quantities of water from frictional melting would be added at the base of the post-Flood ice sheet. Water from surface melting and summer rain would reach the base through crevasses and conduits. With so large an amount of basal water, surges would likely have been common along the periphery. Table 7.3 lists a summary of the variables favoring rapid ice movement along the periphery during the post-Flood ice age.

Table 7.3. Summary of variables favoring rapid motion of the ice at the periphery of the post-Flood ice sheets.

1)	Easily deformable substratum
2)	"Warm" ice
3)	Large amount of impurities
4)	Steep slope at periphery
5)	Large amount of basal water

Oscillations at the margin of a post-Flood ice age would have been greatly affected by the variable input of volcanic dust and aerosols into the stratosphere. Since the dust and aerosols would have been greatest at the beginning, the largest southerly extension of the Laurentide ice sheet, in the continental United States, likely would have occurred at this time. In the north-central United States till, that has been divided into the Nebraskan, Kansan, and Illinoian ice ages, would have been deposited at this time. As volcanism waned, solar melting would have been greatest along the southern portion of the ice sheet. The southern margin would retreat northward to a more-or-less-equilibrium position (the Wisconsin ice edge). Much heavier precipitation than is currently characteristic of the area south of the Wisconsin ice edge would have caused extensive weathering of the surface of the newly exposed till, and formed gumbotil and clay soils in poorly drained areas. The surface would develop an "old," or eroded, appearance in a short time. During the large-scale ice retreat in the north-central United States, plants and animals, some indicating mild conditions as discussed in Chapter 4, would have lived south of the ice sheet and rapidly populated previously glaciated areas.

At the Wisconsin equilibrium position, marginal oscillations would have continued. A high surface slope at the margin, at times, would have aided southward advances and surges. Long-term readvances would have occurred during periods of high volcanic activity. Mild climate plants, and possibly some animal bones, likely would have been buried by these readvances. Scientists finding these remains would naturally postulate warm, interglacial periods.

Ice movement in interior Canada would have been sluggish. The bedrock is mostly hard crystalline rock that does not easily deform. At first, this area would have been relatively warm, and would have received much of its moisture from the Arctic Ocean. Ice velocity would have been faster at this time. As the oceans cooled, so would the atmosphere. The annual available moisture would consequently diminish. The storm tracks would progressively be displaced farther south. Under these conditions, the ice over the interior of the ice sheet would end up relatively thin, with a rather flat surface slope. An ice dome over Keewatin would be favored by the moisture from the Arctic Ocean, while an ice dome over Labrador-Ungava would grow mainly from North Atlantic moisture. Another ice dome may have formed between the Great Lakes and Hudson Bay, and later in the ice age, over the Queen Elizabeth Islands of northeast Canada. A thin ice sheet and relatively cold air temperatures result in cold basal temperatures, with little basal water. Accordingly, the interior portion of the ice sheet likely became frozen to its bed. Because of all these conditions, the ice sheet would move little in interior regions. During deglaciation of the interior region, the margin would oscillate, but with the very cold climate, the rate of motion would have been slow. The net result would be little erosion of the bedrock, and only a thin, coarse-grained, final till cover.

Some glacial geologists, although committed to multiple glaciations, now recognize that one glaciation can form multiple tills, with non-glacial deposits between them. For instance, Derbyshire (1979, p. 77) writes:

Long-standing problems of interpretation of complexly interbedded tills of the Pleistocene glaciations have been resolved as a result of the realization that not all tills are of subglacial origin, and that a formation of several tills interbedded with meltwater stream deposits may be the product of a single advance and retreat of the glacier.

Sugden and John (1976, pp. 135,220,234) and Paul (1983) agree with Derbyshire, and show how several till sheets can develop within the periphery of one ice sheet, due to shearing, or thrusting, of debris-rich basal layers. This process is illustrated in Figure 7.4, and has been observed on a glacier in Greenland (Flint, 1971, p. 107).

Multiple till layers can be formed, at least locally, well to the north of the ice margin. This is accomplished by episodes of erosion, and by discontinuous basal, or lodgement till deposition (Eyles and Menzies, 1983, pp. 38-41). Eyles et al. (1983b, p. 222) indicate how this pattern can lead geologists to postulate multiple glaciations:

In drumlinized terrain ubiquitous 'tripartite' stratigraphies composed of lower till(s), middle sands, gravel and laminated clays and upper till(s) have been used extensively as mapping units and taken to indicate multiple glaciation. Many multiple successions can probably be explained by the former presence of subglacial melt streams coupled with shifting ice divides and changing ice flow directions ....

The controversy over the Scarborough Bluffs section along Lake Ontario, supposedly showing multiple glaciations, has previously been discussed. When challenged on their seemingly unreasonable subdivisions of the stratigraphy of the Scarborough Bluffs, Eyles et al. (1984, p. 896) responded:

We place stratigraphic boundaries 'rather differently' from those of Karrow's original 1:50,000 regional mapping ... simply because the sediments have been looked at in detail. Logging shows that lithological breaks (considered as major stratigraphic boundaries by Karrow) are part of a single depositional sequence with transitional or interbedded contacts between such lithologically, dissimilar beds.

The type-section approach, upon which the multiple glaciation concept was derived years ago, is seen as overly simplified and confusing, in view of newer research, which indicates that one glaciation can deposit multiple till sheets (Eyles, 1983, pp. 15,18). The new three-dimensional view "... sees multiple tills as the normal expectation in glacial sediments" (Paul, 1983, p. 85).

Surging glaciers that stopped at the approximate location of a previous advance, or advanced the margin farther, would cause stacked till sheets and/or multiple moraines. Several major lobes of the Quaternary ice sheets

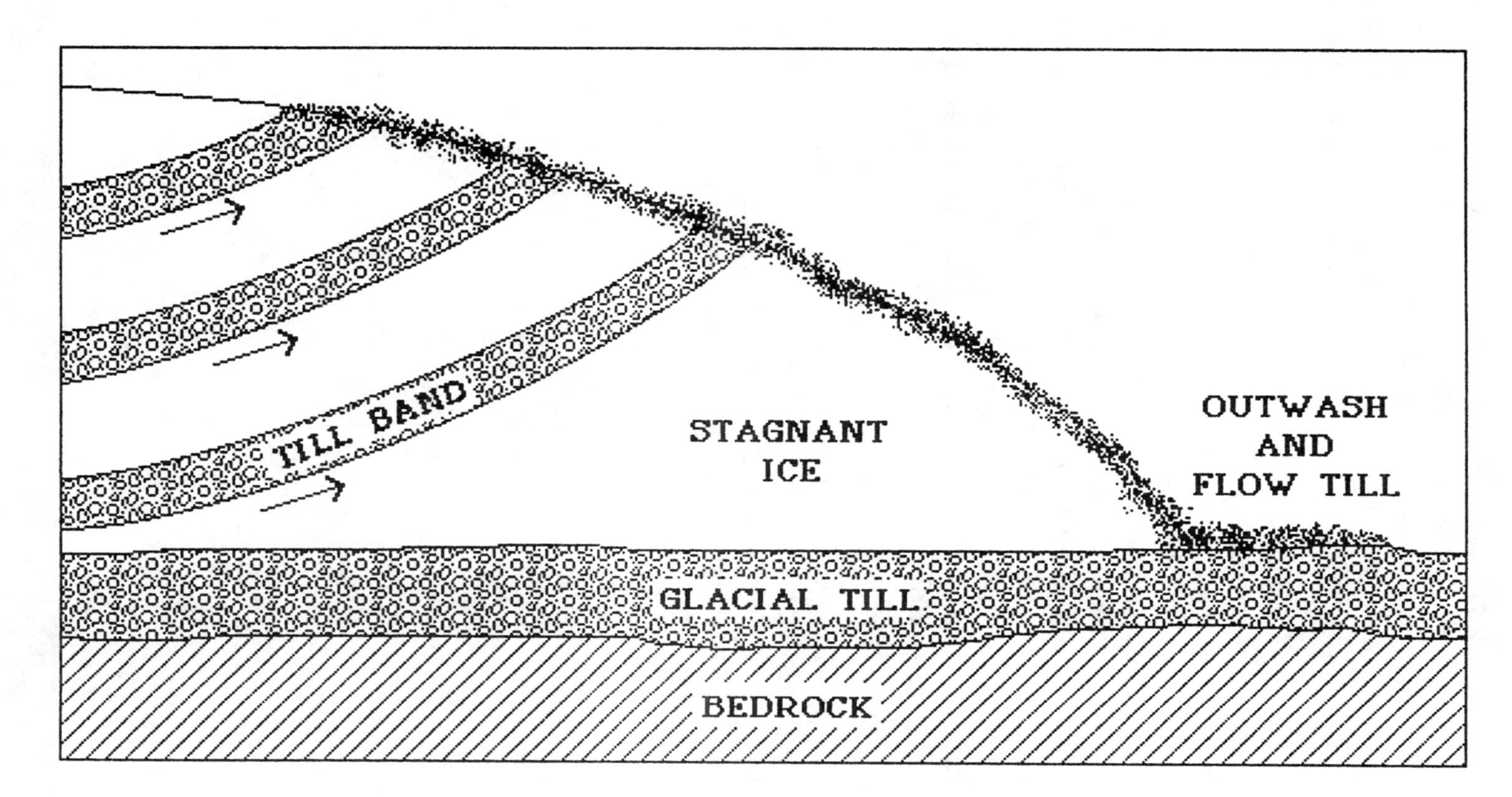

Figure 7.4 Shearing of basal ice and debris at the snout of a glacier. Retreats and advances of the glacier cause a complex mixture of till, flowtill, and outwash deposits after the ice melts that have been mistaken for multiple glaciation.

are now assumed, by many glaciologists, to have advanced by surges (Eyles and Menzies, 1983, pp. 27,28). At least 32 moraine arcs, in Illinois, are believed to have been deposited by repeated surging (Bowen, 1978, pp. 176,177). The landforms produced by modern surging glaciers, are similar to Pleistocene deposits in some areas (Paul, 1983, p. 77). This is as expected along the periphery of the post-Flood ice sheets.

Organic remains may have been engulfed by glacial readvances and surges. Eyles et al. (1983b, p. 222) say that a readvancing ice lobe can sandwich organic material between till sheets. Charlesworth (1957, p. 912) points out that vegetation grows near the snouts of a number of glaciers today. He adds that monoglacialists cannot appeal to this evidence, because vegetation is near modern glaciers only because the glacier forms at high altitude and flows to lower altitude, unlike Pleistocene ice sheets that mostly formed over low terrain. According to Charlesworth, plants could not grow adjacent to the Pleistocene ice sheets, because the climate was too cold, and because some of the vegetation indicates milder temperatures. However, these deductions would not be valid for a mild ice age.

In summary, the post-Flood ice sheets would have been dynamic, and characterized by rapid glacial motion. One ice age can account for the character of the deposits along the periphery, even in the north-central United States. It can also explain the character of the glacial features found over interior regions of the ice sheets.

CHAPTER 8

HOW LONG AGO?

A date for the end of the ice age would be of interest, in itself. But, this date would also indicate the approximate time of the Genesis Flood, and whether the Biblical time framework can be supported objectively. The scientific community predominantly believes that the last ice age peaked about 18,000 years ago, and that the Laurentide and Scandinavian ice sheets melted northward, and completely disappeared about 8,000 years ago. Is there any evidence that would indicate whether the ice melted 8,000 to 18,000 years ago, or in a shorter time—for instance 3,000 to 5,000 years ago?

There is evidence for a relatively recent melting of the ice, but this evidence is mostly qualitative. Unfortunately, our recreation of past phenomenon depends upon assumptions and on backward extrapolation from present measurements of chronological variables. A date for the end of the ice age can be estimated from post-ice-age landscape alterations. Such analysis comes under the classification of geomorphology. Some of these landscape changes include the recession of waterfalls, like Niagara Falls, which formed after the ice left the region; the erosion of till by post-ice-age streams and rivers; and the sediment-filling of lake beds formed in the till. By calculating the current rate of change, and measuring the total erosion, or sedimentation, a date for ice recession can be qualitatively estimated. But approximate calculations are not straightforward. It is highly unlikely that the current rate of change can be extrapolated for all the past. And several other variables, usually not accounted for, affect the accuracy of the calculations.

Very few geomorphologists, today, date the end of the ice age by landscape alterations. Scientists now rely almost exclusively on radiometric and fossil-dating methods (Sibrava et al., 1986). Because these methods are fitted into the popular model for geological time, the model usually determines the dates and the results that are "found." The popular model now is the multiple ice age model, in which 20 or more ice ages are assumed, based on ocean-sediment data. Fitting land sequences of till into such a model is impossible, on the basis of only macroscopic features.

The main sources of data concerning landscape changes that bear on the date when the ice sheets disappeared, are in the earlier literature. Many of these early workers were keen observers, who reported their observations fully, and were not too constrained by existing models. For instance, Antevs and Chalmers, around the turn of the century, claimed that ice moved northward from northern New England down the regional slope and into the St. Lawrence lowlands. This northward movement did not agree with the model of a thick ice sheet that developed in Canada and swept southward into the United States. Consequently, geological surveys, carried out as recently as the 1960s, "firmly established" that the last ice movement in the area was towards the south, or southeast. Now, however, field evidence from glacial-flow indicators shows abundant and overwhelming proof of northward ice flow (Chauvin et al., 1985). The earlier observations were correct, after all—probably because the early glacial geologists were unencumbered by too many assumptions and models.

Most Glacial Features Altered Little

Many investigators have pointed out the old appearance of glacial deposits in the north-central United States, south of the boundary of the "last" glaciation. The deposits are well weathered; the topography is subdued and eroded. This area is called the attenuated border by many glaciologists, and was explained within the context of a rapid ice age in the previous chapter.

Northward from this attenuated border, the glacial deposits look fresh. As stated in Chapter 1, streamlined till can be seen from the air, in many areas. If the drumlins and grooves had not been formed recently, erosion would have smoothed them out. In another instance, G. Fredrick Wright (1911, p. 569), quoting the work of another scientist, writes:

> *On Portland promontory, on the east coast of Hudson's [sic] Bay, in latitude 58°, and southward, the high, rocky hills are completely glaciated and bare. The striae [scratched rock] are as fresh looking as if the ice had left them only yesterday. When the sun bursts upon these hills after they have been wet by the rain, they glitter and shine like the tinned roofs of the city of Montreal.*

Striae should be erased rather quickly after exposure, but their fresh appearance on bare rock east of Hudson Bay and in many other areas, indicates the ice disappeared a relatively short time ago.

Wright, quoting many observers, adds further that little erosion of glacial features has occurred in the state of Wisconsin, and that glacial kames, in

Europe and North America, are only slightly eroded. Charlesworth (1957, pp. 507,508) also notes the abundant signs of very slight post-glacial erosion:

> *... postglacial remodelling is still in its infancy. The decay is often scarcely appreciable on roches moutonnées, grooves and striae as Sefström noticed. Cirque-lakes have frequently only insignificant notches in their outer rim, and even large streams have been able to cut only extremely youthfull trenches in the steps of trough-floors and the lips of hanging valleys. Cirque-cliffs, e.g. the Spiegelwände of Zillertal, are often still fresh and the dismantling of the walls of U-valleys has made little progress since talus cones are few ... Minor and more delicate topographic forms are scarcely touched; moraines stand out as bold and steep embankments; outwash sheets are but slightly dissected .... Drumlins retain their perfect form ....*

Many other writers have made similar comments. The only sound conclusion is that the ice melted from the glaciated area recently.

At the time Wright was writing, geologists believed the ice age ended about 70,000 years ago, because of "... the almost unquestioned acceptance of the astronomical theory ..." (Wright, 1911, p. 532). Wright was primarily writing to show that geomorphological data indicated the ice age did not end 70,000 years ago. As a result, his calculations for the end of the ice age are most likely too old. His estimate was about 10,000 years ago. A contemporary observer, Warren Upham, believed the end of the ice age was 5,000 to 10,000 years ago (Wright, 1911, p. 522).

Estimated Time Based on Erosion

We will take a further look at Wright's data, to see if the date for the end of the ice age can be quantitatively narrowed down.

The most thoroughly investigated post-glacial time indicator is the erosion of Niagara Gorge. From surveys taken over the past 150 years, the average rate of recession of Niagara Falls (Horseshoe Falls) is about five feet/year. If this rate is assumed constant, the ice sheet left this area 7,000 ago. However, several complications make this estimate untrustworthy. First, several other Niagara river channels are known—one of which is filled with glacial drift (Philbrick, 1970; Calkin and Brett, 1978). Second, the Great Lakes probably drained through several other outlets for a short time, greatly reducing the flow of the Niagara River, and the resulting erosion of the Niagara Gorge (Karrow and Calkin, 1985). These complications would increase the real time.

From a rapid ice age perspective, channels now filled with till more likely were cut by the draining Flood waters. Although the Great Lakes probably drained through other outlets, at times, during deglaciation, most of the drainage was by the Niagara River since northern drainage outlets were often blocked by ice. These outlets probably were lower at the end of the ice age, based on north-south tilted shore lines indicating greater isostatic depression north of the Great Lakes. Since the melting rate in a post-Flood ice age is much faster than uniformitarian estimates, the Niagara River, at one time, would have had a flow greatly in excess of modern observations. This would have significantly increased the recession rate.

An analysis of how the Niagara Gorge recedes shows that the river first erodes the soft shale at the bottom of the canyon, causing the hard limestone at the top to break off in blocks (Gilbert, 1907, p. 5). These blocks then protect the soft shale from further erosion until the waterfall wears the limestone away. In high-flow years, the falling water wears away these limestone blocks more rapidly, resulting in a more rapid recession of the gorge.

A quantitative estimate of the effect of high flow can be found by comparing the two branches of Niagara Falls: the Horseshoe Falls and the American Falls. American Falls carries only about 10% of the water, and its average erosion rate for the past 500 years, when the two falls separated, has been 0.32 inches/year. Horseshoe Falls erodes 15 times faster than American Falls. On this basis, the average erosion-rate ratio is about 1.5 times the ratio of flow rate. For a flow rate during deglaciation ten times the current rate, the rate of recession of Niagara Gorge would be 75 feet/year. But if the flow were 50 times more, recession would be 375 feet/year, assuming the 1.5-ratio holds for all flow rates. However, these estimates are conservative, because the ratio of erosion-to-flow rate is probably more an exponential function of the flow ratio. With an exponential relationship, the recession of Niagara Gorge would be much higher than the simple linear estimates given above. Since the gorge is only six miles long, the entire length of the gorge could have been cut in 500 years and 100 years, respectively, at the above linear rates. Of course, we do not know how long the Niagara River was swollen with huge volumes of meltwater, nor how long the ice north of the Great Lakes prevented most of the water from flowing through other outlets. Previous calculations showed the ice would completely melt along the periphery in about 100 years. According to a rapid ice-age model, the cutting of the gorge would have been rapid for perhaps a 100-year period, and then would have slowed to the present average rate for perhaps 3,000 more years. The combination could erode Niagara Gorge in perhaps 3,000 to 4,000 years.

The recession of St. Anthony Falls in Minneapolis, is a similar time indicator. Extrapolating the present recession rate (before the falls were made stationary), the river would have cut the post-glacial gorge in about 7,800 years (Wright, 1911, pp. 552-560). The same considerations regarding a much higher flow rate as were used for Niagara Falls, apply to St. Anthony Falls. Thus, the estimated time for the recession can be reduced, significantly, below 7,800 years.

The estimates of recession of Niagara and St. Anthony Falls, unfortunately, are still more qualitative than quantitative. A more quantitative estimate can be found by estimating the rate at which Niagara Gorge has widened with time. Wright (1911, pp. 548-552) calculated the amount of erosion on the east side of Niagara Gorge near its mouth, which was formed at the time of ice removal from the area. Assuming the 340-foot-high gorge was originally vertical, 388 feet of rock has been horizontally removed from the top since the ice melted (Figure 8.1). How long would this take? This estimate is independent of much higher river flows during deglaciation, and to a first approximation should be constant since the ice melted. This approximation depends primarily on the year-to-year weather patterns since deglaciation, which likely have been similar to the present average-weather conditions. Wright states that if the average rate of removal, by erosion, from the face of the cliff, is only 0.25 inches/year, the material would have been eroded in less than 10,000 years. This is the age he favored.

However, the observed erosion is greater than 0.25 inches/year. A railroad track was laid, in 1854, that gradually climbed the east face of the gorge, from its mouth. Wright actually measured the average amount of erosion of the shale in the 55 years since the track was laid, as 1.5 inches/year. At this rate of erosion, the ice receded only 1,667 years ago.

Wright considered how the above rate could have been slower, in the past. But, he concludes, "... the Niagara shale has not been protected to any extent by a talus, and but slightly by vegetation" (Wright, 1911, p. 552). He did not consider the possible retarding effect of the harder limestone, but the limestone at the top of the gorge, and another smaller limestone layer midway down the gorge, should not slow the overall erosion much. The limestone should fall off as blocks at about the average rate of erosion of the underlying shale. The blocks would fall into the river and offer no protection to the erosion of the shale, unlike the situation for the recession of the waterfall. Unless the rate of erosion was significantly less in the past, this more quantitative conclusion indicates that the ice left the area only about 2,000 years ago.

Plum Creek, in Oberlin, Ohio, developed after the ice melted from the area. It has been eroding entirely through glacial till since its origin. Based on the volume of till eroded and the current rate of erosion, Plum Creek eroded its small valley in about 2,500 years (Wright, 1911, pp. 565-567). Unfortunately, other complicated variables make this estimate rough. For instance, after a reservoir was constructed, and a portion of the stream diverted, the new stream eroded the new channel at only 63% the rate of the undisturbed stream. If the diverted stream erosion rate is the average for Plum Creek since the ice melted, the erosion time would be extended to 4,000 years. A dense forest, which once grew in the Plum Creek drainage basin, would slow the erosion rate. But the forest covered the area for only a short period. Furthermore, the rate of erosion

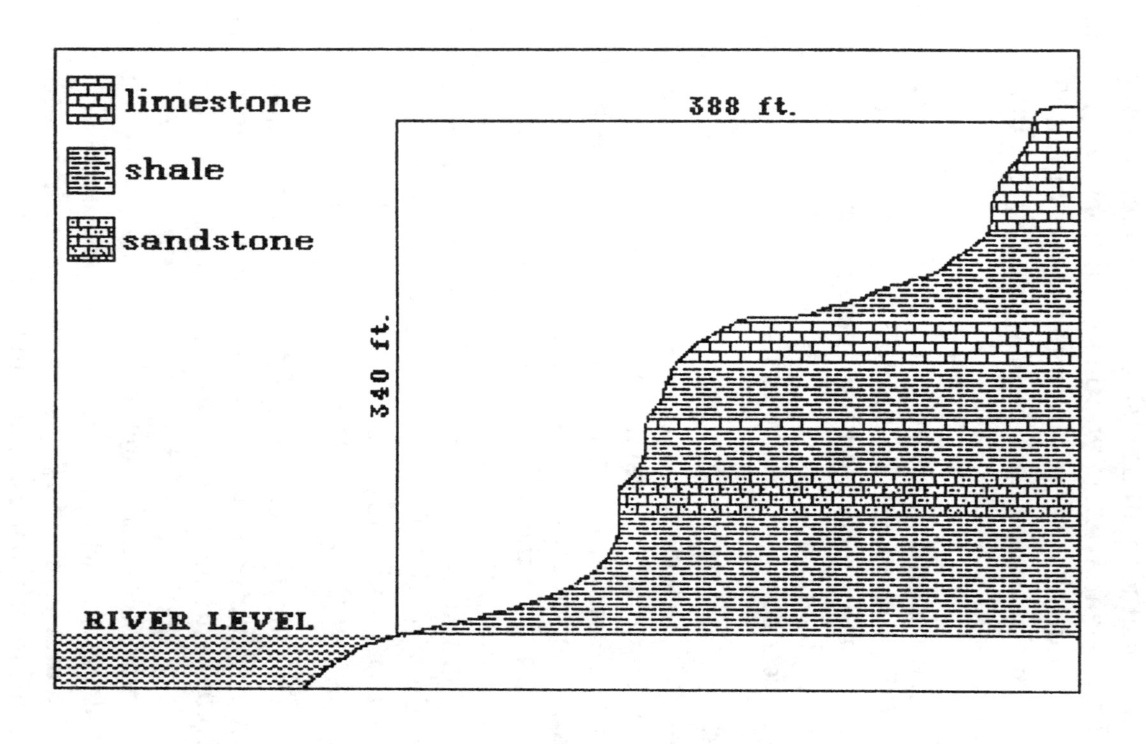

Figure 8.1 East side of Niagara Gorge at its mouth at Lewiston (Wright, 1911).

of Plum Creek, now should be at a minimum. These calculations, although rough, indicate that glacial ice left the area on the order of 3,000 to 4,000 years ago.

In summary, qualitative data for the area north of the line of the "last" glacial advance, in the north-central United States, shows that glacial features were formed relatively recently. Landscape changes since the ice left the region provide the best method for a quantitative estimate of the time when the ice sheet melted. However, little data is available, because of the modern dependence on radiometric and fossil-dating methods. The data that is available is old, but seems to be reliable. Although based on assumptions—some good and some poor—the estimated time since deglaciation is as little as 2,000 years. A more reasonable estimate, for the time since the glacial ice melted, is probably 3,000 to 4,000 years.

Eustasy and Isostasy

The topic of eustasy and isostasy, although briefly alluded to already, will be discussed in more detail, in this section. These phenomena have continued into the post-ice-age period, and even up into modern times.

During the post-Flood ice age, sea level would have lowered rapidly—much more rapidly than has been estimated from the uniformitarian time scale. Melting of the ice sheets within 100 to 200 years would have raised sea level rapidly. This type of sea-level change is called "eustatic." Figure 8.2 is a postulated graph of eustatic sea-level change, compared to today's average sea level, for a post-Flood ice age, and afterwards. Immediately following the Flood, sea level begins about 40 meters higher than at present, since the Antarctic and Greenland ice sheets had not yet formed. If these two ice sheets melted today, 60 meters of water would be added to the ocean. But due to isostatic compression (which will be discussed next), the ocean basins probably would sink enough to limit the total rise in sea level to only 40 meters.

The lowest glacial sea level, of course, occurs at glacial maximum, when the largest volume of water is locked up as ice, on land. Uniformitarian estimates of sea-level lowering, during maximum glaciation, are on the order of -130 meters (Blackwelder et al., 1979, p. 619). Since my estimate of post-Flood ice volume is less than one-half uniformitarian estimates, sea level, in the post-Flood model, is on the order of -50 or -60 meters. Do uniformitarian measurements refute my post-Flood estimate? No, because many of the uniformitarian methods of estimating sea level are faulty, and as explained in Chapter 5, are sometimes based on the assumed ice thickness. Just estimating ancient shore lines above current sea level, is a major problem. Donner (1985) states:

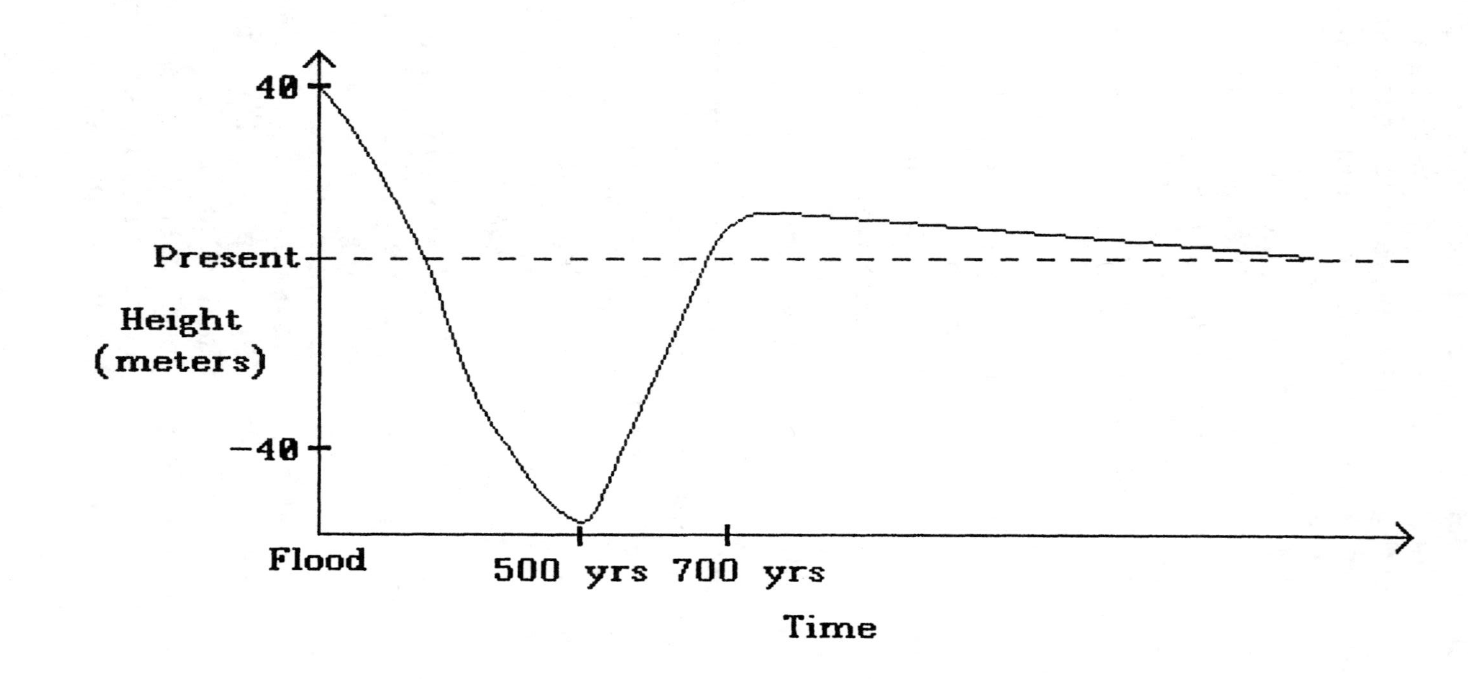

Figure 8.2 Postulated post-Flood sea level curve relative to today.

In following the development of Quaternary shoreline studies the reviewer is reminded of a remark made by the late Professor Auer that the surest way for a Quaternary geologist to lose his reputation is to study shorelines. This remark stems particularly from the observation of how over the years very different height/distance diagrams of shorelines have been presented for the same areas, by connecting morphological features in various ways. It is a problem with which, for instance, Tanner battled over 50 years ago when studying the shorelines of northern Fennoscandia. Reading the chapters on isostatic uplift is fascinating when one knows that the conclusions are likely to change and, further, that they are not always any more correct than earlier ones. In the Baltic region, for instance, there are many examples of a 'fluctuating correctness' sometimes caused by models getting the upper hand in the interpretation.

Although their curve was incomplete, Blackwelder et al. (1979) estimated a sea level at about -50 to -70 meters during maximum glaciation, based on "non-moveable" sea-level indicators. They conclude:

Compared to other sea level curves, our data indicate that substantially less ice was present from 17,000 to 10,000 years B.P. Our data strongly suggest that the late Wisconsinan maximum regression was not as profound as has been indicated in the literature (Blackwelder et al., 1979, p. 620).

Besides eustatic changes in sea level caused by glacial melting, there also would have been isostatic, tectonic, and geoidal changes. All these variables are complicated and difficult to measure and isolate from one another. It is evident that reports of sea-level indicators below 50 or 60 meters cannot really be taken as firm evidence that sea level actually was below that value. In fact, the eustatic component of sea level really cannot be measured at all, as admitted by Dawson and Smith (1983, p. 373):

However, these advances have coincided with the discovery that a global 'eustatic' sea level cannot be measured anywhere ... and that regional differences in Holocene sea-level curves may be explained by ocean floor deformation and geoidal deformation of the ocean surface caused by changing ice and water loads.

After maximum glaciation, the Laurentide and Scandinavian ice sheets would melt rapidly. But the Greenland and Antarctic ice sheet would still be growing at significant rates, due to the relatively warm oceans surrounding them (10°C at glacial maximum). Thus, the post-Flood eustatic sea-level rise, although rapid compared to uniformitarian standards, would be more gradual than estimated from a simple model. Immediately after the Laurentide and Scandinavian ice sheets melted, sea level should have been a little higher than today, because the Antarctic and Greenland ice sheets yet would not have reached their present size (Figure 8.2). Sea level would then slowly descend to near the current value.

Another phenomenon of interest and potential conflict with uniformitarian ice age models, is the depression and rebounding of the earth's crust, due to changes in the amount of either ice, on land, or water, in the ocean. This vertical motion of the earth's crust, due to a changing load, is called isostasy.

Isostatic depression and rebound have been observed directly, and there is excellent evidence for their occurrence in the past. For example, when Lake Mead, in Nevada, was filling with water, the extra weight of the water caused a 20-centimeter subsidence of the crust (Dott and Batten, 1976, p. 117). As discussed in Chapter 4, at the beginning of the ice age, Lake Bonneville was about 285 meters higher than the current Great Salt Lake. Interestingly, the highest shoreline of this ancient lake is bowed upward as much as 70 meters higher towards the middle of the lake, where the lake was the deepest (King, 1965, p. 850). By using only the highest shoreline, arguments as to the exact chronology of lower shorelines is avoided, since shorelines are mostly spotty, and their matching is subjective.

The rebounding of the land during and after the melting of the Laurentide and Scandinavian ice sheets, is well known. Modern sea-level measurements in the Baltic Sea reveal that the land is currently rising at about one centimeter/year. Many recent shorelines are easily visible around Hudson Bay and the Baltic Sea (Fairbridge, 1983; Gudelis and Königsson, 1979). These shorelines are post ice age, and not due to a higher sea level immediately after the Flood, since the glaciers would have obliterated preceding shorelines.

Measurements of the geoid and gravity anomalies reveal that isostatic rebound, in areas formerly glaciated, is likely not yet complete. The geoid is the difference between the actual sea surface and an ideal ellipsoid of the earth's surface. Gravity anomalies are a measure of the deviation from the average gravity of the earth. Both reveal either less or more mass in the earth below the location where the anomaly is measured. Both the smoothed gravity anomalies and the geoid are negative over Hudson Bay and the Baltic Sea (Walcott, 1973; Strahler, 1987, p. 258). This suggests less mass in the earth below, probably due to the weight of the ancient ice sheets having pushed a low viscosity portion of the mantle horizontally outward from the ice-covered area.

But negative gravity anomalies and a negative geoid do not automatically indicate incomplete glacial rebound, since many other variables are involved. Wolcott (1973, p. 20) states: "Since there are examples of regions of positive anomaly that are rising, and negative anomaly that are sinking, it is not certain that the negative anomaly does, in fact, indicate residual vertical movements." Shilts (1980, p. 217) says there is no firm evidence on the origin of the gravity anomalies in the Hudson Bay area. He thinks that part of the negative anomaly may be due to permanent structural features. In general, a negative anomaly usually does mean the crust is slowly rising. But due to the above observation and other complicating variables, the magnitude of the gravity anomaly due to ice load and hence the amount of incomplete isostatic rebound, is not really known (Walcott, 1970, p. 719; 1980, p. 6).

Besides indicating that isostatic rebound probably is incomplete, the negative gravity anomalies imply that mantle rock is probably flowing horizontally, into the negative area, from the surrounding region. This may be why the bottom of the North Sea is slowly subsiding, causing sea level along the coast to rise, and vice versa, in the Baltic Sea. However, some scientists believe that isostatic sinking of the North Sea floor has stopped, and the current subsidence is due to high sediment loading from river input (Fairbridge, 1983, p. 4). This is hard to understand, in view of the postulated isostatic recovery remaining from the last ice age, according to the uniformitarian model.

How fast will the land respond to ice-loading and unloading? Strahler (1987, p. 259) claims the process is much too slow for a rapid ice age:

> *To fit even a single cycle of glaciation into the first 1,000 or 2,000 y. of post-Flood time would require a drastic reduction of the viscosity of the moving mass, something completely removed from serious consideration because of the actual conditions of depth, rock density, and temperature that must have prevailed then, as now.*

Strahler is saying the viscosity of the mantle material that must horizontally flow is too high for significant motion on the time scale envisioned by any post-Flood, ice-age model. However, the real question should be: What really **is** the viscosity of the mantle? Strahler seems to indicate that the viscosity is known from geophysics. Actually, this is not true. The viscosity of the hot mantle is an educated guess, based on other phenomena—the significance of which depends on many assumptions in historical geology. The viscosity of the mantle is mainly inferred from the presumed post-glacial uplift of Hudson Bay and Scandinavia:

> *Historically the subject [isostasy] has been primarily of concern to the geophysical community since studies of the rebound of the crust following deglaciation have provided the only means by which one could infer the effective viscosity of the planetary mantle. The importance of this parameter of course lies in the fact that it is a fundamental ingredient in thermal convection models of the process of continental drift ... (Peltier and Andrews, 1983, p. 299).*

In other words, the viscosity of the mantle, as well as the supposed motion of lithospheric plates, is really derived from glacial isostatic rebound, not the other way around.

The next question is: How is the past rate of isostatic uplift determined? Isostatic uplift rate is determined by the assumed deglaciation history:

> *Geophysical models of glacial unloading for the major ice sheets have now attained a high degree of sophistication. However, their accuracy remains subject to, amongst other factors, the accuracy of inferred deglaciation histories (Dawson and Smith, 1983, p. 374).*

So the assumed deglaciation history determines the rate of isostatic uplift, and not the reverse, as presumed by Strahler. Notice that Dawson and Smith say "amongst other factors," indicating that even more assumptions are needed besides the assumed deglaciation history.

The above example is like so much of historical geology. One conclusion of historical geology is based on assumptions that are further based on other assumptions. A conclusion, or even an assumption, is used to bolster other conclusions and assumptions. Andrews (1982, p. 2) states how, "Sometimes ... the inputs for one approach serve as a verification for another line of inquiry." Consequently, circular reasoning abounds, and it is very difficult to find raw data that are untainted by assumptions, or that are not based on, or fitted into, some model.

An example of isostatic rebound data that is likely based on a model, is given by Mörner (1980a, p. 260), who draws contours of postglacial uplift totaling 820 meters at the presumed center of the Scandinavian ice sheet. This is not based on actual measurements at the center of uplift, since the highest postglacial shoreline is a maximum of 290 meters (Eronen, 1983, p. 188). Values of uplift over most of Scandinavia are actually much less than 290 meters. Mörner's maximum value is probably inferred by an ice sheet believed to have been about 3,000 meters thick. But the thickness of past ice sheets is, in itself, only an educated guess, based on uniformitarian assumptions and models.

Radiometric-dating methods, and, in particular, Carbon-14, are used to bolster the uniformitarian models. Isostatic uplift rates often depend upon Carbon-14 measurements on ancient shorelines. However, there are many references to discarded Carbon-14 dates, and complaints on how inaccurate the dating methods are. As an example, Walcott (1970, p. 719) states that Carbon-14-dated shorelines give an order of magnitude difference in the isostatic recovery time of Hudson Bay. As another example, Mickelson et al. (1983, pp. 12,13) write:

> *We know of several hundred radiocarbon dates from the area and time range being considered here, but only 27 have been used in our chronology. All*

but wood dates have been rejected because of unresolvable contamination problems, and only wood dates that seem to be from stratigraphically significant materials have been used. Other dates could be used to construct other chronologies.

What the authors are inferring is that they are choosing only the dates that agree with their model, and that these are a small percentage of those available. The rejected dates are said to be from contaminated samples. But scientists do not deliberately select organic material that is believed to be contaminated. They are very careful to avoid contamination, since it is a well-known problem. More likely, the Carbon-14 dates did not agree with the model, so the samples were assumed to be contaminated.

Since so many scientists have faith in radiometric dating methods, a third example may be helpful, this time from the topic under discussion. Eronen (1983, pp. 183,184) states:

A substantial improvement in dating methods was achieved by the discovery of the ^{14}C *method of age determination, and it is this method that has come to occupy a crucial position in shoreline displacement research over the last 20 years or so. This has helped to solve many problems, but has still not carried research forward as rapidly as had been initially expected, and many points have arisen which complicate the interpretation of* ^{14}C *dates in embarrassingly many instances.*

Radiocarbon has been used to bolster old models and to develop new models. But this dating method, like all others, is based on unprovable assumptions, and I believe the method is more complicated than researchers state.

In order to find the isostatic rebound rate, and hence mantle viscosity, numerical values from the presumed deglaciation history are needed. One must know how thick the ice sheets were, the time the ice sheets began to melt, how fast they melted, the crustal rebound since ice removal, and the incompleted amount of presumed isostatic recovery. All of these variables are unknown. The rate of uplift is probably a logarithmic function—rapid at first, due to the sudden melting of ice, then slowing with time. Maximum uplift has been about 290 meters for Scandinavia (Eronen, 1983, p. 188), and 315 meters for the Hudson Bay area (Fairbridge, 1983, p. 7). However, the average uplift for the total area glaciated is much lower than the above values. Most ice-age specialists believe the ice sheets were about 3,000 meters thick, and that they didn't begin melting in northeast Canada until about 11,000 years ago. Based on a probable logarithmic decrease in uplift rate since 11,000 years ago, isostatic recovery should be finished in about 20,000 years or more. But this figure depends upon many complicated variables that are poorly understood.

The model presented in this monograph would predict a faster isostatic recovery rate. The ice-sheet thickness proposed here is significantly less than uniformitarian estimates. Based on a thinner ice sheet, isostatic recovery, due to ice unloading, should be almost finished. The time since the ice sheets began to melt, possibly is around 3,000 or 4,000 years. This value indicates complete isostatic recovery, probably in about 5,000 to 10,000 years. A faster isostatic recovery rate also implies a lower mantle viscosity, which may have further ramifications for a geophysical Flood model.

Figure 8.3 is a graph of the presumed change in the land elevation near the "center" of the Laurentide and Scandinavian ice sheets. In Figure 8.3, the land gradually sinks a maximum of about 400 meters in 500 years, which is the time until glacial maximum. Because ice sheets developed so fast, the earth's crust probably never reached isostatic equilibrium before the ice sheets began to melt. Since the ice sheets melted rapidly, isostatic recovery would be rapid at first, then would slow down considerably.

One other variable influencing eustasy and isostasy that has not been discussed yet is vertical, tectonic movements. Tectonic movements have been either observed, or inferred, for most areas of the world. These vertical movements can be either rapid, and associated with earthquakes (likely frequent during the ice age), or gradual subsidence, or emergence, due to an unknown process in the crust, or mantle. Consequently, it is difficult to separate this factor out of shoreline data in order to isolate the eustatic and/or isostatic component.

Gradual upward tectonic movements have been inferred for many tropical islands with coral reef terraces (Broecker et al., 1968; Veeh and Chappell, 1970). These coral-reef terraces, which are as high as 700 meters in New Guinea (Veeh and Chappell, 1970, p. 862), are most likely post-Flood. Many of these coral reefs have been related to the astronomical theory of the ice ages. This is another example of the "reinforcement syndrome," in an effort to prove a theory (Oard, 1985, pp. 178,179). Because of contradictions with plate tectonic models, Nunn (1986) has postulated that the tectonic uplift of tropical islands is either illusory, or slower than calculations have predicted. Investigators have not considered changes in the geoid as a possible mechanism for raising sea level to form these high coral terraces. Regardless of whether sea-level changes are due to migrating geoid anomalies, or to plain, ordinary tectonics, both mechanisms throw considerable confusion on the whole subject of eustasy and isostasy.

Origin of Biogenic Sediments

Modern investigations have revealed that carbonate ooze covers 47% of the ocean bottom, while silaceous ooze covers 15%, and clays, 38%

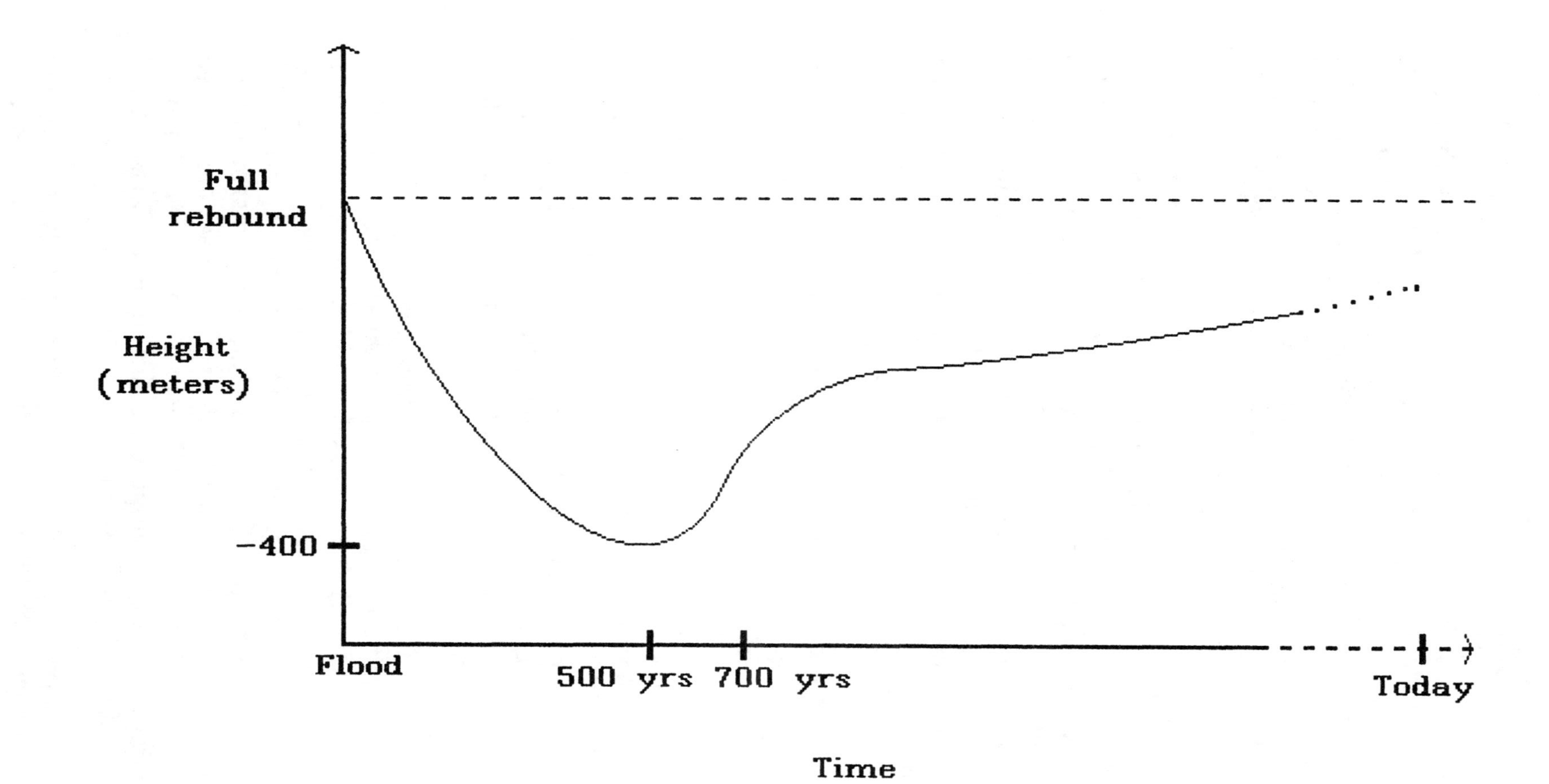

Figure 8.3 Graph of presumed isostatic rebound for the "center" of the Laurentide or Scandinavian ice sheet in a post-Flood ice age.

(Kennett, 1982, p. 457). Most of the surface carbonate ooze consists of the shells of foraminifera. Foraminifera are one-celled organisms that form a series of globular $CaCO_3$ shells. They are mostly less than one millimeter in diameter. An "ooze" is usually defined as a sediment consisting of more than 30% of a particular component, in this case, foraminifera shells. The carbonate ooze below the sediment surface changes from predominantly foraminifera ooze to coccolith ooze (Roth, 1985, pp. 50,51). Coccoliths are microscopic $CaCO_3$ scales that cover coccolithophores—a small planktonic animal.

The current rate of carbonate sedimentation is on the order of 1-3 cm/1000 years (Kennett, 1982, p. 464). Since the average depth of carbonate ooze is 200 meters (Roth, 1985, p. 51), this slow rate of deposition would require millions of years to accumulate the carbonate sediments. How can these carbonate sediments be accounted for within the Biblical time frame? The above sedimentation rate was actually inferred from steady state conditions; the $CaCO_3$ deposition rate is balanced by the amount of new material brought into the ocean by rivers (Kennett, 1982, pp. 459,460; Berger, 1976, p. 299). The above sedimentation rate apparently also has been confirmed recently in some areas of the ocean by observations from sediment traps (Honjo et al., 1982).

Roth (1985) has presented the creationist problem of carbonate oozes, indicating how a catastrophe may alter the deduction of a necessary long period of time. His article inspired this section, which will emphasize several of Roth's key points, and suggest that the catastrophe of the ice age may have been responsible for most biogenic sediments. It shall focus, mainly, on foraminiferal ooze—the major constituent of the biogenic sediments. Siliceous and coccolith oozes are assumed to have been deposited by the same catastrophe, but under different regional conditions. On the other hand, evolutionists have a problem opposite to that of creationists. At the current rates of river-sediment input and supposed subduction of the sea floor, the oceans have too little sediment for the long evolutionary time scale (Roth, 1985, p. 49).

In order to discuss a potential solution to this time problem, we must look at the variables that determine the carbonate sedimentation rate. There are many variables that determine this rate—most of which are poorly known (Berger, 1976). There are four major processes involved (Kennett, 1982, p. 456): 1) the supply of biogenic material, 2) the dissolution of this biogenic material, 3) the dilution of the organic material by non-biogenic sediments, and 4) the diagenetic alteration of the ooze. The third and fourth processes are deemed small in a rapid sedimentation scenario, especially in the open ocean, far away from terrigenous sediment inputs, as proposed in this section. Thus, we need only consider the rate of $CaCO_3$ supply and dissolution.

The supply of $CaCO_3$ from near-surface zooplankton, namely foraminifera and coccolithophores, depends on the primary production of phytoplankton, which in turn depends upon sunlight in the photic zone (the upper 100 meters) and the amount of available nutrients. Davies and Gorsline (1976, pp. 13,14) write: "The production of biogenous sediment is thus determined by the biological productivity of the ocean; this, in turn, is controlled by the available nutrient supply ...." In other words, the number of foraminifera is dependent on the food chain. Sunlight, of course, is not a problem. Given optimum conditions of plentiful food, foraminifera multiply very rapidly. Roth (1985, pp. 51,52) estimates the average depth of calcareous ooze could be produced in less than 1,000 or 2,000 years, under ideal conditions, assuming no dissolution. There is no potential biological reproduction problem.

In today's ocean, three nutrients determine the rate of growth of the phytoplankton. These nutrients are silicon, phosphorus, and nitrogen (Spencer, 1976). At present, these elements are severely depleted in the surface layer, due to biological activity and to their flux into deeper water by sinking foraminifera and coccolithophore shells. On the other hand, the water below the thermocline is overloaded with these nutrients, mostly as a result of dissolution of the zooplankton shells. Accordingly, areas of high biological activity are mainly confined to areas of oceanic upwelling, where the nutrients are transported from the deeper ocean to the surface layer.

The Genesis Flood undoubtedly would supply abundant nutrients to the ocean, making foraminifera and coccolith production rapid at the end of the Flood and the beginning of post-Flood time. But the nutrients would soon be depleted in the photic zone, unless resupplied by rivers and upwelling. In a rapid ice age in which the ocean began uniformly warm, the ocean water would be rapidly mixed (see Chapter 4). This turnover would quickly replenish the nutrients in many areas of the surface layer. Broecker (1971, p. 240) states: "That the accumulation rate of $CaCO_3$ is related to the rates of oceanic mixing has been widely recognized ...."

Two other variables would act to increase biological production. Very high precipitation during the ice age would cause much greater river runoff than occurs today. As the ice sheets rapidly melted, high river runoff would continue. Consequently, nutrients would be added to the ocean more rapidly than is done by modern rivers. The warmer water would aid biological reproduction. Algae, the primary food of foraminifera, reproduce faster in warm water (Berger, 1976, pp. 291,292). Foraminifera abundance and diversity today generally increase from the cool polar ocean to the warm tropical ocean. So there are three variables—rapid oceanic mixing, large nutrient input by rivers, and warm ocean water—that would each contribute to a large, sustained supply of foraminifera and coccoliths during the ice age.

The ice-age catastrophe could produce a large supply of $CaCO_3$, but would the carbonate be dissolved while sinking to the ocean floor? To answer this question, we must first look at the many complex variables influencing carbonate dissolution. This subject is related to the geochemical cycles for calcium and carbon dioxide. Dissolution in the deeper ocean depends upon the corrosiveness of the water, by the production of carbonic acid. Kennett (1982, p. 466) lists five variables. Less dissolution in the deep water is favored by more carbonate ions, warmer temperatures, decreased water flow through the sediments, a low partial pressure of CO_2, and a reduced hydrostatic pressure. Normally, higher temperatures increase chemical reactions, but CO_2 is less soluble in warmer temperatures, so less carbonic acid is formed. The last variable, of course, depends only on ocean depth, and is constant for a given point on the ocean bottom. The other four variables would be acting during the ice age to strongly suppress dissolution.

Carbonate ion content would depend upon the supply of $CaCO_3$ from the photic zone, which would be very high during the ice age. A high supply lowers the calcite compensation depth (CCD) as a result of more carbonate ions. The CCD is the level in the ocean, above which $CaCO_3$ rich sediments are deposited, and below which $CaCO_3$ free sediments accumulate. Berger (1976, p. 308) writes: "Where the shell supply is low, the CCD is in the upper part of this zone [the zone of carbonate corrosion], but it migrates downward, as the supply increases." Due to the large supply of zooplankton, the CCD would be very deep during the ice age. Bottom water temperatures during the ice age were quite warm. Rapid sedimentation would reduce the water flow through the sediments, since they would dewater faster, due to the mass of the accumulating sediments. Also, less time would be available for water flow than within the uniformitarian time frame.

The fourth variable requires further discussion. Carbon dioxide reacts with water to form carbonic acid, which dissolves the shells, so less CO_2 in the water would dissolve less $CaCO_3$. Bottom water CO_2 builds with time, due to the respiration of benthonic, or bottom-dwelling organisms, and to the oxidation of organic remains. In other words, carbon dioxide increases the older the bottom water. The more time the water spends flowing along the bottom, the more its CO_2 will increase by the above two mechanisms. This is why the calcite compensation depth is about 1,000 meters deeper in the Atlantic Ocean than in the Pacific Ocean—Atlantic deep water is young, and Pacific deep water is relatively old. During the ice age, rapid downwelling of ocean surface water in mid and high latitude would constantly replenish the deep ocean with CO_2-depleted surface water. The deep water would have spent much less time circulating on the bottom than modern deepwater has. As a result, the amount of CO_2 in the ice-age deep water would be significantly less than it is today. On the other hand, the increased decay of organic matter due to much more biological activity, would somewhat offset the above depletion of carbon dioxide. The net effect of the first four variables would thus be decreased dissolution, and increased biogenic sediment accumulation.

From these considerations, it is apparent that the rapid ice-age model presented in this monograph, has the potential to account for the depth of biogenic sediments now observed on the ocean bottom. Millions of years are not needed in this model. This example gives hope that many other geophysical features which appear to require long periods of time can be accounted for on a sound scientific basis, within the time limits indicated by the data in Genesis 5, 10, and 11.

The above discussion indicates that all biogenic sediments on the ocean floor, except the most recent, were laid down in the waning stages of the Genesis Flood, and during the ice age. These sediments are dated from the Jurassic to the Pliocene, in the uniformitarian time frame. In a Flood model, sediments in this time range normally are considered to be mostly flood deposits. This may be correct for indurated sediments, but may not hold true for unconsolidated sediments. Unconsolidated ocean sediments are mostly dated by index microfossils, especially foraminifera. The organisms that produced these microfossils could easily have lived during the ice age. Some of these organisms probably became extinct as a result of crucial changes in the ocean water. Others are still living in the modern oceans.

If this is true, why aren't modern plankton fossils found in older oceanic sediments? This brings up the complex subject of taxonomy and biostratigraphy, which is beyond the scope of this monograph and the author's expertise. However, permit a few comments. The above two fields are based on many assumptions from historical geology. Just the classification of oceanic microorganisms is very complex with many problems (Ramsay, 1977). There is a proliferation of different names for the same organism, and much species splitting. Little is known about the biology and ecology of the modern organisms. Looking at the pictures in Ramsay's book (1977) of the various foraminifera from various geological periods, one is impressed by how similar some of them looked to modern foraminifera.

These impressions are reinforced by an article in *Origins*. Tosk (1988) states how foraminifera fossils are often placed in separate biological categories—sometimes even different superfamilies—and are given a different name if they are found at different stratigraphic levels, while if discovered together, they would be considered the same species or genus. So modern foraminifera are likely represented in older sediments of the geological time scale, and are disguised by different names. Evolutionists have called this process "iterative evolution" (similar to parallel, or convergent evolution), whereby the same form supposedly evolved, repeatedly, during geological history. From a statistical point of view, iterative evolution seems incredible for a basically chance process (random mutations). It appears to be a high-sounding term, designed to cover up an embarrassing evolutionary problem. To add to the confusion, foraminifera sometimes display different forms under different ecological conditions. Some of the supposed extinct forms could be only odd varieties of present foraminifera, under critically different conditions. Some pre-Quaternary sediments, so classified according to index microfossils (Hays et al., 1969, p. 1482), are found at the sediment surface, and are probably recent sediments.

In view of the many problems in using microfossils to define geological periods in the oceans, it can be concluded that practically all the biogenic ocean sediments could have been laid down at the end of the Flood, and during the ice age.

CHAPTER 9

CONCLUDING REMARKS

Summary

Over 60 theories of the ice age have been offered in the past, and all have serious deficiencies, including the currently popular astronomical theory. Their major problem is that northern North America and northern Europe possess abundant surface evidence of former ice sheets, yet the present climate cannot glaciate these regions. The requirements for glaciation are a combination of much colder summers and higher snowfall. According to a realistic climate simulation over a snow cover, at least 10-to-12°C summer cooling and twice the snowfall are needed just to glaciate northeast Canada (Williams, 1979). Several solutions to these stringent requirements have been proposed, but these solutions are largely speculation. Many climate simulations have indicated that ice ages can develop easily, with only a small change in higher latitude summer radiation (as proposed by the astronomical theory). But these climate simulations are crude, and glaciation is specified as a response to unrealistic variables.

The only possible way for solving the mystery of the ice age is to develop a new approach, within which to interpret geological and climatological data. It is the purpose of this monograph to make available a theory—a model—a new development, which provides a satisfactory explanation. This new approach is radically different from those which have been utilized for more than 100 years. It is paramount to a paradigm shift in historical science (Kuhn, 1970).

The proposed mechanism is catastrophic, and is not based on the uniformitarian principle. Specifically, the ice age is treated as a consequence of the Genesis Flood, which disrupted the climate to such a degree that an ice age developed immediately afterwards. The Genesis Flood has never been **proved** to be a fable. It has only been assumed so, by some men of science, over the past 200 years or more. There is ample evidence that a gigantic flood once inundated the earth. For example, many sedimentary layers were laid down quickly by huge, powerful currents, with little or no sign of erosion between layers. Well over 100 flood traditions, in cultures from all over the world add support. The Bible clearly specifies that the Flood was global—not regional, or local.

The Genesis Flood provides the initial conditions for the ice age. Since the Flood was associated with extensive volcanicism, a vast shroud of volcanic dust and aerosols would have remained in the atmosphere for several years afterwards. Water for the Flood erupted from below the ground, in the "fountains of the great deep." The hot water from the deep would mix with the pre-Flood ocean, which itself probably was relatively warm compared to today. The tremendous earth upheavals associated with the fountains of the deep, and the draining of the Flood waters, would have mixed the ocean water. Consequently, the ocean would likely have been universally warm from pole to pole, and from top to bottom, at the end of the Flood.

Cooling mechanisms caused by the Flood, in combination with a universally warm ocean, would result in a snowblitz, or a rapid ice age. Volcanic dust and aerosols would provide the main summer cooling over the mid and high-latitude continents, by reflecting a relatively large percentage of the summer sunshine back to space. Once a permanent snow cover becomes established, even more solar radiation is reflected back, reinforcing summer cooling caused by volcanism. Snow-cover cooling is especially effective over barren ground, which would have been characteristic immediately after the Flood. More cloudiness, caused by higher mid and high-latitude moisture, would most likely reinforce the cooler summers. Carbon dioxide, due to volcanism and the decay of vegetation, would have been very high right after the Flood, countering the cooling mechanisms somewhat, but it would have decreased rapidly as the ice age progressed, providing a supplementary cooling mechanism later on as the other cooling mechanisms waned.

The above cooling mechanisms would have acted mainly on land—the oceans would have been least affected. The combination of cold land and warm oceans would have caused the main storm tracks to lie parallel to the east coasts of Asia and North America. These storm tracks would be more-or-less stationary throughout the year. Storm after storm would develop and drop most of its moisture over the colder land. Additionally, the strongest evaporation from the warm ocean would have occurred near the continents, to provide the copious moisture needed for the ice age. Northeastern North America and East Antarctica would be especially favored to develop an ice sheet immediately after the Flood. The mountains of Scandinavia, Greenland, West Antarctica, and western North America, would also have been glaciated at the beginning. However, many areas close to the warm ocean, like the British Isles and the lowlands of northwestern Europe, would be too warm for glaciers at the beginning. Due to at least three factors, the lowlands of eastern Asia and Alaska would have escaped glaciation.

For the ice age to progress, sustained cooling of the mid and high-latitude continents is required. The volcanic dust and aerosols from the Flood would have settled out in a few years, but abundant volcanism, at a much higher rate than we have observed in the recent 200 years, would continue the volcanic cooling. A large array of geological evidence attests to these large ice-age eruptions. The other cooling mechanisms would have continued in operation.

The ocean adjacent to the developing ice sheets, and in the path of storms, would continue warm, due to a vigorous horizontal and vertical ocean circulation. As the water was cooled by evaporation and by contact with cold continental air, it would become more dense, and sink, being replaced by warmer water from deeper in the ocean. Ocean currents, set up along the east coasts of Asia and North America would continually transport warmer water northward. As the deeper ocean cooled, the ocean surface and atmosphere at mid and high latitude would slowly cool, as the ice age progressed and the ice sheets expanded. Mountain icecaps, in many areas, would coalesce and spread to lower elevations.

The unique post-Flood climate would explain a number of long-standing mysteries during the ice age. For instance, a multitude of large lakes filled enclosed basins in now arid or semi-arid regions of the earth. Great Salt Lake was 285 meters deeper, and 17 times the size. Six times more precipitation than in today's climate is needed to account for this lake (Smith and Street-Perrott, 1983). The actual filling of these pluvial lakes was likely due to the Genesis Flood. But there is evidence that they were partially maintained during the ice age. This would be accounted for by at least three times the current precipitation during the post-Flood ice age. Uniformitarian ice age theories usually specify very dry weather during the ice age.

One uniformitarian ice-age puzzle that has lasted for 200 years, is the observation that cold tolerant animals, like the reindeer, lived with warm tolerant animals, like the hippopotamus. The latter even migrated into northern England, France, and Germany during the ice age. A post-Flood ice age can account for this unique distribution of animals, since winters would be mild, and summers cool. And, also, northwest Europe would have been relatively warm at first because of the surrounding warm ocean and the generally westerly onshore flow of air. Land bridges, for instance, across the Bering Strait and the English Channel, would have aided rapid animal dispersion after the Flood.

The climate of Siberia and Alaska would have been mild during the ice age. The Arctic Ocean not only was not covered by sea ice, but it also was relatively warm during the ice age. Temperatures over the surrounding continents would have been significantly warmer than at present as a result (Newson, 1973). The warm North Atlantic and North Pacific also would have contributed to the warmth in these regions, and precipitation would have been higher. Consequently, the woolly mammoth and many other types of animals would have found a suitable home, with adequate food, in Siberia and Alaska.

Due to the unique post-Flood climate, glacial maximum is reached very rapidly—in about 500 years. This figure is based on the length of time the controlling conditions likely operated. The main variable determining this time span is the ocean warmth, which made copious moisture available. Once the ocean cooled to some threshold temperature, the supply of moisture would critically decline, and deglaciation would begin. In Chapter 5, the time needed to cool the ocean was found from the oceanic and atmospheric heat-balance equations applied to the post-Flood climate. Speculation is inherent in such an estimate. As a result, maximum and minimum estimates of the most important variables were used. The initial average ocean temperature following the Flood was assumed to be 30°C, and the threshold temperature, at maximum glaciation, was estimated to be 10°C. The time to reach maximum glaciation ranged from 174 to 1,765 years—very short, compared to uniformitarian estimates. Both these figures are extremes. The best estimate is probably about 500 years.

The available moisture for an ice age not only comes from the warm mid and high-latitude oceans, but also from the poleward transport of water vapor from lower latitudes by the atmospheric circulation. The former was estimated from the heat balance equation of the ocean. The latter was smaller, and found by using the present estimate of poleward transport and adapting it to the post-Flood climate. A maximum and minimum amount of available moisture for the entire ice age was estimated. The next step was to determine how much of this moisture fell on the developing ice sheets. Maximum and minimum areal distributions of the available precipitation were calculated. Ice-depth ranged from 515 meters to 906 meters for the Northern Hemispheric ice sheets, and from 726 meters to 1,673 meters for Antarctica. The best estimate for the average ice depth over the Northern Hemisphere was found to be about 700 meters, and over the Southern Hemisphere, about 1,200 meters.

These numbers are significantly less than uniformitarian estimates, but they are more soundly based than are the uniformitarian estimates. The main method of estimating ice thickness has been by simply assuming that past ice sheets were similar to the Antarctic ice sheet. But a large amount of evidence from the interior and the margin of the Laurentide ice sheet, indicates it actually was comparatively thin. Other methods of estimating ice sheet thickness are faulty, and are often based on circular reasoning.

During deglaciation, summers over mid and high latitudes of the Northern Hemisphere would be warm, but winters would become very cold. The colder winters were due to the continued cooling of the atmosphere by the ice sheets. The cold climate would have caused sea ice to develop on the Arctic Ocean. Sea ice would also have become more extensive than it is today in the North Atlantic and North Pacific Oceans. Due to the cooler temperatures and the greater extent of sea ice, the atmosphere would also become drier than at present. The storm tracks would be displaced southward, with a secondary storm track just south of the ice sheets. Dry, windy storms would track south of the ice sheets, and would often cause blowing dust that would result in extensive sand and loess sheets.

Even in such a climate, the ice sheets would melt in summer. Over a snow cover, and with 10°C colder summer temperatures along the periphery than at present, the energy-balance equation indicates that the ice sheet would melt rapidly—in less than 100 years, at the periphery. The interior would likely melt in under 200 years. The melting rates calculated in this book are close to those observed in the present climate. Consequently, the total time for a post-Flood ice age is only about 700 years.

The rapidly melting ice sheets would cause rivers to overflow and become choked with sediment. Terraces would be cut into deep fills of river-valley alluvium. Large river meanders, close to the ice sheet edge, attest to a large runoff. Some of these geomorphic features formed at the end of the Flood, but the ice age would surely add its imprint.

At this time, the cold, dry climate would stress the abundant megafauna. Many animals would become extinct—with the assistance of man, the hunter, in some cases. The extinction of the megafauna at the end of the ice age is just one of many mysteries unexplainable by uniformitarian assumptions. The woolly mammoth is one of the extinct megafauna. The disappearance of a million or more of them in Siberia and Alaska is especially intriguing. Since only a small percentage of mammoths had soft parts frozen, and most of the other animals managed to flee, the catastrophe seems to be more a result of a gradual, but permanent cooling of the climate. Partially digested stomach contents, in one or two carcasses, is the basis for a regional quick-freeze theory. But since other indicators show the regional freeze was gradual, there probably is a local explanation for the condition of these stomach contents.

Some readers may think the number of glaciations has been firmly established by science. An examination of the history of the multiple-glaciation concept shows that the number has never been established. The glacial sediments are so complex that a case can be made for anywhere from one-to-six or more separate glaciations. Four ice ages were agreed upon in the early 20th century, primarily on the basis of investigations in the Swiss Alps. During the last two decades, glaciologists have come to believe 20 or 30 ice ages developed and dissipated in succession. The fourfold scheme that was worked out in the Alps is now considered to be inadequate, and to have many serious errors. For over 60 years, all research was fitted into the alpine scheme, while it held sway over scientific thinking. This is an example of the reinforcement syndrome that continues to operate strongly in the geological sciences.

Abundant evidence indicates that one ice age is much more probable than many. A major reason for this is that the very radical requirements for one ice age (Williams, 1979) are not likely to be repeated. The ice-age sediments have not been transported far, strongly suggesting only one, thin ice sheet. Combining this evidence with the thin till cover, especially over interior regions, and with the observation that nearly all the till was deposited during the "last" ice age, one ice age is more reasonable. Moreover, two favorable areas along the periphery, called driftless areas, were never glaciated. This is more in line with one, thin ice sheet, than with 20 or more thick ice sheets. Since practically all the ice-age fossils are found south of the former ice sheets, and most major extinctions followed only the "last" ice age, there most likely never were interglacial periods.

Evidence for multiple glaciations comes from the periphery of the ice sheets—evidence such as fossils and ancient soils found between sheets of till. This evidence actually is rare. The properties of ancient soils are used to date various ice ages, but too many poorly known variables make such classification speculative. Just recognizing an ancient soil, is difficult. The evidence for multiple ice ages can be adequately explained by one dynamic ice age. Just like modern glaciers, one ice sheet would advance, retreat, and surge, in accord with variations in climate. Post-Flood ice sheets would move rapidly at the periphery, and slowly, in the interior. Rapid oscillations would cause stacked till sheets, with non-glacial deposits sandwiched between. Even organic remains can be engulfed in this way. Heavy precipitation south of the ice sheet could develop clay-like "soils" in a short time, and high erosion can give the terrain an old appearance.

The ice age ended within the last several millenia. The basis for this qualitative assessment is the freshness of most glacial features. More quantitative estimates, like those based on the rate of recession of Niagara Falls, have unfortunate complications, but nevertheless indicate a short time—especially when the rapid melting of the ice sheets is considered. The erosion along the sides of the Niagara Gorge gives a more dependable estimate of the time—only about 2,000 years. The erosion of till by Plum Creek, in Ohio, provides an estimate of 3,000-to-4,000 years. By adding 700 years, a date for the Flood can be estimated.

During the ice age and afterwards, sea level fluctuated due to the formation and melting of the ice sheets. The maximum lowering of sea level would be significantly less than indicated by uniformitarian estimates, which are based on excessive ice thickness and many other poorly known variables.

The ice sheets caused the crust to depress and then rebound. The amount of rebound, based on the highest observed shore line, and the slow uplift measured today, agree best with a thin ice sheet that melted relatively recently. Uniformitarian estimates claim a much higher amount of isostatic rebound due to a thicker ice sheet. Negative gravity anomalies in Scandinavia and the Hudson Bay area are used to bolster these high values, but the magnitude of the remaining rebound, surmised from these anomalies, is not known because of additional variables, whose effects have not been quantified.

A major time-scale problem is the depth of biogenic sediments on the bottom of the ocean. From present estimates, these sediments would need millions of years to accumulate. But the Flood and a post-Flood ice age can potentially account for these sediments in a short time. Due to a rapid mixing of the ocean during the ice age, a large flux of nutrients would have been available for very large numbers of plankton. Shells, from zooplankton, would not dissolve as fast as they do today, and would have accumulated more rapidly on the bottom of the ocean.

Further Research

It is expected that the reader, who has carefully read the preceding chapters, has now concluded that a post-Flood ice-age model is not only viable but far superior to any uniformitarian ice-age model. It can account for a number of outstanding mysteries of the ice age. A good model also suggests areas for further research. One of these areas is the origin of drumlins.

Drumlins are lens-shaped mounds of glacial deposits, found by the thousands in some areas. Drumlins can sometimes be as long as a mile, and several hundred feet high. They have been moulded and streamlined, with their long axis parallel to glacial movement. They are the last remnants of glaciation, since they are easily erodible, and eskers are sometimes draped over them. The internal composition is variable. Sometimes solid rock forms the core of a drumlin, and at other times, till and even stratified deposits, predominate. How a glacier forms drumlins is a long-standing puzzle (Muller, 1974). Shaw (1988), referring to two recent conferences on the origin of drumlins, writes: "No general agreement appears to have materialized on future research initiatives, and drumlins remain as enigmatic as ever ... [the origin of drumlins is] one of the great unsolved problems in Quaternary geology."

There are two schools of thought on the origin of drumlins (Menzies and Rose, 1987a). One school believes drumlins are formed by subglacial deformation and the sqeezing of till into elliptical mounds (Boulton, 1987a). The other, newer school of thought, believes they are formed by subglacial meltwater (Shaw, 1983; Dardis et al., 1984; Shaw and Kvill, 1984; Shaw and Sharpe, 1987; Shaw, 1989). Unfortunately, the issue is difficult to resolve, because few drumlins have been extensively studied (Boulton, 1987a, p. 65; Dardis, 1987, p. 215). This newer school points to the fact that many drumlins frequently contain stratified deposits ranging from gravels to finely laminated clay (Menzies and Rose, 1987b, p. 2). Most important, these stratified deposits are often undeformed. Shaw (1988, p. 354) states the significance of this observation:

> *It is simply not possible for drumlins to form by pervasive subglacial deformation and, at the same time, contain large thicknesses of undeformed, but highly deformable, fine-grained laminated sediment near the landform surface.*

The second school of thought has theorized that drumlins form in extra-wide subglacial tunnels excavated by water. Then the tunnels fill with sediments that are streamlined by glacial motion. Because the amount of meltwater needed to form drumlins is much higher than most glacial geologists can envision, the two schools radically diverge (Menzies and Rose, 1987b). Boulton (1987b, p. 28) states the problem as follows:

> *If this explanation were correct for many or most drumlins, their high frequency in many areas, and common evidence for their rapid construction would imply that the ice sheets underwent rapid and catastrophic "dewatering" events which would lead to large-scale instability and have a major impact on our concept of the evolution of glacial cycles.*

Catastrophic "dewatering" and rapid formation of drumlins are expected during deglaciation in a post-Flood, ice-age model. Consequently, this model may provide the missing key for explaining the origin of drumlins.

The ice age model presented in this monograph, can possibly provide solutions to many post-Flood creationist puzzles, particularly in trying to account for data sets that appear to need much more time for formation than Scripture allows. The origin of biogenic sediments on the bottom of the ocean, presented in Chapter 8, is but one example. Another example is the origin of limestone caves. According to the creationist paradigm, these caves and their speleothems must have formed in the waning stages of the Genesis Flood and in post-Flood time. Creationists have researched the origin of cave deposits, and can point out that stalactites can sometimes form rapidly (Austin, 1980). Strahler (1987, pp. 279-281) claims that creationist research in this area is flawed, and that much more post-Flood time is required than the Bible allows.

However, Strahler (1987, p. 281) does recognize that cave deposits are climate-dependent. A cavern, or cave, must first be dissolved out of the limestone before speleothems can form. This depends especially on the amount of carbon dioxide in the atmosphere, and in the soil, due to biological processes (Sutcliffe, 1985, p. 79). Limestone solution is most rapid in moist climates, and depends, secondarily, on temperature. In the post-Flood climate, precipitation in non-glaciated areas was at least three times the present precipitation. Higher rainfall would have caused more surface vegetation and ground litter that would contain higher amounts of CO_2, especially in currently semi-arid regions. Atmospheric carbon dioxide would have been quite high at the beginning of the ice age (see Chapter 3). These factors can possibly account for the rapid formation of caves and speleothems during the ice age, especially for those caves in which the present climate is too dry for their formation (Charlesworth, 1957, p. 1112).

Another problem, more for a post-Flood than a uniformitarian model, is the transport of far-traveled, erratic boulders, if, indeed, they are far-traveled. Some of these boulders weigh hundreds of tons, and supposedly traveled hundreds of miles. They are commonly angular, indicating protection from abrasion by bedrock and other boulders in the ice. It is hard to see how a thin ice sheet could transport boulders large distances, although modest distances are possible. But, there are possible solutions to this problem. The actual evidence for far-traveled boulders should first be reexamined. Most "far-traveled" erratics could be classifications based on a model in which ice sheets developed in the far north, and slowly spread to the southern periphery. Given the pervasiveness of this model, it is doubtful that other possibilities have been seriously considered.

Since nearly all till, including most boulders, is local (Feininger, 1971), why should a small minority of the boulders be far-traveled? To protect boulders from the grinding action at the base of a glacier, they must first be thrust well up into the ice from below—a more difficult task than with the finer-grained till. The Laurentide ice sheet developed and mainly moved over flat terrain. There are no mountains from which a boulder could roll down onto the ice sheet, as observed in valley glaciers today. Whillans (1978, pp. 517,518) says that, except for shear planes near the glacier snout (Figure 7.4), no good mechanism exists for transporting basal debris vertically up into the ice. If the boulders could be emplaced upward in the ice, the ice sheet must then transport them hundreds of miles, which the local nature of till makes questionable. As discussed in Chapter 5, the margins of the Laurentide ice sheet were very thin. Mathews (1974, p. 41) questions how ice sheets, with low slopes, could build morainal ridges containing far-traveled erratics.

The source of many unique erratics is not really known. Could the source rock be actually nearby, but covered by till? Possibly a nearby source was completely eroded, except for a few residual outcroppings. Caldwell and Hansen (1986) invoked this explanation to account for "erratic" boulders on Mt. Katahdin that other scientists claim were transported a long distance, and forced uphill to near the top of the mountain.

Some erratic boulders, transported across the Baltic Sea, are believed to have been emplaced by floating ice (Houmark-Nielsen, 1983, p. 201; de Jong and Maarleveld, 1983, p. 353). Erratics, transported eastward across Hudson Bay, are now believed to have been transported by icebergs, or sea ice, since they are found below the marine limit (Andrews, 1982, p. 24). Some far-traveled boulders in the northern Queen Elizabeth Islands, could have been transported by ice rafting (Bird, 1967, p. 108). Extensive pro-glacial lakes and large rivers formed at the boundary of the ice sheets as they melted (Bretz, 1943; Gudelis and Königsson, 1979; Karrow and Calkin, 1985). Icebergs, containing boulders, could have been transported far by these interconnected lakes and large rivers. Erratics also could have been deposited south of the ice sheet boundary by this mechanism. In summary, there are many problems with the concept of far-traveled boulders. Other variables could have been responsible for them. An extensive investigation of these erratics is needed, but still, questions of their origin probably would remain due to the many complications.

Implications

The Genesis Flood is the basis for the post-Flood ice-age model. Since this model can explain the development of ice sheets, and offer viable solutions to many outstanding ice age mysteries, the Flood should offer a firmer foundation for pre-glacial, earth history. After all, if the principle of uniformitarianism cannot explain the last geological period, why should it be the basis for all other geological periods?

Since uniformitarianism is unable to solve many mysteries of the past, it should be discarded, along with its accompanying theories—the theory of evolution and an old earth. A revolution, or paradigm change in historical science would result. Many research conclusions would be rethought. The contribution to science and to life would be overwhelmingly positive.

Uniformitarian scientists are fond of accusing creationists of merely attacking the theory of evolution, without providing positive contributions to science. If a theory has serious problems, a positive alternative is not necessarily needed to advance science. On the basis of the Creation-Flood paradigm, creationists have made significant contributions to scientific problems. The ice-age model, presented in this book, is one such effort. Most evolutionists have had little contact with these contributions.

A post-Flood ice-age model is but one example of an explanation for a phenomenon of natural history using the Creation-Flood paradigm. New scientific data relating to earth history is published each year. Most of these data are incorporated within the uniformitarian paradigm, whether the data fit, or not. Care must be excercised in using these data, since data collection and/or presentation is often biased by theory. Much new, as well as old scientific data, need reinterpreting within a Creation-Flood paradigm. This cannot be accomplished quickly. Thousands of uniformitarian scientists have spent over 150 years, and billions of dollars, on the uniformitarian model of earth history. Patience is needed to decipher the information on a particular subject. Creationists, as well as others, must be careful not to jump to conclusions too quickly. Of course, not every mystery of the past will be solved. But with time, and effort, many aspects of the Creation-Flood paradigm can be filled in, and will result in a far superior model of the prehistoric past.

A post-Flood, rapid ice age, supports the Genesis Flood, which further supports the historicity of the Bible. It also adds credence to the God of the Bible, and to the spiritual message in the Bible. A God who has control of the earth, can cause a global Flood, and allow an ice age is very powerful. He is even more powerful and intelligent for having created the entire universe. He is a master mathematician, engineer, and artist. Only the God of power and love described in the Bible, is up to the task.

APPENDIX 1

DERIVATION OF TIME FOR MAXIMUM GLACIATION

To solve Equation 5.1, we need to first divide the ocean surface into areas of net heating and net cooling in the post-Flood climate. In the present and post-Flood climate, the tropical and subtropical oceans gain heat, while the mid and higher-latitude oceans lose heat. Net cooling of the ocean surface is accomplished by evaporation and conduction. The heat lost by conduction occurs by a similar process, and over a similar area as that for evaporative cooling. The areas of net cooling in the post-Flood climate correspond closely to the areas of moderate-to-strong evaporation, which are estimated for the Northern Hemisphere in Figure 3.9. These areas are for the first half of glaciation, and an average for the entire period of glaciation is needed. As the ice age progressed, areas of moderate and high evaporation would spread out slightly. Another feature to note in Figure 3.9, is that areas of net cooling and heating are not latitudinally symmetrical. High evaporation takes place off the east coast of the continents, while generally light evaporation occurs off the west coasts. For the purpose of estimating the variables in Equation 5.1, the dividing line, between areas of net surface cooling and warming, was assumed to average 40°N in the Northern Hemisphere.

Since the Southern Hemisphere has a much larger ocean, and the continent of Antarctica is the predominant source of cold air, moderate-to-strong evaporative and conductive cooling of the ocean surface was assumed to have taken place in a 10°-latitude strip around Antarctica. This strip of ocean has an average latitude of about 60°S. Therefore, 60°S was assumed to be the boundary latitude between net oceanic warming to the north and net cooling to the south, during the post-Flood ice age. Figure A1.1 shows the heat balance for the partitioned ocean. The only difference for the ocean heat-balance equation—the terms of which are illustrated in Figure A1.1 and Figure 5.2—is that heat flow by ocean currents must be included. Figure A1.1 illustrates this heat flow, and the spreading of the colder water from the higher latitude surface to the deeper ocean.

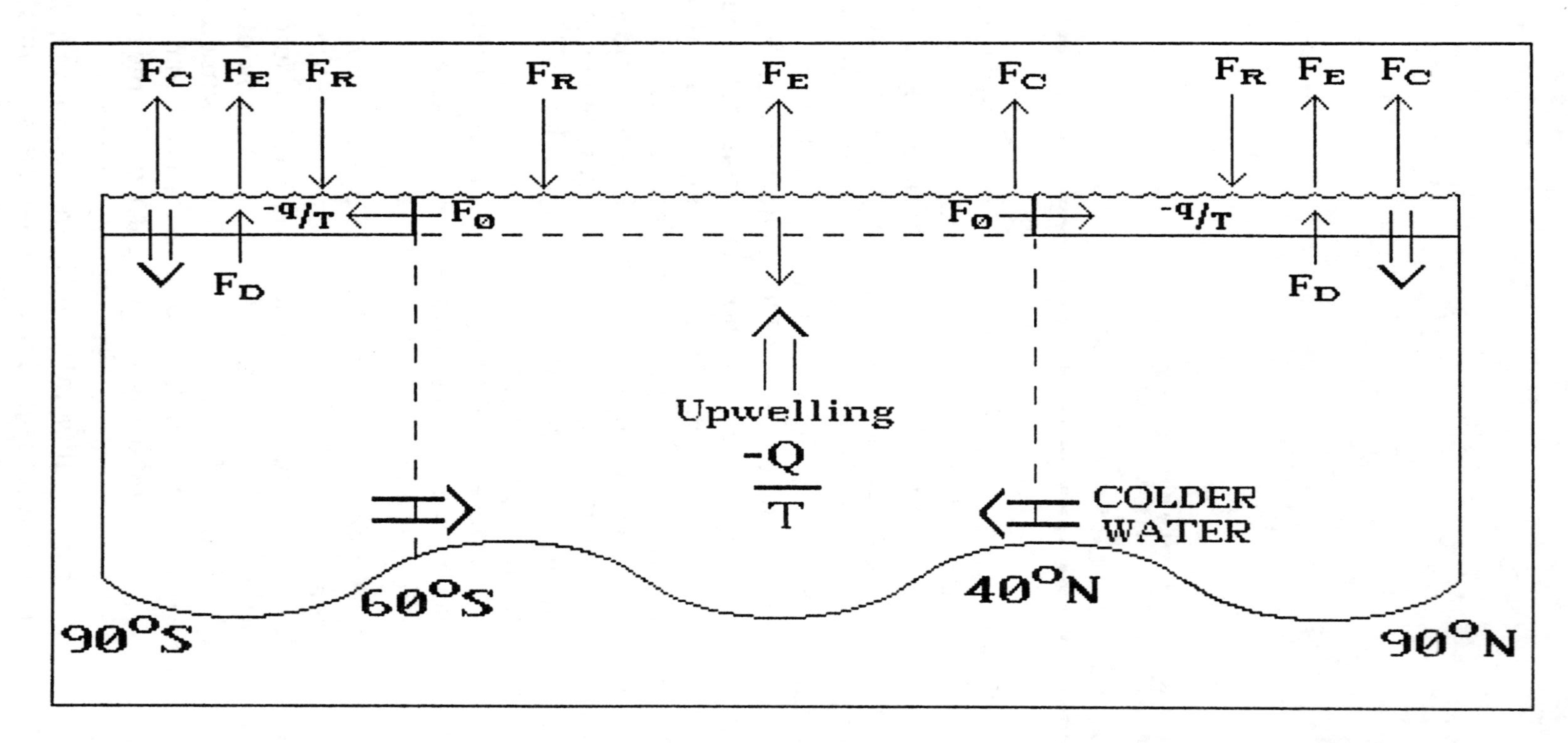

Figure A1.1 The heat balance of the ocean partitioned into areas of net surface heating and cooling in the post-Flood climate. Symbols the same as in Figure 5.1. In addition, double arrows represent the flow of colder water, F_0 is the heat flux by surface ocean currents, F_D is the heat flux from deeper water, and q/T is the rate of heat loss in the higher latitude surface layer.

For the two surface areas of net cooling (shown by the solid boxes in Figure A1.1), Equation 5.1 becomes:

$$F_R - F_E - F_C + F_O + F_D = -q/T \qquad \text{(A1.1)}$$

where F_O is the net rate of higher-latitude heat transport by ocean currents, F_D is the rate of heat added from the deep warm ocean at mid and high latitudes, and q is the heat lost in the higher latitude surface layer in time T. F_R, F_E, and F_C were previously defined in Chapter 5.

Equation A1.1 can be further simplified. F_D is equal to Q/T - q/T added from the deep ocean. This heat from below is equal to the total cooling of the ocean, Q/T, minus the small contribution from the surface layers, q/T. The reason the surface layer value is small, is because it has a much smaller volume, compared to the total volume of the ocean. As previously stated in Chapter 5, the signs of the terms in the balance equations must be watched carefully. If a variable adds heat to the volume under consideration, the sign is positive, and vice versa for a variable that subtracts heat. This is why F_D is positive in Equation A1.1, while Q/T is negative in Equation 5.1. Substituting the above equality and solving for T, Equation A1.1 becomes:

$$T = -Q/(F_R - F_E - F_C + F_O) \qquad \text{(A1.2)}$$

In order to solve this equation, the heat balance of the atmosphere must be included, because F_E and F_C transfer heat from the ocean to the atmosphere. The heat added to the atmosphere will, in turn, influence the rate of heat loss from the ocean. In other words, the atmosphere acts like a regulator, or negative feedback, to the heat flux. If the continental air becomes too cold, evaporative and conductive heating, F_E and F_C, are stronger, as colder, drier, continental air encounters the warm ocean. More atmospheric heating over the ocean, spread around mid and higher latitudes by the atmospheric circulation, will cause the continental air to not be so cold, which then reduces F_E and F_C. Because of the warmth of the mid and high-latitude oceans and the bulk aerodynamic equations for F_E and F_C applied to areas adjacent to cold continents, the transfer of heat to the atmosphere is high. This heat, injected into the higher latitudes, would result in milder, wet winters, especially for areas along the coast. Continental interiors at higher latitude, would, of course, be kept cool by the mechanisms described in Chapter 3.

The equation for the heat balance of the atmosphere north of 40°N, and south of 60°S, in the post-Flood climate, is (Budyko, 1978, p. 86):

$$-F_{RA} + F_E + F_C + F_A = -Q_A/T \qquad \text{(A1.3)}$$

where F_{RA} is the average radiative heat balance for the atmosphere per unit of time, which is negative at higher latitudes; F_A is the higher latitude rate of heat transport by the atmosphere; and Q_A is the total change in heat content of the higher latitude atmosphere, in time T. The atmospheric heat balance for the mid and high latitudes of the Northern Hemisphere is depicted in Figure A1.2. Analogous to F_O, in the ocean heat balance, F_A represents the resultant of the lower-latitude atmospheric-heat balance. Q_A is negative, because the higher latitude atmosphere will gradually cool in the post-Flood climate. Considering the low specific heat and the light weight of air, Q_A will be small compared to the other terms in the equation, and can be neglected.

F_{RA} is difficult to estimate, so can be simplified by the following equation (Budyko, 1978, p. 86):

$$F_{RA} = F_{RE} + F_R \qquad \text{(A1.4)}$$

where F_{RE} is the average radiative heat balance per unit of time at the top of the atmosphere, equal to the difference between the absorbed solar radiation by the earth and atmosphere and the outgoing infrared radiation to space. Substituting into Equation A1.3, and setting Q_A equal to zero:

$$-F_{RE} - F_R + F_E + F_C + F_A = 0 \qquad \text{(A1.5)}$$

F_{RE} and F_R are negative, because they cause the higher-latitude atmosphere to lose heat.

The second, third, and fourth terms in Equation A1.5, are the same terms as in the oceanic-heat-balance Equation A1.2. However, the terms apply to different volumes. Equation A1.5 includes the total volume of atmosphere above the higher latitude oceans, and also the total volume above the higher latitude continents. In order to substitute an expression for the atmospheric heat balance into the oceanic heat balance equation, only those terms common to both the atmosphere and ocean can be exchanged. In other words, we can only substitute F_R, F_E, and F_C for the atmospheric volume above the ocean into Equation A1.2, simplifying the latter. Separating Equation A1.5 into over-land and over-ocean volumes, and rearranging terms, Equation A1.5 becomes:

$$(-F_R + F_E + F_C)_{LAND} + (-F_R + F_E + F_C)_{OCEAN} = F_{RE} - F_A \qquad \text{(A1.6)}$$

The first term in parentheses cancels, because over-land F_R equals $F_E + F_C$ (Budyko, 1978, pp. 86,90). Equation A1.6 then becomes:

$$(-F_R + F_E + F_C)_{OCEAN} = F_{RE} - F_A \qquad \text{(A1.7)}$$

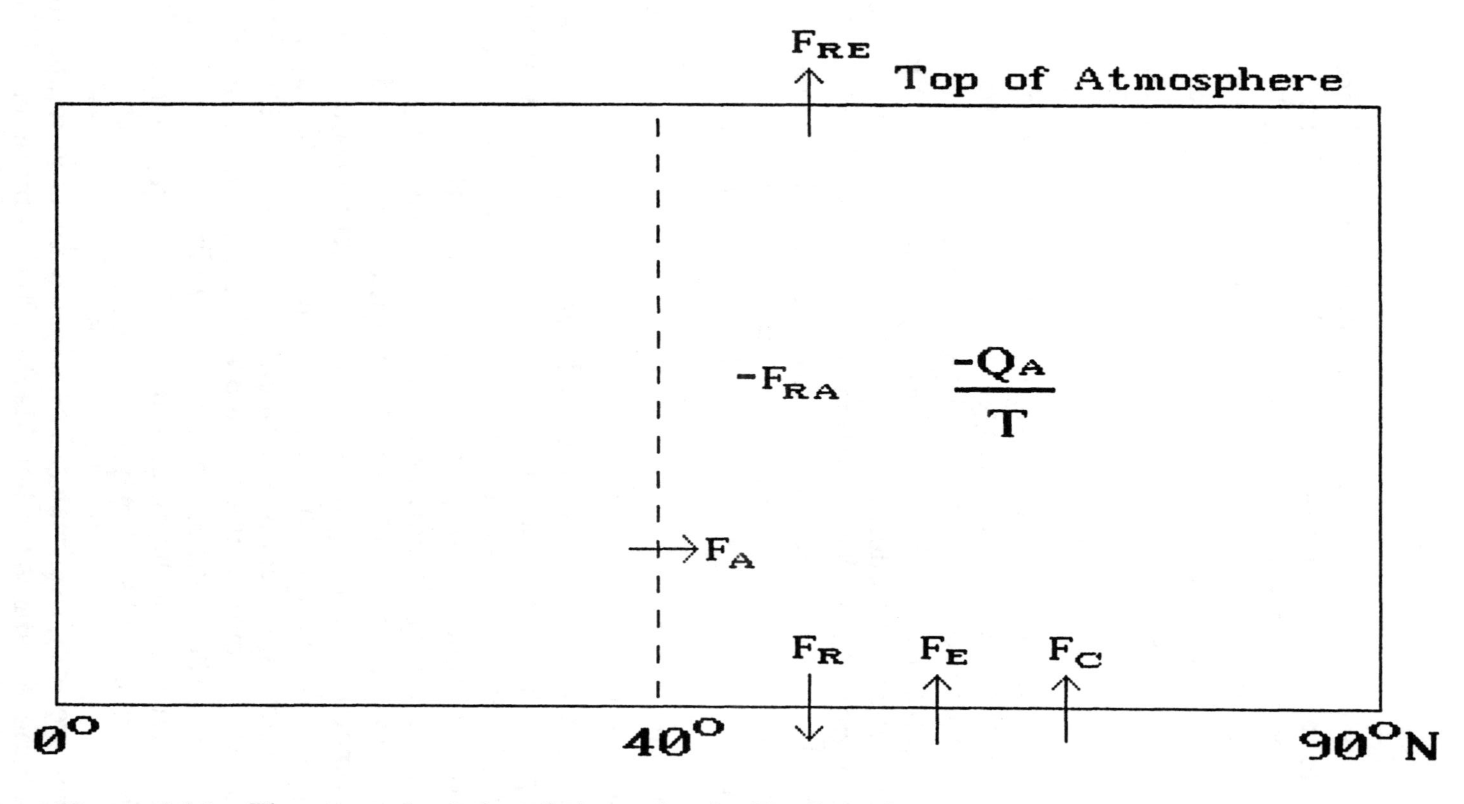

Figure A1.2 The atmospheric heat balance for the Northern Hemisphere north of 40°N.

Substituting Equation A1.7 into Equation A1.2:

$$T = -Q/(-F_{RE} + F_A + F_O) \qquad (A1.8)$$

Equation A1.8 is as far as we can simplify the ocean-heat-balance equation. In today's climate, which is in a steady state, Q is zero, and the terms in the parentheses balance (Carissimo et al., 1985, p. 83). This will later help us estimate post-Flood values of F_A and F_O, together. Now we must estimate the four terms on the right for the post-Flood climate. The values for the terms in parentheses will be in calories/year.

Oceanic Cooling

Q is the total heat lost to the ocean between the Flood and ice-age maximum. It depends upon the initial average temperature and the threshold temperature at glacial maximum. The initial ocean temperature depends upon the average temperature of the pre-Flood ocean, and on the average temperature and volume of subterranean water added to this ocean from the "fountains of the great deep." The temperature of the pre-Flood ocean was probably warm, but depended upon many factors. The temperature of subterranean water, today, varies from the warm temperature of some hot springs, to the very hot temperature of 350°C for many oceanic hydrothermal vents that have been recently discovered along ocean ridges (Kerr, 1987). In general, the average temperature of the subterranean water will depend upon the average depth of the released water.

Since the pre-Flood atmosphere was likely warmer than at present (see Chapter 2), the pre-Flood deep ocean must have been warmer than the current average of 4°C. Therefore, I shall assume the average pre-Flood ocean temperature was 10°C. Since, in the present crust of the earth, the temperature warms with depth at 30°C per kilometer, I will assume the average temperature of the subterranean water was 200°C. This temperature corresponds to a depth of about six kilometers, assuming the same vertical-temperature gradient in the pre-Flood crust. The volume of the ocean now is 1.5×10^9 km^3, with an average depth of four kilometers (Considine, 1983, p. 2045). If the "fountains of the deep" added 10% more water to the pre-Flood ocean, the height of the ocean would have risen 363 meters, if contained only in the ocean basins, with no change in the elevation of the ocean bottom. The average temperature of the ocean, at the end of the Flood, would then be 27°C.

These figures are rough estimates. Possibly, an average temperature of 200°C for subterranean water is too hot. Maybe 100°C is more reasonable. On the other hand, the highest pre-Flood mountain could have been much higher than 363 meters, requiring a greater volume of ocean water to cover the tops of all the highest mountains (Genesis 7:19). Disregarding the assumption that the extra water was contained only in the ocean basin, 363 meters would reduce to around 200 meters, depending upon the proportion of land versus ocean, and the average height of the pre-Flood continents. Although there is no way of knowing the variables that determined the average ocean temperature immediately after the Flood, I can envisage a very warm ocean. The fountains of the deep are a large heat source. Therefore, 30°C, likely an upper boundary, will be assumed as the initial ocean temperature. Initial ocean temperatures of 25°C and 20°C will also be used in calculating the time to reach glacial maximum. A temperature warmer than 30°C would have been a serious threat to marine life as we know it. Although the ocean would be well mixed, small regional differences in ocean temperature would be likely, and surface cooling at higher latitudes would begin soon after the Flood, relieving stress on marine life. In general, a uniformly warm temperature would occur from top to bottom, and from pole to pole, following the Flood.

A source of moisture adequate for an ice age depends upon the ocean surface temperature near the area of ice buildup, which, in turn, depends upon the average temperature of the entire ocean. In today's climate, the ocean temperatures are too cool to supply sufficient moisture for a continental snow cover that would last through a summer. This is because the solar radiation, in summer, as shown in Chapter 6, is very efficient in melting snow. Thus, ice-age maximum would certainly occur at an average ocean temperature higher than at present. Therefore, I will assume the ice-age maximum occurred at a threshold ocean temperature of 10°C. Since the specific heat of ocean water is 1 cal/gm, a 20°C change in temperature, from the end of the Flood to glacial maximum, represents a heat loss of 3.0×10^{25} calories.

Although this loss would be from higher-latitude surface cooling, one significant effect that would slow the oceanic cooling is the upwelling of colder water along the west coast of the continents in the Northern Hemisphere, especially along North America (Budyko, 1978, p. 90). Figure 4.2 shows the estimated areas of upwelling in the North Atlantic. In the present climate, upwelling transports colder, deep water, to near the surface, where it is warmed by solar radiation. At the beginning of the post-Flood ice age, upwelling would transport warm water to the surface. Only after a sufficient pool of cold water developed below the surface, would the upwelling become important. This would occur towards the later stages of the ice buildup, and would, consequently, not be too significant. Therefore, upwelling will be ignored. The effect of including upwelling, would be to make the ice age a little longer. Thus, Q will be set equal to 3.0×10^{25} calories in Equation A1.8.

Radiation Balance at Top of Atmosphere

F_{RE} is the difference between the incoming solar radiation that is absorbed by the earth-atmosphere system and the outgoing infrared radiation at the top of the atmosphere. Both will be strongly affected by the unique post-Flood climate. The amount of solar-radiation energy directed back into space will depend upon the amount of volcanic dust and aerosols trapped in the upper atmosphere, the snow cover, and cloudiness during time T. Since the average reflectivity is unknown, I shall assume a range of values, depending mainly on the volcanic dust and aerosol loading. The eruption of Krakatoa reduced sunlight four percent (Oliver, 1976, p. 936), and the April 1982 eruption of El Chichón, in Mexico, reduced it five percent at Fairbanks, Alaska, during a three-month period the following winter (Wendler and Haar, 1986). Mass and Portman (1989, p. 567) estimate modern-day volcanoes reduce the total sunlight five percent to seven percent for a limited time at higher latitudes. The extensive post-Flood volcanism must have reduced sunlight much more, since eruptions observed during the past 200 years are quite small, compared to ice-age eruptions (Kerr, 1989, p. 128). For a minimum average, I will assume 10% of the present solar radiation energy is redirected back to space. For a maximum possible average, which is unrealistic, I will assume 75% is lost from Earth. Values for a 25% and a 50% loss will also be calculated. Table A1.1 presents the values for the yearly average solar radiation at the top of the atmosphere, for each 10°-latitude band. The data for the present atmosphere was taken from Budyko (1978, p. 91).

The infrared-radiation loss, at the top of the atmosphere, is generally proportional to the surface temperature (Budyko, 1978, pp. 93,94). Infrared radiation will also depend, to a lesser extent, upon the atmospheric distribution of water vapor, clouds, and CO_2. Since latitudes poleward of 60° were significantly warmer in the post-Flood climate, infrared radiation loss must have been higher. Accordingly, I adjusted current values for the high latitudes upward 20%. Values for the latitude band, 40°N to 60°N, were assumed the same as present values, because a warmer average temperature over the ocean would likely be balanced by colder average annual temperatures over the continents. Table A1.2 presents the yearly average infrared-radiation loss in the present and the post-Flood climates, for each 10° latitude band.

Table A1.3 presents the difference between the absorbed solar radiation and the outgoing infrared radiation for the four volcanic-dust and aerosol-loading scenarios. For instance, in Table A1.2, the value for post-Flood outgoing radiation in latitude band 40-50°N, which is 160.2 kcal/cm^2-yr, is subtracted from the values for the four dust loading scenarios for that latitude band, from Table A1.1. The resulting four values are then multiplied by the area of the earth within that latitude band, which is 31.5×10^{16} cm^2. The values in the latitude bands are totaled for each dust-and-aerosol-loading scenario, and these four values represent the range in F_{RE} that will be used to solve Equation A1.8.

Table A1.1. Absorbed solar radiation by the earth-atmosphere system, 40°N to 90°N and 60°S to 90°S, in today's climate, and for various dust and aerosol-loading scenarios in the post-Flood climate. Units are in kcal/cm^2-yr.

Lat. Band	Today	-10%	-25%	-50%	-75%
40-50°N	140.4	126.4	105.4	70.2	35.2
50-60°N	111.6	100.4	83.7	55.8	27.9
60-70°N	79.8	71.8	59.9	39.9	20.0
70-80°N	52.2	47.0	39.2	26.1	13.1
80-90°N	47.4	42.7	35.6	23.7	11.9
60-70°S	54.6	49.1	41.0	27.3	13.7
70-80°S	27.6	24.8	20.7	13.8	6.9
80-90°S	20.4	18.4	15.3	10.2	5.1

Table A1.2. Outgoing infrared radiation, 40°N to 90°N and 60°S to 90°S, for the present atmosphere, and as estimated for the post-Flood atmosphere. Units are in kcal/cm^2-yr.

Lat. Band	Today	Post-Flood
40-50°N	160.2	160.2
50-60°N	150.6	150.6
60-70°N	142.2	170.2
70-80°N	134.4	161.3
80-90°N	129.0	154.8
60-70°S	137.4	164.9
70-80°S	125.4	150.5
80-90°S	114.6	137.5

Table A1.3. The difference in outgoing infrared radiation and incoming solar radiation, 40°N to 90°N and 60°S to 90°S, for various volcanic-dust and aerosol-loading scenarios in the post-Flood climate. Units of area within each latitude band are in 10^{16} cm^2, and radiation difference in 10^{22} cal/yr.

Lat. Band	Area	-10%	-25%	-50%	-75%
40-50°N	31.50	-10.65	-17.26	-28.35	-39.38
50-60°N	25.61	-12.86	-17.13	-24.28	-31.42
60-70°N	18.91	-18.61	-20.86	-24.64	-28.40
70-80°N	11.59	-13.25	-14.15	-15.67	-17.18
80-90°N	3.91	-4.38	-4.66	-5.13	-5.59
60-70°S	18.91	-21.90	-23.43	-26.02	-28.59
70-80°S	11.59	-14.57	-15.04	-15.84	-16.64
80-90°S	3.91	-4.66	-4.78	-4.98	-5.18
Total		-10.1	-11.7	-14.5	-17.2

Poleward Heat Transport

F_A and F_O are the higher-latitude transports of heat by the atmosphere and ocean, respectively. These variables for the post-Flood climate need estimating. Both are residuals of the heat balance of the atmosphere and ocean at lower latitudes. Unfortunately, F_A and F_O are not precisely known, in the present climate, although the general features are understood (Charnock, 1987). The sum of the transports is reasonably known in the present climate, since the sum must balance the higher-latitude-heat deficit, which is F_{RE} (de Szoeke, 1988, p. 585). The sum is what we need for solving Equation A1.8. Minimum and maximum values will again be estimated for the post-Flood climate. The minimum estimate will be zero. The maximum values of F_A and F_O for each hemisphere in the present climate, will be used as the maximum post-Flood estimates, because the post-Flood values would be less than today, as will be shown. An attempt will be made to find a best estimate for the post-Flood heat transports.

Satellite measurements, potentially, are the best method of observing the higher-latitude-heat balance (Vonder Haar and Oort, 1973). However, these estimates do have errors (Hall and Bryden, 1982; Luther and Herman, 1987, p. 134). Recently, improved satellite measurements have been employed to estimate F_A and F_O (Carissimo et al., 1985). The new estimates are not much different from the previous estimates of Sellers (Charnock, 1987), but are a little higher than those of Budyko (1978). The most recent satellite measurements are probably a little high, but will do for our estimate of maximum-heat transport.

Higher latitude heat transport varies with latitude, and is maximum at 40°N and 40°S. The values for the present atmosphere will be taken from Carissimo et al. (1985, p. 91), based on recently improved satellite estimates. The maximum higher latitude transport for both hemispheres is 8.4 x 10^{22} cal/yr, which is the assumed maximum for the post-Flood climate. The current transport poleward, across 40°N and 60°S, is 6.4 x 10^{22} cal/yr.

With an estimate of F_A and F_O for the post-Flood atmosphere and ocean, we will be ready to solve Equation A1.8. The solar and infrared radiation balance in the tropics and subtropics during early post-Flood time, would be smaller than at present, due to volcanic dust. Less radiation available for heating, results in smaller values of F_E and F_C, and, also, probably smaller values for the higher-latitude-heat transports. (See Figure A1.1 for an illustration of the lower-latitude oceanic-heat balance.) The values for F_A and F_O would also vary, according to which dust and aerosol-loading scenario is used. And, the mean latitudinal atmospheric temperature difference would be less than at present, because of the much warmer temperature at higher latitudes. This would cause F_A to be smaller, since it is proportional to the north-south temperature difference (Budyko, 1978, p. 94). A similar argument applies to F_O, since the north-south ocean-temperature difference would be small, especially at the beginning of the ice age. Consequently, I assume the best post-Flood estimate of F_A and F_O to be one-half the percent change in the post-Flood average solar radiation. For instance, if post-Flood solar radiation was reduced 25%, on the average, the higher-latitude-heat transport is assumed reduced 12.5%.

Table A1.4 presents the results for the various combinations of the terms in Equation A1.8. The estimated time for glacial maximum ranges from as little as 174 years, to as much as 1,765 years—both unrealistic—and both very short compared to geological time. In view of the solar-radiation decrease caused by modern volcanic eruptions, the best estimate for an average solar-radiation reduction until glacial maximum, is probably 25%. Therefore, from Table A1.4, the time to reach glacial maximum would be around 500 years.

In the above calculations, Q, and the infrared radiation loss, were not given maximum and minimum ranges. Further calculations, with different values for these variables, have been tried. For instance, if I had used present values for post-Flood infrared radiation loss (Table A1.2), which would be a minimum, in the post-Flood climate, the best estimate for the time to reach post-Flood glacial maximum, would be about 640 years. By reducing the initial ocean temperature immediately after the Flood to 25°C and to 20°C, instead of 30°C, and using the best post-Flood estimates for the other variables, the time to reach glacial maximum would be 370 and 245 years, respectively. A corresponding decrease in ice volume would also occur with these temperatures (see Appendix 2). No matter which values are used for the variables in Equation A1.8, the main conclusion is still the same—glacial maximum is reached in a very short time.

Table A1.4. Values of the time T, to reach glacial maximum for various solar-radiation decreases from the present retention of solar-radiation energy, and for various values of higher-latitude ocean and atmospheric-heat transport. The units are in years.

	-10%	-25%	-50%	-75%
$F_A + F_O$ Zero	297	256	207	174
$F_A + F_O$ Post-Flood	746	492	309	227
$F_A + F_O$ Present	811	566	370	278
$F_A + F_O$ Maximum	1765	909	492	341

APPENDIX 2

DERIVATION OF AVERAGE ICE DEPTH

There are two sources of moisture for a post-Flood, rapid ice age. The first source, M_1, is evaporation from the warm mid and high-latitude ocean. The second source, M_2, is a result of higher-latitude latent-heat transport by the atmosphere (see Figure A1.2 in Appendix 1). Both will be estimated here, as well as the amount of snow expected to fall on the ice sheets.

High and Mid-Latitude Evaporation

We shall begin by rewriting Equation 5.1:

$$F_R - F_E - F_C + F_O = -Q/T \quad \text{(A2.1)}$$

F_E is the variable of interest. We could have started with the heat balance equation for the atmosphere, but either way, F_R cannot be simplified out, and must be estimated, for the post-Flood climate.

The first variable eliminated will be F_C, the heat lost from the ocean by conduction. Evaporative and conductive cooling of the oceans at higher latitudes, takes place by a similar mechanism, as given by the bulk aerodynamic equations (Bunker, 1976, p. 1122). Because of this, they are generally proportional. For the ocean between 40°N and 70°N, Budyko (1978, p. 90) gives the following average relationship:

$$F_C = 0.4F_E \quad \text{(A2.2)}$$

Bunker (1976, p. 1132) finds the same relationship for the Gulf Stream during the cold season, which would be representative of much of the post-Flood higher latitudes all year long. Substituting Equation A2.2 into Equation A2.1 and solving for F_E:

$$F_E = 0.71(Q/T) + 0.71F_R + 0.71F_O \quad \text{(A2.3)}$$

As discussed in Appendix 1, F_O is not well known. There have been, and still are, differences of opinion, on the values of oceanic and atmospheric higher-latitude heat transport in the present climate. As a rough consensus of current scientific opinion, the higher-latitude ocean transport is now considered the same as the atmospheric-heat transport (de Szoeke, 1988, p. 585). Although there are latitudinal differences between the average oceanic and atmospheric heat transports, we shall assume that the present value of F_O is equal to one-half the total higher-latitude heat transport. Then F_O would be 3.2×10^{22} cal/yr north of 40°N and south of 60°S (see Appendix 1). The present value of F_R, from Budyko (1978. p. 90), is 2.0×10^{22} cal/yr. If we solve Equation A2.3, using the present values for the last two terms, $F_E = 8.0 \times 10^{22}$ cal/yr. This can be considered a maximum value, because F_R and F_O would be less in the post-Flood climate.

We shall now estimate a minimum, and a best approximation for the last two terms, in Equation A2.3, during the early post-Flood climate. In Appendix 1, reasons were given why F_O would be less in the post-Flood climate. For a 25% decrease in retention of solar-radiation energy, post-Flood F_O was assumed to be 12.5% less than now. We shall use this percentage as the best post-Flood estimate. Due to compensating processes, F_O likely would not decrease below 25%. So, 25% will be considered the minimum post-Flood value.

F_R is the ocean-surface balance between the absorbed solar radiation and the net infrared-radiation loss. If solar-radiation retention, at the top of the atmosphere is already depleted 25%, then post-Flood F_R would be at least this much less than it is at present. And, the additional amount of water vapor and clouds would absorb or reflect additional sunlight—let us say five percent more, for a total of 30% less, by the time the sunshine hits the ocean surface. Since infrared radiation is roughly proportional to surface temperature, more heat is radiated from the warmer ocean. Some of this heat is reradiated back to the surface, so the net change would be rather small. A five percent increase in infrared radiation loss, seems like a good estimate. Accordingly, the radiation balance at the surface of the post-Flood ocean would be about 35% less than it is under present conditions. For a minimum value, I shall assume F_R is 50% less.

Plugging the above changes for F_O and F_R into Equation A2.3, the best estimate of F_E equals 7.2×10^{22} cal/yr, and the minimum estimate is 6.7×10^{22} cal/yr. The maximum and minimum values, and the best post-Flood estimate, do not differ greatly. Consequently, the exact values of the heat transport and the surface-radiation balance are not particularly important, for an estimate of F_E. The first term in Equation A2.3—the cooling rate of the ocean—is the most important variable.

The moisture evaporated from the surface of the mid and high-latitude ocean, M_1, is related to F_E by the latent heat of evaporation, which is 590 cal/gm—a large amount of heat loss for the evaporation of just one gram of water. Dividing F_E by 590 cal/gm, and multiplying by 500 years, the total evaporation from the mid and high-latitude ocean, during glacial buildup, ranges from a maximum of 6.8×10^{22} grams to a minimum of 5.7×10^{22} grams.

Since the geography of the Northern and Southern Hemispheres is very different, the available moisture will not be equally divided. The amount of M_1, evaporated in the mid and high latitudes of each hemisphere will simply be assumed proportional to the area of ocean from which the moisture is evaporated. The ocean area south of 60°S is 20.3×10^{16} cm^2, and that north of 40°N, is 43.2×10^{16} cm^2 (List, 1951, p. 484). Consequently, 68% of M_1 will be evaporated in the Northern Hemisphere, and 32%, in the Southern Hemisphere. It makes sense, that the Northern-Hemisphere contribution would be higher, because that hemisphere has much more land at mid-and-high latitudes, and, therefore, can generate more cold air for evaporation from the warm water. The maximum, best, and minimum estimates for available post-Flood moisture in each hemisphere, are presented in Table A2.1.

Moisture Transport from Lower Latitudes

The higher latitude-latent heat transport can be found from the modern value and an estimate of the post-Flood difference. F_A is the sum of several heat transports: 1) latent heat, 2) sensible heat, 3) potential energy due to air being warmed while descending from a higher tropical altitude to a lower altitude towards the poles, and 4) kinetic energy (Manabe, 1969, pp. 764,765). The latter is small, and will not be considered (Holloway and Manabe, 1971, p. 360). From the data of Sellers (Charnock, 1987, p. 7), the latent heat transport north of 40°N, and south of 60°S in the current atmosphere, is about 1.6×10^{22} cal/yr. This value is on the high side, because Sellers believed the atmosphere contributes much more to the poleward heat advection than do ocean currents. Since both transports are now generally considered equal, the above value for latent heat transport can be considered a maximum for the post-Flood climate. Since latent heat advection would certainly be less in the post-Flood climate than it is in the present climate, and the maximum value given above is likely high for the present climate, a minimum post-Flood value will be assumed to be 50% lower, and a best post-Flood average 25% lower. Although these estimates are crude, poleward transport of moisture in the form of latent heat, M_2, is significantly less than the evaporation from the higher latitude oceans, M_1, and, therefore, is less crucial in the calculation of total moisture available for an ice age.

We must now split the latent heat transport up into hemispheric components. Similar to the method of the previous section, we will assume that the value for each hemisphere is proportional to the area of the ocean from which the moisture was evaporated. This area would be the lower latitude ocean, whereas, in the previous section, it was the higher-latitude ocean area. Accordingly, 63% of the latent heat is transported across 60°S and 37%, across 40°N (List, 1951, p. 484). The maximum, best, and minimum estimates of the post-Flood available moisture from both sources are presented in Table A2.1.

Table A2.1. Maximum, best, and minimum estimates of available moisture in the Northern Hemisphere (N.H.) and the Southern Hemisphere (S.H.), for the two sources of moisture, M_1 and M_2, in the post-Flood ice age. Units are in 10^{22} grams.

	Maximum	Best	Minimum
N.H. M_1	4.6	4.1	3.9
N.H. M_2	0.5	0.4	0.3
N.H. Total	5.1	4.5	4.2
S.H. M_1	2.2	2.0	1.8
S.H. M_2	0.9	0.6	0.4
S.H. Total	3.1	2.6	2.2

Ice-Depth Estimates

The moisture available for precipitation in each hemisphere is an average value for 500 years. Precipitation is not expected to fall evenly over the entire area. Most of the evaporation from the higher latitude ocean would occur close to the cold continents, particularly in storms, and most of the precipitation would fall in the colder sector of the storm, which would mostly be on land (see Chapter 3). On this basis, the best post-Flood estimate for snowfall on the ice sheets assumes that twice as much of the available moisture falls on the land as falls over the ocean. A minimum estimate for ice depth will assume an even distribution of precipitation; a maximum value will be based on three times as much precipitation falling over land as over water.

A certain amount of the precipitation that falls over non-glaciated land would reevaporate and fall over the ice sheets. However, in a mild ice age, summer runoff would deplete some of the ice sheet volume, especially near the warm water and along the lower latitude ice margins. I shall assume, for the sake of simplicity, that these two effects compensate each other, and therefore will include no runoff in the calculations. In the Northern

Hemisphere, north of 40°N, 53% of the area is land, and 62% of this was glaciated (Flint, 1971, p. 84). Consequently, for all combinations, the average ice depth ranges from 515 to 906 meters, with the best estimate 718 meters. These values are presented in Table A2.2. The average depth in a uniformitarian treatment of the ice age is 1,700 meters (Flint, 1971, p. 84).

In the Southern Hemisphere, 41% of the area south of 60°S is land or ice, and practically all of this area was covered by ice at maximum glaciation. Neglecting the effect of isostatic depression while the ice sheets were nonexistent or thin, the ice depth on Antarctica, therefore, ranges from 726 to 1,673 meters, with a best estimate at 1,208 meters. The uniformitarian estimate of average Antarctica ice depth is 1,880 meters, the same as at present (Flint, 1971, p. 84).

Table A2.2. Estimated ice depths in the Northern and Southern Hemispheres for a 500-year post-Flood ice age, as determined from a range of estimates for total available moisture and land/ocean precipitation distribution. Ice depths are in meters.

Precipitation Ratio Land/Water	Estimated Values of Total Available Post-Flood Moisture		
	Maximum	Best	Minimum
N.H. Precip. Even	625	552	515
N.H. Precip. Twice	806	718	670
N.H. Precip. Thrice	906	800	746
S.H. Precip. Even	1,022	858	726
S.H. Precip. Twice	1,438	1,208	1,022
S.H. Precip. Thrice	1,673	1,403	1,188

APPENDIX 3

DERIVATION OF ICE MELTING TIME

We shall begin by first rewriting Equation 6.2, which applies to the ablation season:

$$Q_M = F_R + F_E + F_C \qquad \text{(A3.1)}$$

To solve this equation, F_R must be broken up into its solar and infrared radiation components. Therefore, Equation A3.1 becomes:

$$Q_M = F(1\text{-}a) - F_I + F_E + F_C \qquad \text{(A3.2)}$$

where F is the solar radiation that reaches the surface per unit of time, a is the albedo, or reflectivity of the surface, and F_I is the net infrared radiation balance at the surface, in unit time. F_I is the difference between outgoing infrared radiation from the surface, and infrared radiation, either reflected back by clouds and/or reemitted downward by the atmosphere. The first two terms on the right of Equation, A3.2, the radiation balance, are the dominant terms in the equation (Paterson, 1981, p. 313). These two terms are illustrated in Figure A3.1. The last two terms on the right are impossible to calculate with any precision, because they vary considerably from glacier to glacier, and with the weather pattern (Kuhn, 1979, p. 264). They are smaller terms than the radiation balance, and will be treated by finding their average value compared to the radiation balance.

Data for an entire summer on the Karsa Glacier in Sweden, and for 24 glaciers from a wide variety of climatic regimes, indicate F_C is about 30% of the radiation balance, and F_E is about 10% (Paterson, 1969, pp. 56-61). Kuhn (1979, p. 270) reports that 57% of the melting during a 100-day period on a glacier in the Alps was due to the radiation balance; the other 43% came from F_E and F_C. During a 17-day period on a glacier in New Zealand, 52% of the melted ice was accounted for by net absorption of radiation (Hay and Fitzharris, 1988, p. 149), but the observational period was too short for an accurate average.

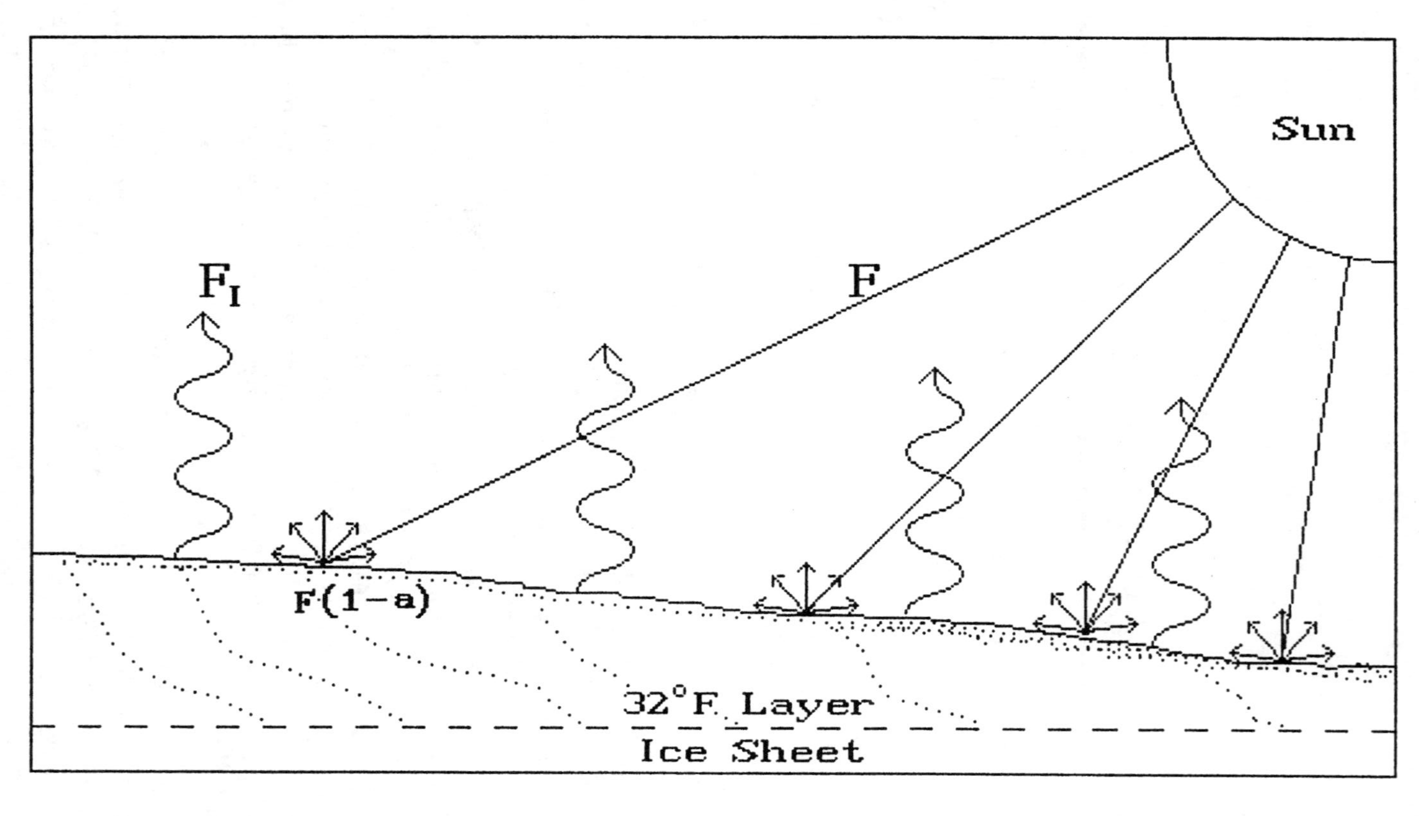

Figure A3.1 The main component in melting snow: Solar radiation (solid lines) minus the net infrared radiation (wavy lines). Dots are flowing water.

The relationship reported by Paterson, for a wide variety of glaciers, seems like a good approximation, and will be used here. Equation A3.2 then simplifies to the following:

$$Q_M = 1.67[F(1\text{-}a) - F_I] \qquad \text{(A3.3)}$$

Central Michigan was chosen as the location to estimate the terms in Equation A3.3. The ice depth of the Laurentide ice sheet likely varied considerably, being thickest near the Atlantic Coast and thinnest in the western portion. Central Michigan would represent a good average ice depth for the Northern Hemisphere, as calculated in Chapter 5. This location is also about 450 kilometers inward from the edge of the ice sheet at maximum extension, but still close enough to represent the periphery. Central Michigan is fairly cloudy, and has about the lowest yearly average radiation in the United States. For this area, any postulated increase in cloudiness after glacial maximum, should not significantly alter the results.

The melt season for the ice sheet was assumed to begin May 1 and to end September 30, which is probably too short, and, therefore, conservative. The first of May was chosen because the winter snow, which would be lighter than today in the drier late glacial climate, should have melted by then. I also assumed that a sufficient depth of the ice sheet near the periphery, had been raised to 0°C by May 1, so that additional heat would be expended in melting snow and ice. The melt-season temperature was assumed 10°C colder than a comparable present average, which seems like a good ice-age estimate for summer, on an ice sheet about 700 meters thick, and is relatively consistent with model results (Pollard, 1980, p. 385). After subtracting 10°C from the current average (as shown in Table A3.1), the post-Flood warm season temperature averages 8.4°C.

Some readers may think the winter snow would not melt before May 1, with the temperature still below 0°C in spring. Net melting actually can occur well below freezing in spring and summer, so the ablation season could begin around March 1. The reason snow can melt below freezing, is because solar radiation, during spring and summer, is intense at mid and high latitudes. This is well known to inhabitants of northerly latitudes, when, after a spring snow storm, the sun may start melting the snow at air temperatures well below freezing. Pickard (1984) has observed melting on the Antarctic ice sheet at 15°C below zero, and considers the ablation season to begin when the air temperature warms above -10°C.

The average cloud-base temperature, which determines the infrared back-radiation to the ice sheet, was assumed to average 5°C during the ablation season. This value was chosen because there would be a strong inversion over the ice sheet, and upper air temperatures would be controlled more by the general circulation of the mid-latitude atmosphere (Manabe and Broccoli, 1985b, pp. 2179-2181). Consequently the lapse rate, or change in temperature with altitude, would be less than the assumed average of -6°C/1,000 meters in current-day models. Some researchers believe such a lower lapse rate is highly likely over an extensive snow cover (Williams, 1979, p. 448).

To simplify the calculations, other weather variables, like relative humidity, cloudiness, and surface wind speed, were assumed similar to their present values. In Pollard's (1980, p. 385) estimation, during an ice age there would be more cloudiness (which is questionable), higher winds, and more humidity. The latter two effects would add a significant amount of heat to the ice sheet. However, these differences will be neglected, and, consequently, the results will be even more conservative.

The solar and infrared radiation balance depend especially on the amount of clouds and the surface albedo. Clouds have a high albedo. They not only reflect solar radiation back to space, they also absorb and retransmit infrared radiation back to the ice sheet. Although the effect of clouds is very complicated, the net result is less snowmelt than under sunny skies. Since the cloud and albedo conditions over the melting ice sheet in central Michigan are not known, extreme ranges for these variables will be used in the calculations. Maximum melting would occur under completely clear skies, and minimum melting under completely cloudy skies. The melting rate under variable cloudiness similar to the current weather conditions will be interpolated using the present value of solar radiation.

The interpolation is necessary because the net infrared radiation at the surface is impossible to estimate with any precision under variable cloud conditions for a five-month period. In completely clear skies, the infrared radiation from the atmosphere depends upon the vertical temperature and moisture profile of the atmosphere. However, the lower layers of the atmosphere can be used for the estimate, since they have the warmest temperatures and a greater moisture content than the middle and upper atmosphere (U.S. Army Corp of Engineers, 1956, p. 157). In general, the infrared radiation balance causes a loss of about 4.2 langleys/hour under clear skies, at an average temperature of 8.4°C (U.S. Army Corp of Engineers, 1956, pp. 141-191, Plate 5-3, Figure 4). A langley is 1 cal/cm^2. The infrared radiation balance, under cloudy skies, is simply the difference in the black-body radiation at the temperature of the ice-sheet surface (0°C) and the bottom of the clouds (5°C). The average solar radiation, under current conditions of cloudiness for East Lansing, Michigan, is presented in Table A3.1, along with average monthly temperatures (Crabb, 1950, p. 37).

Table A3.1. Maximum, minimum, and average monthly temperature in degrees Celsius, and total monthly solar radiation in langleys for East Lansing, Michigan.

	May	June	July	Aug.	Sept.	Avg.
Monthly Max. Temp.	20.1	25.8	28.1	27.3	22.8	24.8
Monthly Min. Temp.	7.5	13.2	15.1	14.3	10.2	12.1
Monthly Avg. Temp.	13.8	19.5	21.6	20.8	16.5	18.4
Solar Radiation	11,780	13,800	14,700	13,330	9,600	12,642

The albedo of fresh snow is 0.7 to 0.9, for firm or melting snow, 0.4 to 0.6, and for glacier ice, 0.2 to 0.4 (Paterson, 1981, p. 305). The lower albedo for melting snow (0.4) is reached after about two weeks of melting (U.S. Army Corp of Engineers, 1956, Plate 5-2, Figure 4). The reason for the drop in albedo is because of the large increase in size of the ice crystals (Wiscombe and Warren, 1980). If ice is exposed, which is very likely as the ablation season progresses, the albedo will drop below 0.4. From these considerations, the maximum albedo for the five-month period will be assumed to be 0.4.

Due to several other mechanisms, the albedo can drop significantly below 0.4 along the periphery while the ice melts. One of these is dust (loess) that would collect at the surface from strong, dry winds during deglaciation. As previously discussed, a good indication of this is the loess sheets found just south of, and even within, the ice sheet periphery (Flint, 1971, pp. 251-266). The albedo over a permanent snow field in Japan was observed to drop to 0.15 during the summer, after 4,000 ppm of pollution dust had collected on the surface (Warren and Wiscombe, 1980, p. 2736). During winter, dust would be covered by fresh snow. But, after snow melt in the spring, the dust layer is reexposed. And while the ice melts during summer, the dust tends to remain concentrated at the surface, resulting in a low albedo (Warren and Wiscombe, 1985, p. 469). Anyone living in a snowy climate where the streets are sanded and plowed, can observe this. When the snow is piled up by the side of the road and melts, the sand becomes concentrated at the surface of the melting mound.

A second mechanism that lowers the albedo is a positive feedback mechanism caused by crevassing. In crevasses, more ice is exposed, and causes multiple reflection of solar and atmospheric infrared radiation, so that more radiation is absorbed. Because of the tripling of the surface area of the Jakobshanvs Glacier in West Greenland due to crevassing, the observed average melting rate was 0.3 meters/day, for a total ablation-season thinning of 55 meters (Hughes, 1986). Crevassing would likely be extensive along the periphery of the Laurentide and Scandinavian ice sheets due to its temperate locality, rapid velocity with surges, and the many proglacial lakes and marine bays. Paterson (1981, p. 169) writes:

> *Entry of the sea into areas that are now Hudson Bay and the Baltic Sea played a large part in the rapid disintegration of the Laurentide and Fennoscandian Ice Sheets. Calving of icebergs into extensive ice-dammed lakes around the southern margins also contributed significantly.*

All factors considered, I chose a minimum value of 0.15 for the albedo. The best estimate for albedo would lie between the extremes, but probably closer to the minimum value.

Table A3.2 presents the results from Equation A3.3 for East Lansing, Michigan, for the maximum and minimum values of cloudiness and surface albedo. A melting rate of about 10.4 meters/year, with cloudiness equivalent to present Michigan, and with an albedo interpolated between the extremes, is considered to be the best estimate. But no matter what the cloud conditions or the albedo, the melting rate is still high. In Chapter 5, the average ice depth for the Northern Hemisphere was calculated to range from 515 meters to 906 meters. At 10.4 meters/year, the ice would melt in 50 to 87 years. This is very short, and based on a conservative estimate of the melting rate. Even if the albedo was 0.4, melting would still occur in about 105 years.

The interior of the ice sheets would, of course, disappear more slowly, due to colder temperatures and less solar radiation. However, the radiation would not be greatly reduced, because, in summer, the sunshine lasts for a longer period of the day than it does farther south. The albedo would be higher than at the periphery, because the blowing dust likely would not significantly penetrate that far north. A value of 0.4 seems like a good value for the average albedo. Table A3.2 shows that with an albedo of 0.4, and with the radiation equivalent to cloudy skies in central Michigan, the ice would melt at about seven meters/year. Observations from glaciers in the high Arctic support a melting rate near this value. Beget (1987, p. 85) states:

> *A compilation of ablation gradients on active glaciers ... suggests that glaciers at 69 to 71°N latitude typically have ablation rates of 5 to 7 m yr^{-1} at low elevations, and ablation rates of 1.5 to 3.0 m yr^{-1} at elevations of a kilometer ....*

Altogether, an estimate of 200 years to melt the interior ice is conservative, especially considering that in this model, the interior ice was much thinner than specified in uniformitarian models. The total time for a rapid post-Flood ice age, from the end of the Flood to when most of the ice disappeared, is on the order of 700 years.

Table A3.2. Solar and net infrared radiation in langleys for five months at East Lansing, Michigan for clear skies, present cloudiness, and completely cloudy skies. Corresponding melting rates in meters/year are given for a maximum and minimum albedo.

	Solar Rad.	Net Infrared Rad.	Albedo 0.4	Albedo 0.15
Clear	108,860	-15,422	11.4	17.7
Present	63,210	—	8.6	12.1
Cloudy	39,190	7,711	7.2	9.4

BIBLIOGRAPHY

Agenbroad, L.D., 1984. New World Mammoth Distribution. in *Quaternary Extinctions: A Prehistoric Revolution*, P.S. Martin and R.G. Klein, eds., The University of Arizona Press, Tucson, pp. 90-108.

Ager, D.V., 1973. *The Nature of the Stratigraphical Record*. Macmillan Press Ltd., London.

Alley, R.B. et al., 1986. Deformation of Till Beneath Ice Stream B, West Antarctica. *Nature*, 322, pp. 57-59.

Anderson, E., 1984. Who's Who in the Pleistocene: A Mammalian Bestiary. in *Quaternary Extinctions: A Prehistoric Revolution*, P.S. Martin and R.G. Klein, eds., The University of Arizona Press, Tucson, pp. 40-89.

Andrews, J., 1979. The Present Ice Age: Cenozoic. in *Winters of the World*, B.S. John, ed., John Wiley and Sons, New York, pp. 173-218.

Andrews, J.T., 1982. On the Reconstruction of Pleistocene Ice Sheets: A Review. *Quaternary Science Reviews*, 1, pp. 1-30.

Andrews, J.T. and G.H. Miller, 1985. Discussion on the Paper by Denton and Hughes (1983). *Quaternary Research*, 24, pp. 361-364.

Andrews, J.T. and S. Funder, 1985. Introduction to Quaternary Studies. in *Quaternary Environments Eastern Canadian Arctic, Baffin Bay and Western Greenland*, J.T. Andrews, ed., Allen and Unwin, Boston, pp. 1-25.

Andrews, J.T., Clark, P., and J.A. Stravers, 1985. The Patterns of Glacial Erosion Across the Eastern Canadian Arctic. in *Quaternary Environments Eastern Canadian Arctic, Baffin Bay and Western Greenland*, J.T. Andrews, ed., Allen and Unwin, Boston, pp. 69-92.

Andrews, J.T., Shilts, W.W., and G.H. Miller, 1983. Multiple Deglaciations of the Hudson Bay Lowlands, Canada, Since Deposition of the Missinaibi (Last-Interglacial?) Formation. *Quaternary Research*, 19, pp. 18-37.

Andrews, J.T., Shilts, W.W., and G.H. Miller, 1984. Reply to A.S. Dyke's Discussion. *Quaternary Research*, 22, pp. 253-258.

Angell, J.K., 1988. Impact of El Niño on the Delineation of Tropospheric Cooling Due to Volcanic Eruptions. *Journal of Geophysical Research*, 93, D4, pp. 3697-3704.

Angell, J.K. and J. Korshover, 1985. Surface Temperature Changes Following the Six Major Volcanic Episodes Between 1780 and 1980. *Journal of Climate and Applied Meteorology*, 24, pp. 937-951.

Anonymous, 1978. *Geological Perspectives on Climatic Change*. National Academy of Sciences, Washington, D.C.

Anonymous, 1986. Volcanoes, El Niños: Climatic Ties? *Science News*, 129, p. 185.

Anonymous, 1988. Global Concentrations of Carbon Dioxide Shows 25 Percent Increase. *Bulletin of the American Meteorological Society*, 69, p. 1362.

Austin, S.A., 1980. Origin of Limestone Caves. *ICR Impact Series No. 79*, pp. i-viii.

Austin, S.A., 1986. Mount St. Helens and Catastrophism. *Proceedings of The First International Conference on Creationism*, Volume 1, Creation Science Fellowship, Pittsburgh, pp. 3-9.

Baker, V.R., 1978. The Spokane Flood Controversy and the Martian outflow Channels. *Science*, 202, pp. 1249-1256.

Baker, V.R., 1983. Late-Pleistocene Fluvial Systems. in *Late-Quaternary Environments of the United States*, Volume 1, H.E. Wright, Jr., ed., University of Minnesota Press, Minneapolis, pp. 115-129.

Baldwin, E.M., 1964. Geology of Oregon. University of Oregon Cooperative Book Store, Eugene, Oregon.

Ball, T.F., 1986. Historical Evidence and Climatic Implications of a Shift in the Boreal Forest Tundra Transition in Central Canada. *Climatic Change*, 8, pp. 121-134.

Barnett, T.P., 1978. Ocean Temperatures: Precursors of Climatic Change? *Oceanus*, 21 (4), pp. 27-32.

Barry, R.G., 1966. Meteorological Aspects of the Glacial history of Labrador-Ungava with Special Reference to Atmospheric Vapour Transport. *Geographical Bulletin*, 8, pp. 319-340.

Barry, R.G., Ives, J.D., and J.T. Andrews, 1971. A Discussion of Atmospheric Circulation During the Last Ice Age. *Quaternary Research*, 1, pp. 415-418.

Barry, R.G., Andrews, J.T., and M.A. Mahaffy, 1975. Continental Ice Sheets: Conditions for Growth. *Science*, 190, pp. 979-981.

Beardsley, T., 1986. Has Winter Become Fall? *Nature*, 320, p. 103.

Beget, J.E., 1986. Modeling the Influence of Till Rheology on the Flow and Profile of the Lake Michigan Lobe, Southern Laurentide Ice Sheet, U.S.A. *Journal of Glaciology*, 32 (111), pp. 235-241.

Beget, J., 1987. Low Profile of the Northwest Laurentide Ice Sheet. *Arctic and Alpine Research*, 19, pp. 81-88.

Bentley, C.R., 1965. The Land Beneath the Ice. in *Antarctica*, T. Hatherton, ed., Frederick A. Praeger Publishers, New York, pp. 259-277.

Berger, W.H., 1976. Biogenous Deep Sea Sediments: Production, Preservation and Interpretation. in *Chemical Oceanography*, 2nd Edition, Volume 5, J.P. Riley and R. Chester, eds., Academic Press, New York, pp. 265-388.

Berger, W.H. and J.V. Gardner, 1975. On the Determination of Pleistocene Temperatures from Planktonic Foraminifera. *Journal of Foraminiferal Research*, 5, pp. 102-113.

Birch, L.C. and P.R. Ehrlich, 1967. Evolutionary History and Population Biology. *Nature*, 214, pp. 349-352.

Birchfield, G.E., 1984. Climate Models With an Ice Sheet. in *Milankovitch and Climate*, A. Berger, ed., D. Reidel Publishing Co., Dordrecht, Holland, pp. 854-859.

Birchfield, G.E., Weertman, J., and A.T. Lunde, 1981. A Paleoclimate Model of Northern Hemisphere Ice Sheets. *Quaternary Research*, 15, pp. 126-142.

Bird, J.B., 1967. *The Physiography of Arctic Canada*. Johns Hopkins Press, Baltimore.

Bird, W.R., 1989. *The Origin of Species Revisited—The Theories of Evolution and of Abrupt Appearance,* Volume II. Philosophical Library, New York.

Birkeland, P.W., 1984. *Soils and Geomorphology.* Oxford University Press, New York.

Bjorlykke, K., 1985. Glaciations, Preservation of Their Sedimentary Record and Sea Level Changes. *Palaeogeography, Palaeoclimatology, Palaeoecology,* 51, pp. 197-207.

Blackwelder, B.W., Pilkey, O.H., and J.D. Howard, 1979. Late Wisconsinan Sea Levels on the Southeast U.S. Atlantic Shelf Based on In-Place Shoreline Indicators. *Science,* 204, pp. 618-620.

Blankenship, D.D. et al., 1986. Seismic Measurements Reveal a Saturated Porous Layer Beneath an Active Antarctic Ice Stream. *Nature,* 322, pp. 54-57.

Bloom, A.L., 1971. Glacial-Eustatic and Isostatic Controls of Sea Level. in *The Late Cenozoic Glacial Ages,* K.K. Turekian, ed., Yale University Press, New Haven, pp. 355-379.

Boardman, J., 1985. Comparison of Soils in Midwestern United States and Western Europe with the Interglacial Record. *Quaternary Research,* 23, pp. 62-75.

Bolin, B., 1986. Requirements for a Satisfactory Model of the Global Carbon Cycle and Current Status of Modeling Efforts. in *The Changing Carbon Cycle: A Global Analysis,* J.R. Trabalka and D.E. Reichle, eds., Springer-Verlag, New York, pp. 403-424.

Bonneau, M. C., Vergnaud-Grazzini, C., and W.H. Berger, 1980. Stable Isotope Fractionation and Differential Dissolution in Recent Planktonic Foraminifera from Pacific Box-Cores. *Oceanologica Acta,* 3, pp. 377-382.

Borns, Jr., H.W., Lasalle, P., and W.B. Thompson, 1985. *Late Pleistocene History of Northeastern New England and Adjacent Quebec.* The Geological Society of America Special Paper 197, Boulder, Colorado.

Boulton, G.S., 1986. A Paradigm Shift in Glaciology? *Nature,* 322, p. 18.

Boulton, G.S., 1987a. A Theory of Drumlin Formation by Subglacial Sediment Deformation. in *Drumlin Symposium,* J. Menzies and J. Rose, eds., Balkema, Rotterdam, pp. 25-80.

Boulton, G.S., 1987b. Progress in Glacial Geology During the Last Fifty Years. in *Journal of Glaciology,* Special Issue, pp. 25-32.

Boulton, G.S. and A.S. Jones, 1979. Stability of Temperate Ice Caps and Ice Sheets Resting on Beds of Deformable Sediment. *Journal of Glaciology,* 24 (90), pp. 29-43.

Bowen, D.Q., 1978. *Quaternary Geology A Stratigraphic Framework for Multidisciplinary Work.* Pergamon Press, New York.

Bower, B., 1987. Extinctions on Ice. *Science News,* 132, pp. 284,285.

Bradley, D.C., 1981. Late Wisconsinan Mountain Glaciation in the Northern Presidential Range, New Hampshire. *Arctic and Alpine Research,* 13, pp. 319-327.

Bradley, R.S., 1985. *Quaternary Paleoclimatology.* Allen and Unwin, Boston.

Bradley, R.S., 1988. The Explosive Volcanic Eruption Signal in Northern Hemisphere Continental Temperature Records. *Climatic Change,* 12, pp. 221-243.

Bray, J.R., 1976. Volcanic Triggering of Glaciation. *Nature,* 260, pp. 414,415.

Bretz, J.H., 1943. Keewatin End Moraines in Alberta, Canada. *Geological Society of America Bulletin* , 54, pp. 31-52.

Brewer, P.G., 1978. Carbon Dioxide and Climate. *Oceanus,* 21 (4), pp. 13-17.

Brewer, P.G., Bradshaw, A.L., and R.T. Williams, 1986. Measurements of Total Carbon Dioxide and Alkalinity in the North Atlantic Ocean in 1981. in *The changing Carbon Cycle: A Global Analysis,* J.R. Trabalka and D.E. Reichle, eds., Springer-Verlag, New York, pp. 348-370.

Broecker, W.S., 1971. Calcite Accumulation Rates and Glacial to Interglacial Changes in Oceanic Mixing. in *The Late Cenozoic Glacial Ages,* K.K. Turekian, ed., Yale University Press, New Haven, pp. 239-265.

Broecker, W.S. and J. van Donk, 1970. Insolation Changes, Ice Volumes, and the 0^{18} Record in Deep-Sea Cores. *Reviews of Geophysics and Space Physics,* 8, pp. 169-198.

Broecker, W.S. et al., 1968. Milankovitch Hypothesis Supported by Precise Dating of Coral Reefs and Deep-Sea Sediments. *Science,* 159, pp. 297-300.

Bryan, K., 1978. The Ocean Heat Balance. *Oceanus,* 21 (4), pp. 19-26.

Bryson, R.A., 1985. On Climatic Analogs in Paleoclimatic Reconstruction. *Quaternary Research,* 23, pp. 275-286.

Budyko, M.I., 1978. The Heat Balance of the Earth. in *Climatic Change,* J. Gibbin, ed., Cambridge University Press, London, pp. 85-113.

Budyko, M.I. and M.C. MacCracken, 1987. US-USSR Meeting of Experts on Causes of Recent Climate Change. *Bulletin of the American Meteorological Society,* 68, pp. 237-243.

Bunker, A.F., 1976. Computations of Surface Energy Flux and Annual Air-Sea Interaction Cycles of the North Atlantic Ocean. *Monthly Weather Review,* 104, pp. 1122-1140.

Byers, R.H., 1959. *General Meteorology,* 3rd Edition. McGraw-Hill, New York.

Calder, N., 1974. *The Weather Machine.* The Viking Press, New York.

Caldwell, D.W. and L.S. Hanson, 1986. The Nunatak Stage on Mt. Katahdin, Northern Maine, Persisted Through the Late Wisconsinan. *Abstracts with Programs,* Geological Society of America, 18, p. 8.

Caldwell, D.W., Hanson, L.S., and W.B. Thompson, 1985. Styles of Deglaciation in Central Maine. in *Late Pleistocene History of Northeastern New England and Adjacent Quebec,* H.W. Borns, Jr., P. LaSalle, and W.B. Thompson, eds., The Geological Society of America Special Paper 197, Boulder, Colorado, pp. 45-57.

Calkin, P.E. and C.E. Brett, 1978. Ancestral Niagara River Drainage: Stratigraphic and Paleontologic Setting. *Geological Society of America Bulletin,* 89, pp. 1140-1154.

Carey, S.N. and H. Sigurdsson, 1982. Influence of Particle Aggregation on Deposition of Distal Tephra from the May 18, 1980, Eruption of Mount St. Helens Volcano. *Journal of Geophysical Research,* 87 (B8), pp. 7061-7072.

Carissimo, B.C., Oort, A.H., and T.H. Vonder Haar, 1985. Estimating the Meridional Energy Transports in the Atmosphere and Ocean. *Journal of Physical Oceanography,* 15, pp. 82-91.

Carlson, P.R. and H.A. Karl, 1984. Discovery of Two New Large Submarine Canyons in the Bering Sea. *Marine Geology,* 56, pp. 159-179.

Catchpole, A.J.W. and M.A. Faurer, 1983. Summer Sea Ice Severity in Hudson Strait, 1751-1870. *Climatic Change*, 5, pp. 115-139.

Charlesworth, J.K., 1957. *The Quaternary Era*. Edward Arnold, London.

Charnock, H., 1987. Ocean Currents and Meridional Transfers. *Quarterly Journal of the Royal Meteorological Society*, 113, pp. 3-18.

Chauvin, L., Martineau, G., and P. LaSalle, 1985. Deglaciation of the Lower St. Lawrence Region, Quebec. in *Late Pleistocene History of Northeastern New England and Adjacent Quebec*, H.W. Borns, Jr., P. LaSalle, and W.B. Thompson, Eds., The Geological Society of America Special Paper 197, Boulder, Colorado, pp. 111-123.

Chen, S.C., 1986. *Steady State Planetary Wave Response to Wave-Coupled Orographic Lower Boundary Forcing and Diabatic Heating in the Northern Hemisphere*. National Center for Atmospheric Research, Boulder, Colorado.

Chervin, R.M. et al., 1980. Response of the NCAR General Circulation Model to Prescribed Changes in Ocean Surface Temperature. Part II: Midlatitude and Subtropical Changes. *Journal of the Atmospheric Sciences*, 37, pp. 308-332.

Churcher, C.S., 1984. Panel Discussion. in *Quaternary Dating Methods*, W.C. Mahaney, ed., Elsevier, New York, pp. 407-415.

Clark, H.W., 1968. *Fossils, Flood, and Fire*. Outdoor Pictures, Escondido, California.

Clayton, L., Teller, J.T., and J.W. Attig, 1985. Surging of the Southwestern Part of the Laurentide Ice Sheet. *Boreas*, 14, pp. 235-241.

Coffin, H.G., 1969. *Creation—Accident or Design?* Review and Herald Publishing Association, Washington, D.C.

Considine, D.M., ed., 1983. *Van Nostrand's Scientific Encyclopedia*, 6th Edition. Van Nostrand Reinhold Co., New York.

Cook, A.H., 1973. *Physics of the Earth and Planets*. John Wiley and Sons, New York.

Covey, C., Schneider, S.H., and S.L. Thompson, 1984. Global Atmospheric Effects of Massive Smoke Injections from a Nuclear War: Results from General Circulation Model Simulations. *Nature*, 308, pp. 21-25.

Crabb, Jr., G.A., 1950. *Solar Radiation Investigations in Michigan*. U.S. Department of Agriculture Technical Bulletin 222.

Crowley, T.J., 1984. Atmospheric Circulation Patterns During Glacial Inception: A Possible Candidate. *Quaternary Research*, 21, pp. 105-110.

Damon, P.E., 1968. The Relationship Between Terrestrial Factors and Climate. in *Causes of Climatic Change*, J.M. Mitchell, Jr., ed., Meteorological Monograph 8 (30), American Meteorological Society, Boston, pp. 106-111.

Dardis, G.F., McCabe, A.M., and W.I. Mitchell, 1984. Characteristics and Origins of Lee-Side Stratification Sequences in Late Pleistocene Drumlins, Northern Ireland. *Earth Surface Processes and Landforms*, 9, pp. 409-424.

Dardis, G.F., 1987. Sedimentology of Late-Pleistocene Drumlins in South-Central Ulster, Northern Ireland. in *Drumlin Symposium*, J. Menzies and J. Rose, eds., Balkema, Rotterdam, pp. 215-224.

Davies, T.A. and D.S. Gorsline, 1976. Oceanic Sediments and Sedimentary Processes. in *Chemical Oceanography*, 2nd Edition, Volume 5, J.P. Riley and R. Chester, eds., Academic Press, New York, pp. 1-73.

Dawson, A.G. and D.E. Smith, 1983. Shorelines and Isostasy: Retrospect and Prospect. in *Shorelines and Isostasy*, D.E. Smith and A.G. Dawson, eds., Academic Press, New York, pp. 369-377.

de Jong, J.D. and G.C. Maarleveld, 1983, The Glacial History of the Netherlands. in *Glacial Deposits in North-West Europe*, J. Ehlers, ed., A.A. Balkema, Rotterdam, pp. 353-356.

Denton, G.H. and T.J. Hughes, eds., 1981. *The Last Great Ice Sheets*. John Wiley and Sons, New York.

Denton, M., 1985. *Evolution: A Theory in Crisis*. Harper and Row, Scranton, Pennsylvania.

Derbyshire, E., 1979. Glaciers and Environment. in *Winters of the World*, B.S. John, ed., John Wiley and Sons, New York, pp. 58-106.

de Szoeke, R.A., 1988. Heat Flux in the Antarctic. *Nature*, 332, pp. 585,586.

Devine, J.D., Sigurdsson, H., and A.N. Davis, 1984. Estimates of Sulfur and Chlorine Yield to the Atmosphere from Volcanic Eruptions and Potential Climatic Effects. *Journal of Geophysical Research*, 89 (B7), pp. 6309-6325.

Dillow, J.C., 1981. *The Waters Above: Earth's Pre-Flood Vapor Canopy*. Moody Press, Chicago.

Dirks, R.A., Kuettner, J.P., and J.A. Moore, 1988. Genesis of Atlantic Lows Experiment (GALE): An Overview. *Bulletin of the American Meteorological Society*, 69, pp. 148-160.

Dixon, E.J., 1983. Pleistocene Proboscidean Fossils from the Alaskan Continental Shelf. *Quaternary Research*, 20, pp. 113-119.

Donelan, M.A., 1986. Report on The Sixth Conference on Ocean-Atmosphere Interaction 14-17 January 1986, Miami, Florida. *Bulletin of the American Meteorological Society*, 67, pp. 1278-1283.

Donn, W.L. and M. Ewing, 1968. The Theory of an Ice-Free Arctic Ocean. in *Causes of Climatic Change*, J.M. Mitchell, Jr., ed., Meteorological Monographs, 8 (30), American Meteorological Society, Boston, pp. 100-105.

Donn, W.L. and D.M. Shaw, 1977. Model of Climate Evolution Based on Continental Drift and Polar Wandering. *Geological Society of America Bulletin*, 88, pp. 390-396.

Donner, J., 1985. Book Review of *Shorelines and Isostasy*, D.E. Smith and A.G. Dawson, eds., *Boreas*, 14, pp. 257,258.

Dott, Jr., R.H. and R.L. Batten, 1976. *Evolution of the Earth*, 2nd Edition. McGraw-Hill, New York.

Drewry, D., 1986. *Glacial Geologic Processes*. Edward Arnold, London.

Dubrovo, N.A. et al., 1982. Upper Quaternary Deposits and Paleogeography of the Region Inhabited by the Young Kirgilyakh Mammoth. *International Geology Review*, 24, pp. 621-634.

Dury, G.H., 1976. Discharge Prediction, Present and Former, from Channel Dimensions. *Journal of Hydrology*, 30, pp. 219-245.

Dury, G.H., 1977. Peak Flows, Low Flows, and Aspects of Geomorphic Dominance. in *River Channel Changes*, K.J. Gregory, ed., John Wiley and Sons, New York, pp. 61-74.

Ehlers, J., 1983. The Glacial History of North-West Germany. in *Glacial Deposits in North-West Europe*, J. Ehlers, ed., A.A. Balkema, Rotterdam, pp. 229-238.

Ellsaesser, H., 1986. Comments on "Surface Temperature Changes Following the Six Major Volcanic Episodes Between 1780 and 1980." *Jounal of Climate and Applied Meteorology*, 25, pp. 1184,1185.

Erez, J., 1979. Modification of the Oxygen-Isotope Record in Deep-Sea Cores by Pleistocene Dissolution Cycles. *Nature*, 281, pp. 535-538.

Ericson, D.B. and G. Wollin, 1967. *The Ever-Changing Sea*. Albert A. Knopf, New York.

Ericson, D.B. and G. Wollin, 1968. Pleistocene Climates and Chronology in Deep-Sea Sediments. *Science*, 162, pp. 1227-1234.

Eriksson, E., 1968. Air-Ocean-Icecap Interactions in Relation to Climatic Fluctuations and Glaciation Cycles. in *Causes of Climatic Change*, J.M. Mitchell, Jr., ed., Meteorological Monographs, 8 (30), American Meteorological Society, Boston, pp. 68-92.

Eronen, M., 1983. Late Weichselian and Holocene Shore Displacement in Finland. in *Shorelines and Isostasy*, D.E. Smith and A.G. Dawson, eds., Academic Press, New York, pp. 183-207.

Eyles, C.H. and N. Eyles, 1983. Sedimentation in a Large Lake: A Reinterpretation of the Late Pleistocene Stratigraphy at Scarborough Bluffs, Ontario, Canada. *Geology*, 11, pp. 146-152.

Eyles, N., 1983. Glacial Geology: A Landsystems Approach. in *Glacial Geology*, N. Eyles, ed., Pergamon Press, New York, pp. 1-18.

Eyles, N. and J. Menzies, 1983. The Subglacial Landsystem. in *Glacial Geology*, N. Eyles, ed., Pergamon Press, New York, pp. 19-70.

Eyles, N., Eyles, C.H., and A.D. Miall, 1983a. Lithofacies Types and Vertical Profile Models: An Alternative Approach to the Description and Environmental Interpretation of Glacial Diamict and Diamictite Sequences. *Sedimentology*, 30, pp. 393-410.

Eyles, N., Dearman, W.R., and T.D. Douglas, 1983b. The Distribution of Glacial Landsystems in Britian and North America. in *Glacial Geology*, N. Eyles, ed., Pergamon Press, New York, pp. 213-228.

Eyles, N., Miall, A.D., and C.H. Eyles, 1984. Reply—Lithofacies Types and Vertical Profile Models: An Alternative Approach to the Description and Environmental Interpretation of Glacial Diamict and Diamictite Sequences. *Sedimentology*, 31, pp. 891-898.

Fiarbridge, R.W., 1983. Isostasy and Eustasy. in *Shorelines and Isostasy*, D.E. Smith and A.G. Dawson, eds., Academic Press, New York, pp. 3-28.

Farrand, W.R., 1961. Frozen Mammoths and Modern Geology. *Science*, 133, pp. 729-735.

Feininger, T., 1971. Chemical Weathering and Glacial Erosion of Crystalline Rocks and the Origin of Till. *U.S. Geological Survey Professional Paper 750-C*, U.S. Government Printing Office, Washington, D.C., pp. C65-C81.

Felix-Henningsen, P., 1983. Palaeosols and Their Stratigraphical Interpretation. in *Glacial Deposits in North-West Europe*, J. Ehlers, ed., A.A. Balkema, Rotterdam, pp. 289-295.

Fisher, D.A. and R.M. Koerner, 1986. On the Special Rheological Properties of Ancient Microparticle-Laden Northern Hemisphere Ice as Derived from Bore-Hole and Core Measurements. *Journal of Glaciology*, 32 (112), pp. 501-510.

Fix, W.R., 1984. *The Bone Peddlers*. Macmillan Publishing Co., New York.

Flam, F., 1989. Questioning the Cooling Effects of Volcanoes. *Science News*, 135, p. 359.

Fletcher, J.O., 1968. The Influence of the Arctic Pack Ice on Climate. in *Causes of Climatic Change*, J.M. Mitchell, Jr., ed., Meteorological Monographs, 8 (30), American Meteorological Society, Boston, pp. 93-99.

Flint, R.F., 1971. *Glacial and Quaternary Geology*. John Wiley and Sons, New York.

Folland, C. and F. Kates, 1984. Changes in Decadally Averaged Sea Surface Temperature over the World 1861-1980. in *Milankovitch and Climate*, A. Berger, ed., D. Reidel Publishing Co., Dordrecht, Holland, pp. 721-727.

Follmer, L.R., 1983. Sangamon and Wisconsinan Pedogenesis in the Midwestern United States. in *Late-Quaternary Environments of the United States*, Volume 1, H.E. Wright, Jr., ed., University of Minnesota Press, Minneapolis, pp. 138-144.

Fong, P., 1982. Latent Heat of Melting and Its Importance for Glaciation Cycles. *Climatic Change*, 4, pp. 199-206.

Frakes, L.A., 1979. *Climates Throughout Geologic Time*. Elsevier, New York.

Fristrup, B., 1966. *The Greenland Ice Cap*. University of Washington Press, Seattle.

Froggatt, P.C. et al., 1986. An Exceptionally Large Late Quaternary Eruption from New Zealand. *Nature*, 319, pp. 578-582.

Fung, I.Y., 1986. Analysis of the Seasonal and Geographical Patterns of Atmospheric CO_2 Distributions with a Three-Dimensional Tracer Model. in *The Changing Carbon Cycle: A Global Analysis*, J.R. Trabalka and D.E. Reichle, eds., Springer-Verlag, New York. pp. 459-473.

Gage, M., 1970. The Tempo of Geomorphic Change. *Journal of Geology*, 78, pp. 619-625.

Gerath, R.F., Fowler, B.K., and G.M. Hoselton, 1985. The Deglaciation of the Northern White Mountains of New Hampshire. in *Late Pleistocene History of Northeastern New England and Adjacent Quebec*, H.W. Borns, Jr., P. LaSalle, and W.B. Thompson, eds., The Geological Society of America Special Paper 197, Boulder, Colorado, pp. 21-28.

Gilbert, G.K., 1907. Rate of Recession of Niagara Falls. *U.S. Geological Survey Bulletin 306*, U.S. Government Printing Office, Washington, D.C.

Goldthwait, R.P., 1974. Rates of Formation of Glacial Features in Glacier Bay, Alaska. in *Glacial Geomorphology*, D.R. Coates, ed., George Allen and Unwin Ltd., London, pp. 163-185.

Gould, S.J., 1965. Is Uniformitarianism Necessary? *American Journal of Science*, 263, pp. 223-228.

Gould, S.J., 1987. *Time's Arrow, Time's Cycle*. Harvard University Press, Cambridge, Massachusetts.

Graham, R.W. and E.L. Lundelius, Jr., 1984. Coevolutionary Disequilibrium and Pleistocene Extinctions. in *Quaternary Extinctions: A Prehistoric Revolution*, P.S. Martin and R.G. Klein, eds., The University of Arizona Press, Tucson, pp. 223-249.

Grassé, P.P., 1977. *Evolution of Living Organisms,* Academic Press, New York.

Grayson, D.K., 1984a. Nineteenth-Century Explanations of Pleistocene Extinctions: A Review and Analysis. in *Quaternary Extinctions: A Prehistoric Revolution,* P.S. Martin and R.G. Klein, eds., The University of Arizona Press, Tucson, pp. 5-39.

Grayson, D.K., 1984b. Explaining Pleistocene Extinctions. in *Quaternary Extinctions: A Prehistoric Revolution,* P.S. Martin and R.G. Klein, eds., The University of Arizona Press, Tucson, pp. 807-823.

Gudelis, V. and L.K. Königsson, eds., 1979. *The Quaternary History of the Baltic.* University of Uppsala, Uppsala, Sweden.

Guthrie, R.D., 1984. Mosaics, Allelochemics and Nutrients. in *Quaternary Extinctions: A Prehistoric Revolution,* P.S. Martin and R.G. Klein, eds., The University of Arizona Press, Tucson, pp. 259-298.

Haldorsen, S., 1983. The Characteristics and Genesis of Norwegian Tills. in *Glacial Deposits in North-West Europe,* J. Ehlers, ed., A.A. Balkema, Rotterdam, pp. 11-18.

Hall, M.M. and H.L. Bryden, 1982. Direct Estimates and Mechanisms of Ocean Heat Transport. *Deep-Sea Research,* 29, pp. 339-359.

Hansen, J.E., Wang, W. C., and A.A. Lacis, 1978. Mount Agung Eruption Provides Test of a Global Climatic Perturbation. *Science,* 199, pp. 1065-1068.

Hapgood, C.H., 1970. *The Path of the Pole.* Chilton Book Co., New York.

Hasselmann, K., 1976. Stochastic Climate Models Part I. Theory. *Tellus,* 28, pp. 473-484.

Hay, J.E. and B.B. Fitzharris, 1988. A Comparison of the Energy-Balance and Bulk-Aerodynamic Approaches for Estimating Glacier Melt. *Journal of Glaciology,* 34 (117), pp. 145-153.

Hays, J.D. et al., 1969. Pliocene-Pleistocene Sediments of the Equatorial Pacific: Their Paleomagnetic, Biostratigraphic, and Climatic Record. *Geological Society of America Bulletin,* 80, pp. 1481-1514.

Hays, J.D., Imbrie, J., and N.J. Shackleton, 1976. Variations in the Earth's Orbit: Pacemaker of the Ice Ages. *Science,* 194, pp. 1121-1132.

Held, I.M., 1983. Stationary and Quasi-Stationary Eddies in the Extratropical Troposphere: Theory. in *Large-Scale Dynamical Processes in the Atmosphere,* B.J. Hoskins and R.P. Pearce, eds., Academic Press, New York, pp. 127-168.

Herman, G.F. and W.T. Johnson, 1978. The Sensitivity of the General Circulation to Arctic Sea Ice Boundaries: A Numerical Experiment. *Monthly Weather Review,* 106, pp. 1649-1664.

Hess, S.L., 1959. *Introduction to Theoretical Meteorology. Holt, Rinehart and Winston, New York.*

Hillaire-Marcel, C., Grant, D.R., and J.S. Vincent, 1980. Comments and Reply on Keewatin Ice Sheet—Re-Evaluation of the Traditional Concept of the Laurentide Ice Sheet and Glacial Erosion and Ice Sheet Divides, Northeastern Laurentide Ice Sheet, on the Basis of the Distribution of Limestone Erratics. *Geology,* 8, pp. 466,467.

Himmelfarb, G., 1962. *Darwin and the Darwinian Revolution.* W.W. Norton & Co., New York.

Holloway, Jr., J.L. and S. Manabe, 1971. Simulation of Climate by a Global General Circulation Model 1. Hydrologic Cycle and Heat Balance. *Monthly Weather Review,* 99, pp. 335-370.

Horgan, J., 1988. Ice House. *Scientific American*, 259 (5), p. 30.

Holton, J.R., 1972. *An Introduction to Dynamic Meteorology*. Academic Press, New York.

Honjo, S., Manganini, S.J., and J.J. Cole, 1982. Sedimentation of Biogenic Matter in the Deep Ocean. *Deep-Sea Research*, 29, pp. 609-625.

Hooper, P.R., 1982. The Columbia River Basalts. *Science*, 215, pp. 1463-1468.

Hopkins, D.M. et al., eds., 1982. *Paleoecology of Beringia*. Academic Press, New York.

Hoskins, B.J., 1983. Modelling of the Transient Eddies and Their Feedback on the Mean Flow. in *Large-Scale Dynamical Processes in the Atmosphere*, B.J. Hoskins and R.P. Pearce, eds., Academic Press, New York, pp. 169-199.

Houmark-Nielsen, M., 1983. The Compositional Features of Danish Glacial Deposits. in *Glacial Deposits in North-West Europe*, J. Ehlers, ed., A.A. Balkema, Rotterdam, pp. 199-202.

Hoyle, F., 1981. *Ice the Ultimate Human Catastrophe*. Continuum, New York.

Hughes, P., 1979. The Year Without a Summer. *Weatherwise*, 32, pp. 108-111.

Hughes, T., 1986. The Jakobshanvs Effect. *Geophysical Research Letters*, 13, pp. 46-48.

Hyde, W.T. and W.R. Peltier, 1985. Sensitivity Experiments with a Model of the Ice Age Cycle: The Response to Harmonic Forcing. *Journal of the Atmospheric Sciences*, 42, pp. 2170-2188.

Idso, S.B., 1987. A Clarification of My Position on the CO_2/Climate Connection. *Climatic Change*, 10, pp. 81-86.

Imbrie, J. and K.P. Imbrie, 1979. *Ice Ages Solving the Mystery*. Enslow Publishers, New Jersey.

Izett, G.A., 1981. Volcanic Ash Beds: Recorders of Upper Cenozoic Silicic Pyroclastic Volcanism in the Western United States. *Journal of Geophysical Research*, 86 (B11), pp. 10200-10222.

John, B., 1979. Ice Ages: A Search for Reasons. in *Winters of the World*, B.S. John, ed., John Wiley and Sons, New York, pp. 29-57.

Johnson, C.M., 1980. Wintertime Arctic Sea Ice Extremes and the Simultaneous Atmospheric Circulation. *Monthly Weather Review*, 108, pp. 1782-1791.

Jones, P.D. et al., 1989. The Effect of Urban Warming on the Northern Hemisphere Temperature Average. *Journal of Climate*, 2, pp. 285-290.

Karl, T.R. and P.D. Jones, 1989. Urban Bias in Area-Averaged Surface Air Temperature Trends. *Bulletin of the American Meteorological Society*, 70, pp. 265-270.

Karrow, P.F. and P.E. Calkin, eds., 1985. *Quaternary Evolution of the Great Lakes*. Geological Association of Canada Special Paper 30, St. John's, Newfoundland.

Karrow, P.F., 1984. Discussion—Lithofacies Types and Vertical Profile Models; An Alternative Approach to the Description and Environmental Interpretation of Glacial Diamict and Diamictite Sequences. *Sedimentology*, 31, pp. 883,884.

Kemmis, T.J. and G.R. Hallberg, 1984. Discussion—Lithofacies Types and Vertical Profile Models; An Alternative Approach to the Description and Environmental Interpretation of Glacial Diamict and Diamictite Sequences. *Sedimentology*, 31, pp. 886-890.

Kemp, R.A., 1986. Pre-Flandrian Quaternary Soils and Pedogenic Processes in Britian. in *Paleosols Their Recognition and Interpretation,* V.P. Wright, ed., Blackwell Scientific Publications, London, pp. 242-262.

Kennett, J.P., 1982. *Marine Geology*. Prentice-Hall, Englewood Cliffs, New Jersey.

Kerr, R.A., 1984. Climate Since the Ice Began to Melt. *Science,* 226, pp. 326,327.

Kerr, R.A., 1987. Ocean Hot Springs Similar Around Globe. *Science,* 235, p. 435.

Kerr, R.A., 1988. New Ways to Chill Earth. *Science,* 241, pp. 532,533.

Kerr, R.A., 1989a. Did the Roof of the World Start an Ice Age? *Science,* 244, pp. 1441,1442.

Kerr, R.A., 1989b. Volcanoes Can Muddle the Greenhouse. *Science,* 245, pp. 127,128.

King, M.D., 1987. Summary of the Sixth Conference on Atmospheric Radiation. *Bulletin of the American Meteorological Society,* 68, pp. 346-355.

King, P.B., 1965. Tectonics of Quaternary Time in Middle North America. in *The Quaternary of the United States,* H.E. Wright, Jr., and D.G. Frey, eds., Princeton University Press, Princeton, New Jersey, pp. 831-870.

Krishtalka, L., 1984. The Pleistocene Ways of Death. Book Review of *Quaternary Extinctions: A Prehistoric Revolution,* P.S. Martin and R.G. Klein, eds., *Nature,* 312, pp. 225,226.

Kuhn, M., 1979. On the Computation of Heat Transfer Coefficients from Energy-Balance Gradients on a Glacier. *Journal of Glaciology,* 22 (87), pp. 263-272.

Kuhn, T.S., 1970. *The Structure of Scientific Revolutions,* 2nd Edition. The University of Chicago Press, Chicago.

Kukla, G.J., 1975. Loess Stratigraphy of Central Europe. in *After the Australopithecines,* K.W. Butzer and G.L. Isaac, eds., Mouton Publishers, Paris, pp. 99-188.

Kukla, G.J., 1977. Pleistocene Land-Sea Correlations 1. Europe. *Earth Science Reviews,* 13, pp. 307-374.

Kutzbach, J.E. and H.E. Wright, Jr., 1985. Simulation of the Climate of 18,000 Years BP: Results for the North American/North Atlantic/European Sector and Comparison with the Geological Record of North America. *Quaternary Science Reviews,* 4, pp. 147-187.

Lamarche, R.Y., 1971. Northward Moving Ice in the Thetford Mines Area of Southern Quebec. *American Journal of Science,* 271, pp. 383-388.

Lamb, H.H. and A. Woodruffe, 1970. Atmospheric Circulation During the Last Ice Age. *Quaternary Research,* 1, pp. 29-58.

Lammerts, W.E., 1988. Concerning Disjunct Populations of Mammals and Plants. *Creation Research Society Quarterly,* 25, pp. 126-128.

Landsburg, H., 1958. *Physical Climatology,* 2nd Edition. Gray Printing Co., DuBois, Pennsylvania.

Lang, W., 1984. A Response on Psalm 104:8. *Bible-Science Newsletter,* 22 (9), pp. 10,15.

Ledley, T.S., 1984. Sensitivities of Cryospheric Models to Insolation and Temperature Variations Using a Surface Energy Balance. in *Milankovitch and Climate,* A. Berger, ed., D. Reidel Publishing Co., Dordrecht, Holland, pp. 581-597.

Leet, L.D. and S. Judson, 1965. *Physical Geology*, 3rd Edition. Prentice-Hall, Englewood Cliffs, New Jersey.

Lemke, R.W. et al., 1965. Glaciated Area East of the Rocky Mountains. in *The Quaternary of the United States*, H.E. Wright, Jr., and D.G. Frey, eds., Princeton University Press, Princeton, New Jersey, pp. 15-26.

Lewin, R., 1987. Domino Effect Invoked in Ice Age Extinctions. *Science*, 238, pp. 1509,1510.

List, R.J., 1951. *Smithsonian Meteorological Tables*, 6th Edition. Smithsonian Institution, Washington, D.C.

Loewe, F., 1971. Considerations on the Origin of the Quaternary Ice Sheet of North America. *Arctic and Alpine Research*, 3, pp. 331-344.

Lorenz, E.N., 1967. *The Nature and Theory of the General Circulation of the Atmosphere*. World Meteorological Organization, Geneva.

Lougee, R.J. and C.R. Lougee, 1976. *Late-Glacial Chronology*. Vantage Press, New York.

Lundqvist, J., 1983a. The Glacial History of Sweden. in *Glacial Deposits in North-West Europe*, J. Ehlers, ed., A.A. Balkema, Rotterdam, pp. 77-82.

Lundqvist, J., 1983b. Tills and Moraines in Sweden. in *Glacial Deposits in North-West Europe*, J. Ehlers, ed., A.A. Balkema, Rotterdam, pp. 83-90.

Lundqvist, J., 1986. Stratigraphy of the Central Area of the Scandinavian Glaciation. in *Quaternary Glaciations in the Northern Hemisphere*, V. Sibrava, D.Q. Bowen, and G.M. Richmond, eds., Pergamon Press, New York, *Quaternary Science Reviews*, 5, pp. 251-268.

Luther, F.M. and B.M. Herman, 1987. Summer Course on Radiation as it Relates to Climate, 14-19 July 1986, Boulder, Colorado. *Bulletin of the American Meteorological Society*, 68, pp. 131-135.

Macbeth, N., 1971. *Darwin Retried: An Appeal to Reason*. Gambit, Ipswich, Massachusetts.

Mahaney, W.C., ed., 1984. *Quaternary Dating Methods*. Elsevier, New York.

Manabe, S., 1969. Climate and the Ocean Circulation 1. The Atmospheric Circulation and the Hydrology of the Earth's Surface. *Monthly Weather Review*, 97, pp. 739-774.

Manabe, S. and A.J. Broccoli, 1985a. A Comparison of Climate Model Sensitivity with Data from the Last Glacial Maximum. *Journal of the Atmospheric Sciences*, 42, pp. 2643-2651.

Manabe, S. and A.J. Broccoli, 1985b. The Influence of Continental Ice Sheets on the Climate of an Ice Age. *Journal of Geophysical Research*, 90 (C2), pp. 2167-2190.

Mangerud, J., 1983. The Glacial History of Norway. in *Glacial Deposits in North-West Europe*, J. Ehlers, ed., A.A. Balkema, Rotterdam, pp. 3-10.

Mass, C.F. and D.A. Portman, 1989. Major Volcanic Eruptions and Climate: A Critical Evaluation. *Journal of Climate*, 2, pp. 566-593.

Marshall, L.G., 1984. Who Killed Cock Robin? in *Quaternary Extinctions: A Prehistoric Revolution*, P.S. Martin and R.G. Klein, eds., The University of Arizona Press, Tucson, pp. 785-806.

Martin, P.S. and R.G. Klein, eds., 1984. *Quaternary Extinctions: A Prehistoric Revolution*. The University of Arizona Press, Tucson.

Mathews, W.H., 1974. Surface Profiles of the Laurentide Ice Sheet in Its Marginal Areas. *Journal of Glaciology,* 13 (67), pp. 37-43.

Matthews, Jr., J.V., 1982. East Beringia During Late Wisconsin Time: A Review of the Biotic Evidence. in *Paleoecology of Beringia,* D.M. Hopkins and Others, eds., Academic Press, New York, pp. 127-150.

McCauley, J.F. et al., 1982 Subsurface Valleys and Geoarcheology of the Eastern Sahara Revealed by Shuttle Radar. *Science,* 218, pp. 1004-1020.

McDonald, J.N., 1984. The Reordered North American Selection Regime and Late Quaternary Megafaunal Extinctions. in *Quaternary Extinctions: A Prehistoric Revolution,* P.S. Martin and R.G. Klein, eds., The University of Arizona Press, Tucson, pp. 404-439.

Menzies, J. and J. Rose, eds., 1987a. *Drumlin Symposium.* Balkema, Rotterdam.

Menzies, J. and J. Rose, 1987b. Introduction. in *Drumlin Symposium,* Balkema, Rotterdam, pp. 1-5.

Mickelson, D.M. et al., 1983. The Late Wisconsin Glacial Record of the Laurentide Ice Sheet in the United States. in *Late-Quaternary Environments of the United States,* Volume 1, H.E. Wright, Jr., ed., University of Minnesota Press, Minneapolis, pp. 3-37.

Mintz, Y., 1968. Very Long-Term Global Integration of the Primitive Equations of Atmospheric Motion: An Experiment in Climate Simulation. in *Causes of Climatic Change,* Meteorological Monographs, 8 (30), J.M. Mitchell, Jr., ed., American Meteorological Society, Boston, pp. 20-36.

Monastersky, R., 1987. On the Edge Between Water and Ice. *Science News,* 131, p. 280.

Monastersky, R., 1989a. Clouds Clearing from Climate Predictions. *Science News,* 135, p. 6.

Monastersky, R., 1989b. Global Change: The Scientific Challenge. *Science News,* 135, pp. 232-235.

Mörner, N. A., 1980a. The Fennoscandian Uplift: Geological Data and Their Geodynamical Implication. in *Earth Rheology, Isostasy and Eustasy,* N. A. Mörner, ed., John Wiley and Sons, New York, pp. 251-284.

Mörner, N. A., ed., 1980b. *Earth Rheology, Isostasy and Eustasy.* John Wiley and Sons, New York.

Morton, G.R., 1986. *The Geology of the Flood.* G.R. Morton, Dallas.

Muller, E.H., 1974. Origins of Drumlins. in *Glacial Geomorphology,* D.R. Coates, ed., George Allen and Unwin Ltd., London, pp. 187-204.

Namias, J., 1972. Experiments in Objectively Predicting Some Atmospheric and Oceanic Variables for the Winter of 1971-72. *Journal of Applied Meteorology,* 11, pp. 1164-1174.

Namias, J. and D.R. Cayan, 1981. Large-Scale Air-Sea Interactions and Short-Period Climatic Fluctuations. *Science,* 214, pp. 869-876.

Nevins, S.E., 1974. Post-Flood Strata of the John Day Country, Northeastern Oregon. *Creation Research Society Quarterly,* 10, pp. 191-204.

Newson, R.L., 1973. Response of a General Circulation Model of the Atmosphere to Removal of the Arctic Ice-Cap. *Nature,* 241, pp. 39,40.

Nielsen, P.E., 1983. The Lithology and Genesis of the Danish Tills. in *Glacial Deposits in North-West Europe,* J. Ehlers, ed., A.A. Balkema, Rotterdam, pp. 193-196.

Nilsson, T., 1983. *The Pleistocene. Geology and Life in the Quaternary Ice Age*. D. Reidel Publishing Co., Boston.

Nunn, P.D., 1986. Implications of Migrating Geoid Anomalies for the Interpretation of High-Level Fossil Coral Reefs. *Geological Society of America Bulletin*, 97, pp. 946-952.

Oard, M.J., 1982. Book Review of *The Waters Above: Earth's Pre-Flood Vapor Canopy*, J.C. Dillow. *Creation Research Society Quarterly*, 19, pp. 73-75.

Oard, M.J., 1984a. Ice Ages: The Mystery Solved? Part I: The Inadequacy of a Uniformitarian Ice Age. *Creation Research Society Quarterly*, 21, pp. 66-76.

Oard, M.J., 1984b. Ice Ages: The Mystery Solved? Part II: The Manipulation of Deep-Sea Cores. *Creation Research Society Quarterly*, 21, pp. 125-137.

Oard, M.J., 1985. Ice Ages: The Mystery Solved? Part III: Paleomagnetic Stratigraphy and Data Manipulation. *Creation Research Society Quarterly*, 21, pp. 170-181.

Occhietti, S., 1983. Laurentide Ice Sheet: Oceanic and Climatic Implications. *Palaeogeography, Palaeoclimatology, Palaeoecology*, 44, pp. 1-22.

Oliver, R.C., 1976. On the Response of Hemispheric Mean Temperature to Stratospheric Dust: An Empirical Approach. *Journal of Applied Meteorology*, 15, pp. 933-950.

Oommen, T.V., 1976. In Search of the Ideal World. *Bible-Science Newsletter*, 14 (12), pp. 1-3.

Otterman, J., Chou, M. D., and A. Arking, 1984. Effects of Nontropical Forest Cover on Climate. *Journal of Climate and Applied Meteorology*, 23, pp. 762-767.

Pachur, H. J. and S. Kröpelin, 1987. Wadi Howar: Paleoclimatic Evidence from an Extinct River System in the Southeastern Sahara. *Science*, 237, pp. 298-300.

Panofsky, H.A. and G.W. Brier, 1965. *Some Applications of Statistics to Meteorology*. The Pennsylvania State University Press, University Park, Pennsylvania.

Parker, D.E., 1980. Book Review of *Ice Ages: Solving the Mystery*, J. Imbrie and K.P. Imbrie. *Meteorological Magazine*, 109, pp. 185,186.

Paterson, W.S.B., 1969. *The Physics of Glaciers*, 1st Edition. Pergamon Press, New York.

Paterson, W.S.B., 1981. *The Physics of Glaciers*, 2nd Edition. Pergamon Press, New York.

Paul, M.A., 1983. The Supraglacial Landsystem. in *Glacial Geology*, N. Eyles, ed., Pergamon Press, New York, pp. 71-90.

Pawluk, S., 1978. The Pedogenic Profile in the Stratigraphic Section. in *Quaternary Soils*, W.C. Mahaney, ed., Geo Abstracts Ltd., University of East Anglia, Norwich, England, pp. 61-75.

Peltier, W.R. and J.T. Andrews, 1983. Glacial Geology and Glacial Isostasy of the Hudson Bay Region. in *Shorelines and Isostasy*, D.E. Smith and A.G. Dawson, eds., Academic Press, New York, pp. 285-319.

Peters, R.H., 1976. Tautology in Evolution and Ecology. *American Naturalist*, 110, pp. 1-12.

Peterson, I., 1989. Publication Bias: Looking for Missing Data. *Science News*, 135, p. 5.

Philbrick, H.S., 1970. Horizontal Configuration of the Rate of Erosion of Niagara Falls. *Geological Society of America Bulletin*, 81, pp. 3723-3732.

Pickard, J., 1984. Comments on "Wastage of the Klutlan Ice-Cored Moraines, Yukon Territory, Canada" by Driscoll (1980). *Quaternary Research*, 22, p. 259.

Pollard, D., 1980. A Simple Parameterization for Ice Sheet Ablation Rate. *Tellus*, 32, pp. 384-388.

Porter, S.C., 1981. Recent Glacier Variations and Volcanic Eruptions. *Nature*, 291, pp. 139-142.

Potter, J.G., 1965. *Snow Cover*. Climatological Series, No. 3, Department of Transport, Meteorological Branch, Toronto.

Pye, K., 1987. *Aeolian Dust and Dust Deposits*. Academic Press, New York.

Raaflaub, V.A., 1984. Translating Psalm 104:8. *Bible-Science Newsletter*, 22 (9), p. 10.

Raman, S. and A.J. Riordan, 1988. The Genesis of Atlantic Lows Experiment: The Planetary-Boundary-Layer Subprogram of GALE. *Bulletin of the American Meteorological Society*, 69, pp. 161-172.

Ramanathan, V. et al., 1989. Cloud-Radiative Forcing and Climate: Results from the Earth Radiation Budget Experiment. *Science*, 243, pp. 57-63.

Rampino, M.R., Stothers, R.B., and S. Self, 1985. Climatic Effects of Volcanic Eruptions. *Nature*, 313, p. 272.

Ramsay, A.T.S., ed., 1977. *Oceanic Micropalaeontology*, Volume 1. Academic Press, New York.

Reeh, N., 1985. Was the Greenland Ice Sheet Thinner in the Late Wisconsinan Than Now? *Nature*, 317, pp. 797-799.

Richmond, G.M. and D.S. Fullerton, 1986. Summation of Quaternary Glaciations in the United States of America. in *Quaternary Glaciations in the Northern Hemisphere*, V. Sibrava, D.Q. Bowen, and G.M. Richmond, eds., *Quaternary Science Reviews*, 5, pp. 183-196.

Roth, A.A., 1985. Are Millions of Years Required to Produce Biogenic Sediments in the Deep Ocean? *Origins*, 12, pp. 48-56.

Roth, A.A., 1988. Those Gaps in the Sedimentary Layers. *Origins*, 15, pp. 75-92.

Ruddiman, W.F. and A. McIntyre, 1979. Warmth of the Subpolar North Atlantic Ocean During Northern Hemisphere Ice-Sheet Growth. *Science*, 204, pp. 173-175.

Ruellan, A., 1971. The History of Soils: Some Problems of Definition and Interpretation. in *Paleopedology: Origin, Nature and Dating of Paleosols*, D.H. Yaalon, ed., Israel University Press, Jerusalem, pp. 1-14.

Ruhe, R.V., 1983. Depositional Environment of Late Wisconsin Loess in the Midcontinental United States. in *Late-Quaternary Environments of the United States*, Volume 1, H.E. Wright, Jr., ed., University of Minnesota Press, Minneapolis, pp. 130-137.

Schermerhorn, L.J.G., 1974. Late Precambrian Mixtites: Glacial and/or Nonglacial? *American Journal of Science*, 274, pp. 673-824.

Schlesinger, W.H., 1986. Changes in Soil Carbon Storage and Associated Properties with Disturbance and Recovery. in *The Changing Carbon Cycle: A Global Analysis*, J.R. Trabalka and D.E. Reichle, eds., Springer-Verlag, New York, pp. 194-220.

Schneider, S.H., 1983. Volcanic Dust Veils and Climate: How Clear is the Connection?—An Editorial. *Climatic Change*, 5, pp. 111-113.

Schneider, S.H., 1984. Energy Balance Models (EBM) (Report). in *Milankovitch and Climate*, A. Berger, ed., D. Reidel Publishing Co., Dordrecht, Holland, pp. 845-854.

Schumm, S.A., 1967. Meander Wavelength of Alluvial Rivers. *Science*, 157, pp. 1549,1550.

Schumm, S.A., 1977. *The Fluvial System*. John Wiley and Sons, New York.

Schweger, C.E., 1982. Primary Production and the Pleistocene Ungulates—The Productivity Paradox. in *Paleoecology of Beringia*, D.M. Hopkins and Others, eds., Academic Press, New York, pp. 219-221.

Schweger, C.E. et al., 1982. Paleoecology of Beringia—A Synthesis. in *Paleoecology of Beringia*, D.M. Hopkins and Others, eds., Academic Press, New York, pp. 425-444.

Shaw, J., 1983. Drumlin Formation Related to Inverted Melt-Water Erosional Marks. *Journal of Glaciology*, 29 (103), pp. 461-479.

Shaw, J., 1988. Book Review of *Drumlin Symposium*, J. Menzies and J. Rose, eds., *Quaternary Research*, 30, pp. 354,355.

Shilts, W.W., 1980. Flow Patterns in the Central North American Ice Sheet. *Nature*, 286, pp. 213-218.

Shilts, W.W., Cunningham, C.J., and C.A. Kaszycki, 1979. Keewatin Ice Sheet—Re-Evaluation of the Traditional Concept of the Laurentide Ice Sheet. *Geology*, 7, pp. 537-541.

Sibrava, V., Bowen, D.Q., and G.M. Richmond, eds., 1986. *Quaternary Glaciations in the Northern Hemisphere. Quaternary Science Reviews*, 5.

Smalley, I.J., ed., 1975. *Loess Lithology and Genesis*. Benchmark Papers in Geology 26, Dowden, Hutchinson and Sons, London.

Smith, G.I. and F.A. Street-Perrott, 1983. Pluvial Lakes of the Western United States. in *Late-Quaternary Environments of the United States*, Volume 1, H.E. Wright, Jr., ed., University of Minnesota Press, Minneapolis, pp. 190-212.

Spaulding, W.G., 1985. Vegetation and Climates of the Last 45,000 Years in the Vicinity of the Nevada Test Site, South-Central Nevada. *U.S. Geological Survey Professional Paper 1329*, U.S. Government Printing Office, Washington, D.C.

Spaulding, W.G., Leopold, E.B., and T.R. Van Devender, 1983. Late Wisconsin Paleoecology of the American Southwest. in *Late-Quaternary Environments of the United States*, Volume 1, H.E. Wright, Jr., ed., University of Minnesota Press, Minneapolis, pp. 259-293.

Spencer, C.P., 1976. The Micronutrient Elements. in *Chemical Oceanography*, 2nd Edition, Volume 2, J.P. Riley and R. Chester, eds., Academic Press, New York, pp. 245-300.

Stephens, G.L. and P.J. Webster, 1981. Clouds and Climate: Sensitivity of Simple Systems. *Journal of the Atmospheric Sciences*, 38, pp. 235-247.

Stewart, J.M., 1977. Frozen Mammoths from Siberia Bring the Ice Ages to Vivid Life. *Smithsonian*, 8, pp. 60-69.

Stewart, J.M., 1979. A Baby That Died 40,000 Years Ago Reveals a Story. *Smithsonian*, 10, pp. 125,126.

Stewart, R.W., 1978. The Role of Sea Ice in Climate. *Oceanus*, 21 (4), pp. 47-57.

Stothers, R.B. et al., 1986. Basaltic Fissure Eruptions, Plume Heights, and Atmospheric Aerosols. *Geophysical Research Letters*, 13, pp. 725-728.

Strahler, A.N., 1987. *Science and Earth History—The Evolution/Creation Controversy*. Prometheus Books, Buffalo, New York.

Suarez, M.J. and I.M. Held, 1976. Modeling Climatic Response to Orbital Parameter Variations. *Nature*, 263, pp. 46,47.

Suarez, M.J. and I.M. Held, 1979. The Sensitivity of an Energy Balance Climate Model to Variations in the Orbital Parameters. *Journal of Geophysical Research*, 84 (C8), pp. 4825-4836.

Sugden, D.E. and B.S. John, 1976. *Glaciers and Landscape*. Edward Arnold, London.

Sundquist, E.T., 1987. Ice Core Links CO_2 to Climate. *Nature*, 329, pp. 389,390.

Sutcliffe, A.J., 1985. *On the Track of Ice Age Mammals*. Harvard University Press, Cambridge, Massachusetts.

Tarling, D.H., 1978. The Geological-Geophysical Framework of Ice Ages. in *Climatic Change*, J. Gribbin, ed., Cambridge University Press, London, pp. 3-24.

Thaxton, C.B., Bradley, W.L., and R.L. Olsen, 1984. *The mystery of Life's Origin: Reassessing Current Theories*. Philosophical Library, New York.

Tolmachoff, I.P., 1929. The Carcasses of the Mammoth and Rhinoceros Found in the Frozen Ground of Siberia. *Transactions of the American Philosophical Society*, 23, pp. 11-74.

Toon, O.B. et al., 1982. Evolution of an Impact-Generated Dust Cloud and Its Effects on the Atmosphere. *Geological Society of America Special Paper 190*, pp. 187-200.

Tosk, T., 1988. Foraminifers in the Fossil Record: Implications for an Ecological Zonation Model. *Origins*, 15, pp. 8-18.

Trabalka, J.R. and D.E. Reichle, eds., 1986. *The Changing Carbon Cycle: A Global Analysis*. Springer-Verlag, New York.

Trewartha, G.T. and L.H. Horn, 1980. *An Introduction to Climate*, 5th Edition. McGraw-Hill, New York.

Turco, R.P. et al., 1983. Nuclear Winter: Global Consequences of Multiple Nuclear Explosions. *Science*, 222, pp. 1283-1292.

U.S. Army Corps of Engineers, 1956. *Snow Hydrology*, Portland, Oregon.

Udd, S.V., 1975. The Canopy and Genesis 1:6-8. *Creation Research Society Quarterly*, 12, pp. 90-93.

Untersteiner, N., 1984. The Cryosphere. in *The Global Climate*, J.T. Houghton, ed., Cambridge University Press, Cambridge, pp. 121-140.

Valentine, K.W.G. and J.B. Dalrymple, 1976. Quaternary Buried Paleosols: A Critical Review. *Quaternary Research*, 6, pp. 209-222.

vanLoon, H. and J. Williams, 1976a. The Connection Between Trends of Mean Temperature and Circulation at the Surface: Part I. Winter. *Monthly Weather Review*, 104, pp. 365-380.

vanLoon, H. and J. Williams, 1976b. The Connection Between Trends of Mean Temperature and Circulation at the Surface: Part II. Summer. *Monthly Weather Review*, 104, pp. 1003-1011.

Vardiman, L., 1986. The Sky Has Fallen. *Proceedings of The First International Conference on Creationism*, Volume 1, Creation Science Fellowship, Pittsburgh, pp. 113-119.

Veeh, H.H. and J. Chappell, 1970. Astronomical Theory of Climatic Change: Support from New Guinea. *Science*, 167, pp. 862-865.

Vereshchagin, N.K. and G.F. Baryshnikov, 1982. Paleoecology of the Mammoth Fauna in the Eurasian Arctic. in *Paleoecology of Beringlia*, D.M. Hopkins and Others, eds., Academic Press, New York, pp. 267-279.

Vereshchagin, N.K. and G.F. Baryshnikov, 1984. Quaternary Mammalian Extinctions in Northern Eurasia. in *Quaternary Extinctions: A Prehistoric Revolution*, P.S. Martin and R.G. Klein, eds., The University of Arizona Press, Tucson, pp. 483-516.

Vonder Haar, T.H. and A.H. Oort, 1973. New Estimates of Annual Poleward Energy Transport by Northern Hemisphere Oceans. *Journal of Physical Oceanography*. 3, pp. 169-172.

Vreeken, W.J., 1984. Relative Dating of Soils and Paleosols. in *Quaternary Dating Methods*, W.C. Mahaney, ed., Elsevier, New York, pp. 269-281.

Wagner, W.P., 1970. Pleistocene Mountain Glaciation, Northern Vermont. *Geological Society of America Bulletin*, 81, pp. 2465-2470.

Wagner, W.P., 1971. Pleistocene Mountain Glaciation, Northern Vermont: Reply. *Geological Society of America Bulletin*, 82, pp. 1761,1762.

Waisgerber, W., Howe, G.F., and E.L. Williams, 1987. Mississippian and Cambrian Strata Interbedding: 200 Million Years Hiatus in Question. *Creation Research Society Quarterly*, 23, pp. 160-169.

Waitt, R.B. and P.T. Davis, 1988. No Evidence for Post-Icesheet Cirque Glaciation in New England. *American Journal of Science*, 288, pp. 495-533.

Walcott, R.I., 1970. Isostatic Response to Loading of the Crust in Canada. *Canadian Journal of Earth Science*, 7, pp. 716-727.

Walcott, R.I., 1973. Structure of the Earth from Glacio-Isostatic Rebound. *Annual Review of Earth and Planetary Sciences*, 1, pp. 15-37.

Walcott, R.I., 1980. Rheological Models and Observational Data of Glacio-Isostatic Rebound. in *Earth Rheology, Isostasy and Eustasy*, N. A. Mörner, ed., John Wiley and Sons, New York, pp. 3-10.

Wallace, J.M. and M.L. Blackmon, 1983. Observations of Low-Frequency Atmospheric Variability. in *Large-Scale Dynamical Processes in the Atmosphere*, B.J. Hoskins and R.P. Pearce, eds., Academic Press, New York, pp. 55-94.

Warren, S.G. and W.J. Wiscombe, 1980. A Model for the Spectral Albedo of Snow. II: Snow Containing Atmospheric Aerosols. *Journal of the Atmospheric Sciences*, 37, pp. 2734-2745.

Warren, S.G. and W.J. Wiscombe, 1985. Dirty Snow after Nuclear War. *Nature*, 313, pp. 467-470.

Warshaw, M. and R.R. Rapp, 1973. An Experiment on the Sensitivity of a Global Circulation Model. *Journal of Applied Meteorology*, 12, pp. 43-49.

Washburn, A.L., 1980. Focus on Polar Research. *Science*, 209, pp. 643-652.

Watkins, N.D., 1972. Review of the Development of the Geomagnetic Polarity Time Scale and Discussion of Prospects for Its Finer Definition. *Geological Society of America Bulletin*, 83, pp. 551-574.

Wendler, G. and Y. Kodama, 1986. Effect of the El Chichón Volcanic Cloud on the Surface Radiative Regime in Central Alaska. *Journal of Climate and Applied Meteorology*, 25, pp. 1687-1694.

Weisburd, S., 1987. Volcanoes and Extinctions: Round Two. *Science News*, 131, pp. 248-250.

West, R.G., 1968. *Pleistocene Geology and Biology*. Longmans, Green and Co. Ltd., London.

Whillans, I.M., 1978. Erosion by Continental Ice Sheets. *Journal of Geology*, 86, pp. 516-524.

Whitcomb, Jr., J.C. and H.M. Morris, 1961. *The Genesis Flood*. Baker Book House, Grand Rapids, Michigan.

Williams, G.P., 1986. River Meanders and Channel Size. *Journal of Hydrology*, 88, pp. 147-164.

Williams, G.P., 1988. Paleofluvial Estimates from Dimensions of Former Channels and Meanders. in *Flood Geomorphology*, V.R. Baker, R.C. Kochel, and P.C. Patton, eds., John Wiley and Sons, New York, pp. 321-334.

Williams, J. and H. vanLoon, 1976. The Connection Between Trends of Mean Temperature and Circulation at the Surface: Part III. Spring and Autumn. *Monthly Weather Review*, 104, pp. 1591-1596.

Williams, L.D., 1975. Effects of Insolation Changes on Late Summer Snow Cover in Northern Canada. *Proceedings of the WMO/IAMAP Symposium on Long-Term Climatic Fluctuations*, World Meteorological Organization, Geneva, pp. 287-292.

Williams, L.D., 1978. Ice-sheet Initiation and Climatic Influences of Expanded Snow Cover in Arctic Canada. *Quaternary Research*, 10, pp. 141-149.

Williams, L.D., 1979. An Energy Balance Model of Potential Glacierization of Northern Canada. *Arctic and Alpine Research*, 11, pp. 443-456.

Wiscombe, W.J. and S.G. Warren, 1980. A Model for the Spectral Albedo of Snow. I: Pure Snow. *Journal of the Atmospheric Sciences*, 37, pp. 2712-2733.

Wright, G.F., 1911. *The Ice Age in North America*. Bibliotheca Sacra Co., Oberlin, Ohio.

Zuckerman, S., 1970. *Beyond the Ivory Tower*. Taplinger Publishing Co., New York.